STOCK PATTERNS *for* DAY TRADING

2

ADVANCED TECHNIQUES

Barry Rudd

To my grandmother
Elsie Tee (Ma) Rudd
for East Texas home-cooked meals
and acres of countryside to which this trader
must occasionally escape

Serving Traders Since 1975

Publishers of:

A Complete Guide to Trading Profits (Paris)
A Professional Look at S&P Day Trading (Trivette)
Ask Mr. EasyLanguage (Tennis)
Beginner's Guide to Computer Assisted Trading (Alexander)
Channels and Cycles: A Tribute to J.M. Hurst (Millard)
Chart Reading for Professional Traders (Jenkins)
Commodity Spreads: Analysis, Selection and Trading Techniques (Smith)
Comparison of Twelve Technical Trading Systems (Lukac, Brorsen, & Irwin)
Day Trading with Short Term Price Patterns (Crabel)
Exceptional Trading: The Mind Game (Roosevelt)
Fibonacci Ratios with Pattern Recognition (Pesavento)
Geometry of Stock Market Profits (Jenkins)
Harmonic Vibrations (Pesavento)
How to Trade in Stocks (Livermore)
Hurst Cycles Course (J.M. Hurst)
Jesse Livermore: Speculator King (Sarnoff)
Magic of Moving Averages (Lowry)
Pit Trading: Do You Have the Right Stuff? (Hoffman)
Planetary Harmonics of Speculative Markets (Pesavento)
Point & Figure Charting: The Complete Guide (Aby)
Point & Figure Charting: Commodity and Stock Trading Techniques (Zieg)
Profitable Grain Trading (Ainsworth)
Profitable Patterns for Stock Trading (Pesavento)
Reminiscences of a Stock Operator (Lefevre)
Stock Market Trading Systems (Appel & Hitschler)
Stock Patterns for Day Trading (Rudd)
Study Helps in Point & Figure Techniques (Wheelan)
Technically Speaking (Wilkinson)
Technical Trading Systems for Commodities and Stocks (Patel)
The Professional Commodity Trader (Kroll)
The Taylor Trading Technique (Taylor)
The Traders (Kleinfeld)
*The Trading Rule That Can Make You Rich** (Dobson)
Traders Guide to Technical Analysis (Hardy)
Trading Secrets of the Inner Circle (Goodwin)
Trading S&P Futures and Options (Lloyd)
Understanding Bollinger Bands (Dobson)
Understanding Fibonacci Numbers (Dobson)
Viewpoints of a Commodity Trader (Longstreet)
Wall Street Ventures & Adventures Through Forty Years (Wyckoff)
Winning Market Systems (Appel)

STOCK PATTERNS
for
DAY TRADING

2

ADVANCED TECHNIQUES

by
Barry Rudd

ISBN: 0-934-380-57-0

TRADERS PRESS, INC.®
PO Box 6206
Greenville, SC 29606

Books and Gifts for Traders and Investors

Traders Press, Inc. stocks hundreds of titles of interest to investors and traders in stocks, options, and futures. In addition, we carry a full line of gift items for investors. Please contact us and we will gladly forward you our current *TRADERS CATALOG* by return mail.

Serving Traders Since 1975

800-927-8222
Fax 864 298 0222
Tradersprs@aol.com
http://Traderspress.com

ACKNOWLEDGMENTS

Thanks goes to Matt Rudd, my brother, training partner and patient trader who has helped to further develop our trading ideas and improve our training course immensely.

Also, I want to thank my parents William and Dianna Rudd for their encouragement in all of my efforts to complete this book...and for helping proofread it as well. Any mistakes are mine, not theirs.

I wish to express special gratitude to my friend, Albert Butler, who provided me a venue to grow both my own trading...and market profits, and to test new market strategies. Thanks, old codger!

Of course, Ed Dobson and everyone at Traders Press more than deserves my appreciation. It is refreshing to work with the kind of people where "gentlemen's agreements" are not a thing of the past.

Thanks to my friends and accomplished traders Ty Henderson and Kyle Bell who enjoy "talking shop" into the evening hours over a few beers.

I would be remiss if I did not collectively thank all of the clients that I have trained. They helped force me into better codifying and communicating my trading strategies, and were the real genesis of this book.

AUTHOR'S NOTE

This book, *"Stock Patterns for Day Trading 2 – Advanced Techniques,"* originally existed as two separate, unpublished manuals titled: *"Stock Patterns for Day Trading 2"* and *"The Psychology and Discipline of Day Trading."* During the course of writing both manuals, I occasionally made reference to my first published book, *"Stock Patterns for Day Trading."*

I have not changed the original text of the material that you currently hold in your hands. Therefore, anytime in this book that the word "manual" is used, it refers to this book, *"Stock Patterns for Day Trading 2 – Advanced Techniques."*

Any references on these pages using the words "the book," *"Stock Patterns,"* or *"Stock Patterns for Day Trading"* apply to my prior published book available in hardback from Traders Press.

Although it is not necessary that you own the first book, it would help to provide you with a fuller understanding of the ideas presented herein.

I hope that this clears up any possible confusion as you read and study this text.

FOREWORD

As a stock day trader, I have spent countless hours trying to identify and codify specific ways to consistently trade successfully. My book, *"Stock Patterns for Day Trading,"* evolved as my material for training other stock day traders. The strategies and techniques from that book came from my own personal experience as well as that of other successful traders. It became one of the first published books devoted to distinctive methodologies for day trading stocks with level II quotes on the NASDAQ market.

This manual takes these methods to an advanced level and also presents additional techniques that I implement in my own trading. It will help if you have read and digested the information from the *"Stock Patterns"* book since this course builds upon some of the same concepts. While the book included many annotated charts, this manual communicates expanded strategies that I believe do not require as many chart examples, except after a few selected sections.

Stock day trading is not a clean, cold and purely systematic endeavor. Instead, it's a "roll your sleeves up, get down and dirty" activity which puts you in tune with the market. You have to actually reach into its chest and grasp hold of the heart of the market as you uncover its rhythms and discern its character. That is what this manual has been designed to do for you. Consider yourself a certified market surgeon once you achieve the ability to put these ideas and techniques into practice on a daily basis.

While this material will work with New York issues, the genesis and evolution of these strategies grew from trading NASDAQ stocks. Therefore, they work most effectively with the intraday character of this market's individual stock movements, and the structure of the NASDAQ market including its order execution capabilities.

Both the intraday trend trading and scalping approach are covered, with guidance for which style will work best for you. Devote yourself to assimilating all of this information into your trading, and customize it to fit your own trading personality.

Three components will dictate your success or failure as a stock day trader. First, you must have a quality methodology. Second, a quality money management strategy must guide your trading. You hold in your hands both of these. Third, you must cultivate unwavering ***discipline*** to implement the first two components to succeed.

I cannot overemphasize the role of discipline. Without it you will fail, guaranteed. Of all of the people I've trained, this has been the common denominator of those that are now employed elsewhere. The rest have survived to excel and grow in their trading endeavors.

And yes, I still do make my living trading the markets. It is a true joy to take an avocation and turn it into your vocation. I believe that this course provides you all of the tools that will allow you to do the same.

Sincerely,

Barry Rudd

CONTENTS

OVERVIEW

Since this manual builds upon *"Stock Patterns for Day Trading,"* it is organized in a coherent fashion by initially expanding upon some of the patterns in the book. More trading enhancements and additional techniques then follow to carry you progressively forward. The sections are divided under three main headings listed below.

Consider every bit of information as a puzzle piece to be fully understood. The manual will then help you put the puzzle together where each piece relates to another in the overall picture of day trading.

The sections are presented in the following order:

Parts of each section overlap with other sections to help you connect all of the analysis as a whole. This dovetailing of information is intentional and integral to fully understanding and implementing the overall methodology in your day-to-day trading.

Also, read *"The Psychology and Discipline of Day Trading"*. No trader can succeed without hands-on knowledge in this area. It was written specifically for stock day traders to provide insight and solutions into issues uniquely associated with stock day trading. It describes effective ways "to tame that thing we call a brain."

The psychology manual's style and approach are somewhat unconventional and hopefully entertaining. Otherwise it would probably end up on a shelf somewhere collecting dust. Read it. Enjoy it. Find yourself described on its pages, and do whatever it takes to mentally achieve the level of trading success that you desire.

I

PRIMARY TRADING STRATEGIES

WIDE RANGE DAYS,

WITH EXTREME CLOSE

WIDE RANGE DAYS, EXTREME CLOSE

"An enhancement: going from "cookie-cutter" patterns to principles"

This setup pattern is referred to as either a Wide Range *day* or Wide Range *bar*. The names are used interchangeably to describe the same thing. It is a day whose range from high to low is greater than the typical range for a particular stock. It also must close at or near its high or low. At or near means within 10 - 15% of its high or within 10 – 15% of its low. A stock whose average daily range is 1 point may have a day that trades 1 1/2 points from high to low during the course of that trading session. This represents a wide range. For it to qualify as an extreme close, the close must be no less than 1/4 point below its high or no greater than 1/4 point above its low. The open of that bar must also be at or near the opposite end of the close. A wider range bar of several points can have its close 3/8 to 1/2 point from the high or low. It should look similar to the bars below:

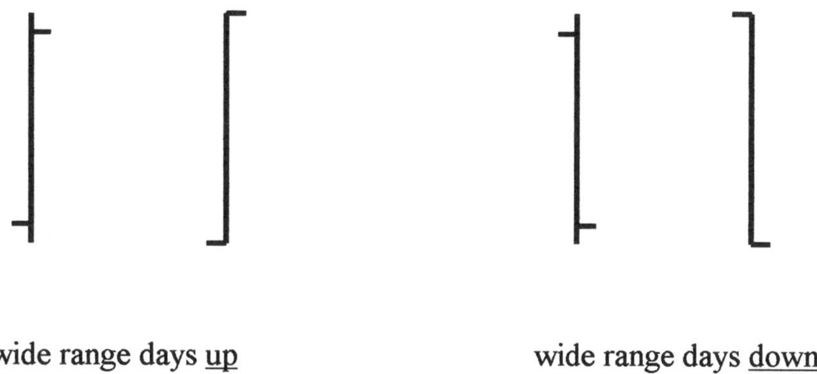

The *"Stock Patterns"* book covers this setup beginning on page 65 and describes how to trade the next day based on 4 different scenarios. These scenarios are determined by where the stock opens the next day in relation to the wide range day's close. The 4 playable opens are shown below.

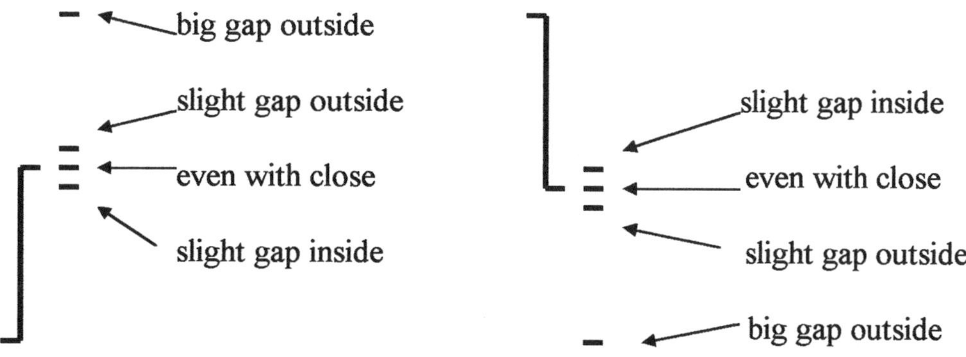

The slight gaps inside or outside must be 3/8 or less away from the close (sometimes 1/2 to 5/8 in higher priced stocks). The big gap outside should be roughly 3 - 5% of the stock's price and at least greater than 1 point. The *"Stock Patterns"* book describes how to play these 4 opens in more detail. As a quick review, the following diagram shows how each open should be traded.

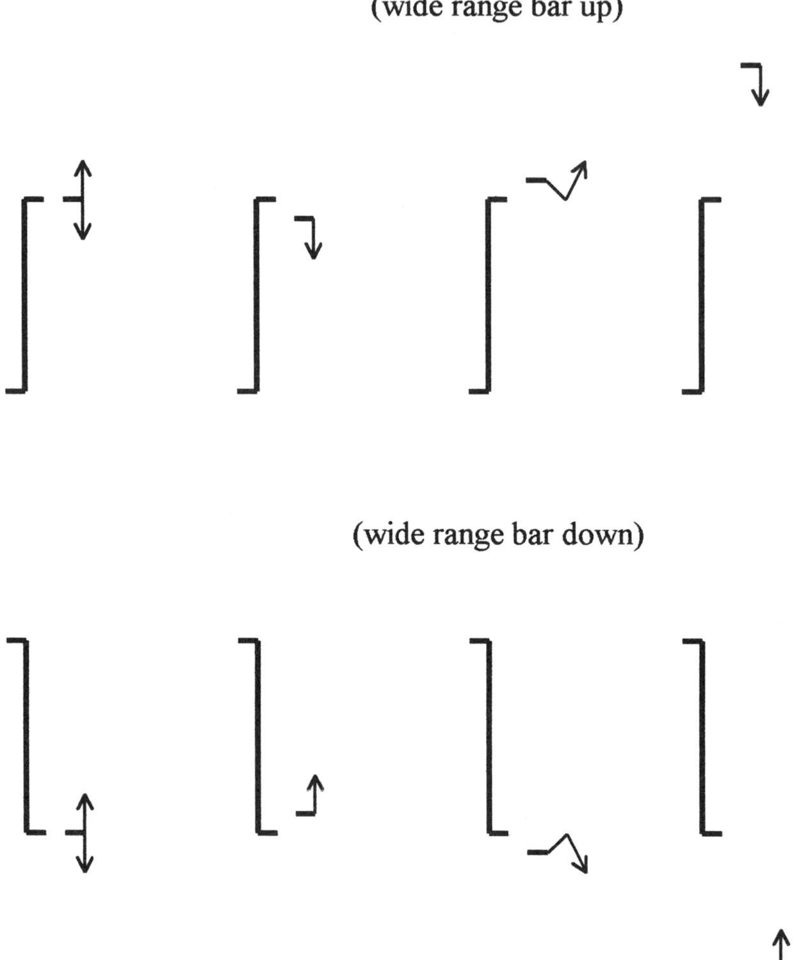

These are specific "cookie-cutter" patterns. There are actually several other ways to play these 4 opens. We're going to the advanced level and trade them based on some underlying principles.

TRADING THE PRINCIPLES OF W/R DAYS

Wide range days are typically followed by a day that also has good directional follow-through with decent price movement. The only problem is that they may go long or short. You won't know until the trading session begins to unfold. Also, **this setup is very dependent upon the direction of the intraday market indices** that should be followed on a 5 minute chart (the NASDAQ composite and SP-500 futures).

Just as price support and resistance can be seen on a historical daily bar chart, the same phenomenon occurs on a micro scale with wide range days. Specifically, the close of the wide range day serves as support/resistance. This fact opens the door to many possibilities as you observe how the price action reacts early in the trading session to the close of the wide range day. This applies only to the 3 opening setups that are near to the prior day's close. The big gap outside operates on a different principle covered later.

The best way to think of the open is to ask yourself, "is there anything in the way to hinder movement to the upside or the downside?" That "thing" which might be in the way is the wide range day's close. If the stock opens slightly inside of a wide range bar up, then the close of the prior day represents a micro resistance point if the stock begins to move to the upside. To the downside there is nothing in the way to prohibit it moving down in an attempt to retrace the wide range day.

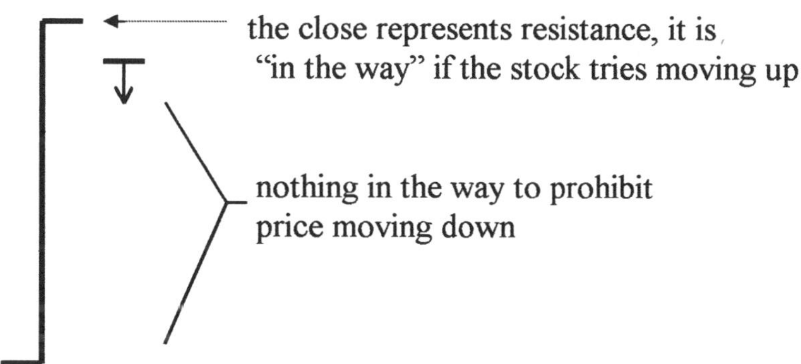

Does this mean that you can only play this stock short? Definitely not! There are 3 playable scenarios with the *slight gap inside* which are based on the principles of micro support/resistance of the wide range day's close (in this case representing resistance). Here they are:

(slight gap inside)

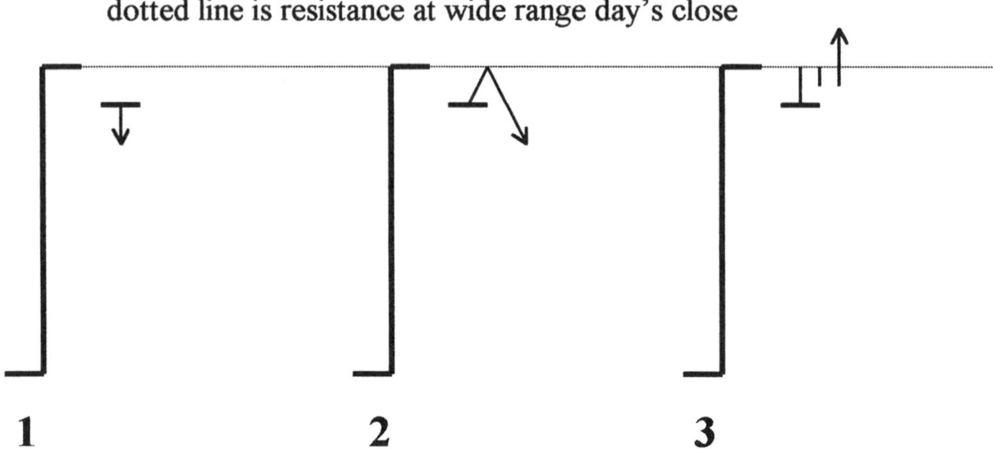

1) The stock opens and immediately begins to move down. It is a good sell no further than 3/8 of a point from the open. Nothing is in the way to halt a down move.

2) The stock opens and immediately moves up only to encounter resistance at the prior day's close. It *reacts quickly* off of this price level and begins to immediately sell off. It is a sell as it penetrates down through its open from a few minutes earlier. The key factor here is that the resistance was confirmed by a quick reaction off of the prior day's close followed by a reverse in direction downward. Direction was further confirmed by its penetration down through the open. Now there is nothing in the way to halt movement to the downside.

3) The stock opens and immediately moves up to resistance at the prior day's close. It presses up against this level for 5 to 15 minutes where it penetrates as a breakout to the upside. This is a buy candidate as it breaks this price level. The key factor in this instance is that the *stock moved up immediately and pressed up against the resistance level* showing strength. It must spend at least 5+ minutes pressing against this level to be a good *long* play. If it trades right up through this level off of the open then it is not a good trade setup and will usually show less follow-through.

Let's distill the principles behind the dynamics of price action from the scenarios shown above:

- If a stock begins to move in a direction where nothing is in the way, it has higher odds of continuing in that direction.
- If a resistance (or support) level is tested and immediately reacted off of, then odds point to that level remaining intact. The move back through the open confirms the most likely direction of follow-through for the stock.
- If a resistance (or support) level is immediately tested off of the open, then it must press against that level for a short time (5+ minutes, but preferably 10+) to indicate its strength in that direction. A penetration of that level confirms the likely direction of that stock with higher odds of significant follow-through.

These are the underlying principles that affect price on the open after a wide range day with extreme close. Remember them well! They apply to the 3 opening setups: slightly inside, slightly outside, and even with the close. These principles must be acted upon in conjunction with the direction of the market indices.

Can you see how this allows you to evaluate a stock and the market, and to react to what it is telling you? The price action based on these principles allows you to enter a high probability trade <u>either long or short</u>. You aren't limited to a "cookie-cutter" entry pattern that will only permit you to trade in one direction. This is part of the art of trading.

We've looked at the slight gap inside. Now let's cover the other openings for potential trades based upon these principles that are all diagrammed for you. Focus on understanding the dynamics of price action following the wide range day setup.

(open is even with w/r day close)

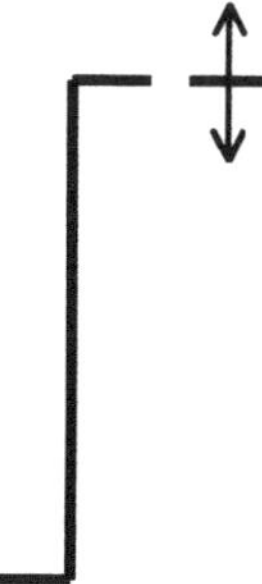

This one is simple. It could move either long or short with nothing in the way to halt its move since it opened at the same price as the wide range day's close. Make sure the direction of the market indices are confirming the stock's direction.

(slight gap outside)

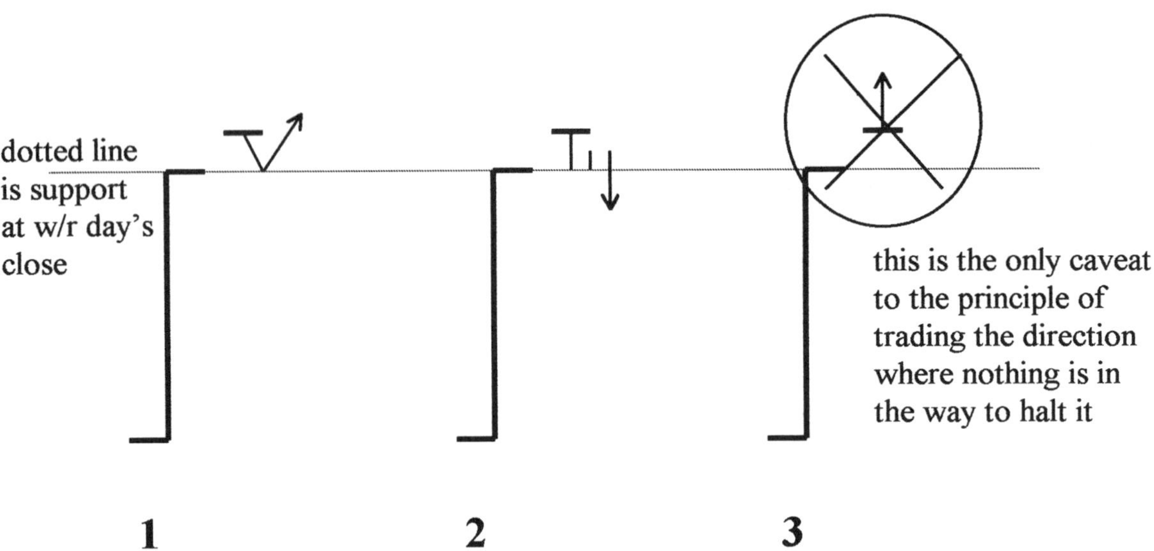

1) The stock opens and immediately sells down only to encounter support at the prior day's close. It *reacts quickly* off of this price level and begins an immediate rally. It is a buy as it penetrates up through its open from a few minutes earlier. The key factor here is that the support was confirmed by a quick reaction off of the prior day's close followed by a reverse in direction upward. Direction was further confirmed by its penetration up through the open. Now there is nothing in the way to halt movement to the upside.

2) The stock opens and immediately moves down to support at the prior day's close. It presses down against this level for roughly 10+ minutes where it penetrates as a breakout to the downside. This is a sell candidate as it breaks this price level. The key factor here is that the *stock moved down immediately and pressed down against the support level* showing weakness. It must spend at least 5+ minutes pressing against this level to be a good short play. If it trades right down through this level off of the open then it is not a good trade setup and will usually show less follow-through.

3) But it gapped up slightly and it's moving up immediately, there's nothing in the way, can't I buy it? It is best if you don't. This is the only instance where the "principles" do not apply as effectively to the wide range day opening setups. This trade usually will not follow through long. One possibility is to wait for 10+ minutes and look to the 5 minute bar chart to see if it shows price hugging up against the current high of the day. If the market indices start moving long, then you might consider a breakout entry based on the 5 minute chart…but only after 10 minutes into the session. Do not play this long immediately off the open based on the wide range day setup…look to the 5 minute chart further into the session for the intraday setup.

Can you understand the principles at work? Watch these stock setups in the morning, and you will see this taking place on a regular basis. These are high probability trades unfolding for you to find the moment to climb aboard. Take advantage of them.

This brings up an early morning 5 minute bar chart setup from the *"Stock Patterns"* book (page 33, setup #12). It is the "flashback" pattern. Flashbacks take place usually within 10 - 30 minutes of the opening bell. Review this pattern from the book and then go back over the wide range opening setups we've just covered (flashbacks are also covered later in this manual). You will notice how the flashback pattern fits in as an integral part of the morning plays for wide range setups.

What about the 4th opening scenario for the w/r day, extreme close: the big gap outside?

(big gap outside)

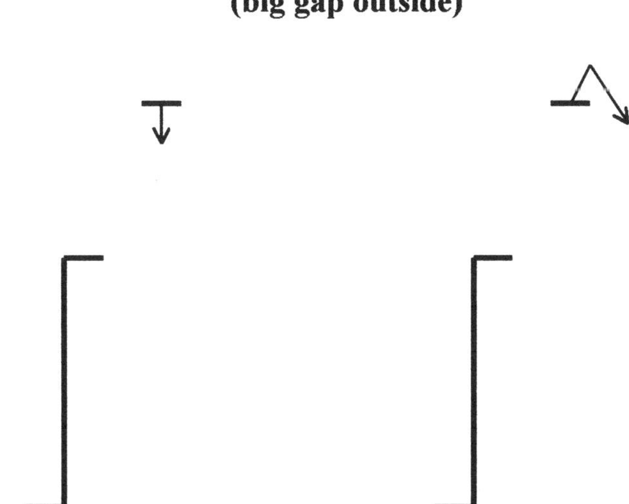

The big gap outside takes place based on some kind of positive news or overall market euphoria for a wide range day up. Vice versa for a big gap outside on a wide range day down. In the above illustration, there are so many buy orders to be filled on the open that the market makers bid the stock up. Since the market makers have to take the other side of the trade, they will be short the stock. Therefore, they bid it up to a level where they are "comfortable" being short the stock. This should tell you something. If they are comfortable being short, it usually means the stock is going down and may fill the gap.

The converse is true on negative news for a wide range down day that has a big gap down. The market makers have opened the stock far enough down to be "comfortable" being long the stock. That means it will usually go up in an attempt to fill the gap. This isn't the case with just wide range days, but is a general market occurrence for stocks that gap significantly up or down on the open. As in the first example above, it could move down immediately for a good shorting opportunity. But sometimes it may have a slight bump up in price off of the open which fails within 15 - 30 minutes as it trades down through its low where a sell-off usually ensues. The converse is true for the big gaps down.

SUMMARY FOR W/R DAYS

It shouldn't be too difficult to make the transition from applying "cookie-cutter" patterns to understanding the principles behind trading wide range days. If you only had a template provided to you, it would limit your trading options for a stock that has the high probability of making a significant move on the day.

By showing you the underlying principles and price dynamics of this daily setup pattern, you have an understanding of what price is doing…and can act on it as a day trader. As the market evolves and rules change (as they always will), you'll be better equipped to evolve along with the market and adjust your trading strategies and techniques.

I cannot overemphasize how important it is to trade this setup and its 4 open scenarios in the direction of the market indices. You are stacking the odds in your favor. If everything isn't lining up like it should for a trade then simply pass it up. It's okay. Trade with quality, don't get sloppy.

Practice recognizing these trades because speed is of the essence. The morning trades often yield explosive opportunities of strong price moves driven by strong morning volume. But do not chase these trades beyond the appropriate entry point. You can refer back to the "*Stock Patterns*" book which further details the entry price levels on these opening scenarios with the wide range bar pattern (beginning on page 65).

The next page summarizes w/r day trades (based on principles) with diagrams as a quick reference source for you.

ADVANCED W/R DAY ENTRIES – Summary Graphs

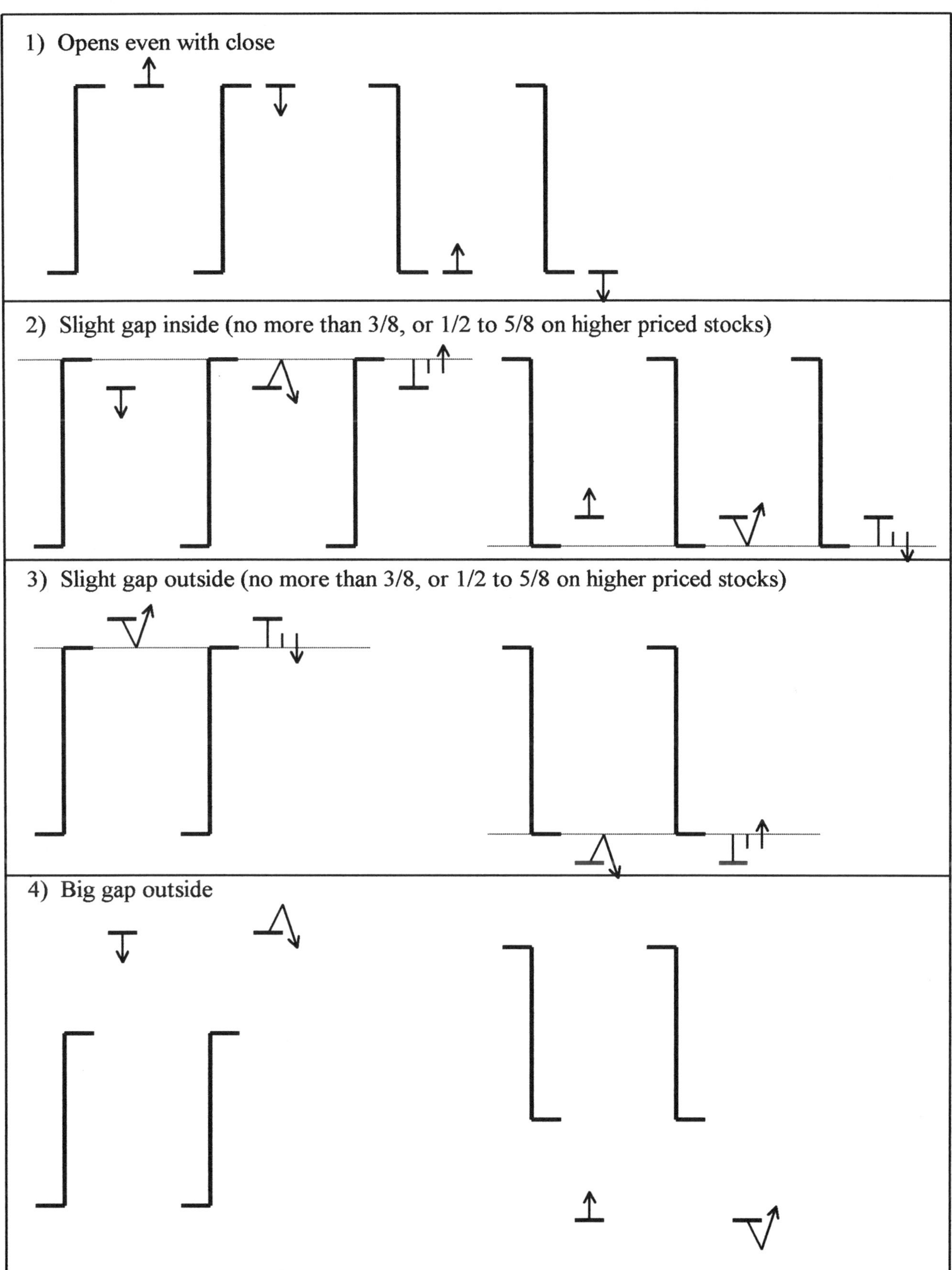

AN ADDITIONAL NUANCE TO W/R DAY TRADES

You have seen how the close of the w/r day serves as micro support and resistance. The same phenomenon occurs with the w/r day's high or low in a few specific instances with the 3 setups that open nearest the w/r day's close. In the wide range day up , it is the high of the w/r day that may serve as support/resistance. In the wide range day down , it is the low that may provide the micro support/resistance. Each tradable scenario is diagrammed below. Support/resistance is indicated by the dashed line.

(wide range days up)

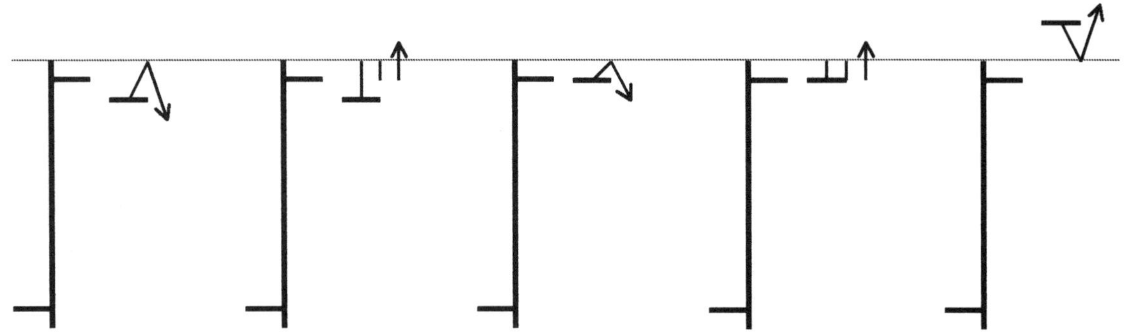

(wide range days down)

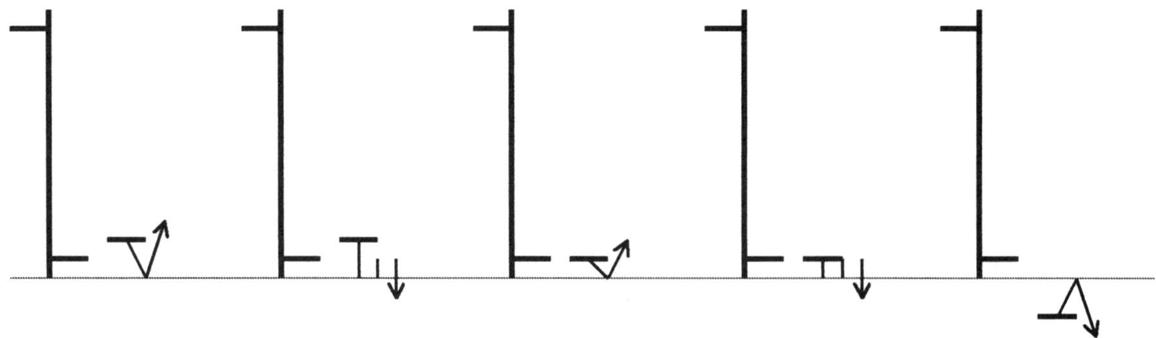

As you can tell, the principles are the same with micro support and resistance at the high and low of the w/r day. These price dynamics dovetail perfectly with using the close as a support/resistance point. None of the patterns contradict, they simply offer additional trading scenarios as you watch the price action unfold in the morning.

Again, the key is your flexibility and speed of interpretation to respond to these principles of price movement. Acting quickly to enter a trade from this pattern isolates a low risk entry point and high probability day trade that can provide good follow-through.

NOW LET'S TAKE IT ONE STEP FURTHER

Since both the close and high (of a w/r day up) or low (of a w/r day down) act as support and resistance areas, you can also consider them as micro support and resistance **zones**. A stock's move does not always have to react off of the exact price level of the w/r day's close, high or low. Because the close is so near the high or low of the w/r day, they can create a zone for price to react (bounce) off of, indicating that particular price *area* has halted and reversed the stock's movement.

This zone is that "something that's in the way" referred to earlier. If a stock trades up to or down to that zone and pushes against it for 5 to 10 minutes or more in the first 30 minutes to 1 hour of trading, be ready for a potential breakout trade. The 5 minute bar chart will aid you in seeing this as the trading session unfolds. This is a more conceptual, yet specific way to trade the w/r days. As always, make sure the market indices favor the direction of any trade you choose to enter.

To help you visualize how these zones appear on a chart, I've taken the previous page and substituted ellipses as opposed to the hard and fast dashed line drawn at the specific price level of the w/r day's high, low and close. Watch how this phenomenon plays out on your daily and 5 minute bar charts in real time trading.

The diagrams of these zones are on the following page.

W/R DAY MICRO SUPPORT & RESISTANCE AS ***ZONES***

In the wide range day up , it is the close and high of the w/r day that may serve as a support/resistance zone. In the wide range day down , it is the low and close that may provide the micro support/resistance zone. Each tradable scenario is diagrammed below. Support/resistance zones are indicated by the ellipses.

(wide range days up)

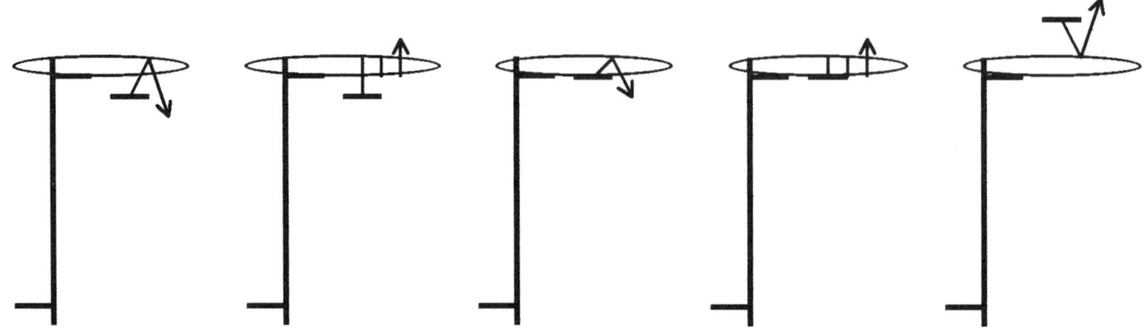

(wide range days down)

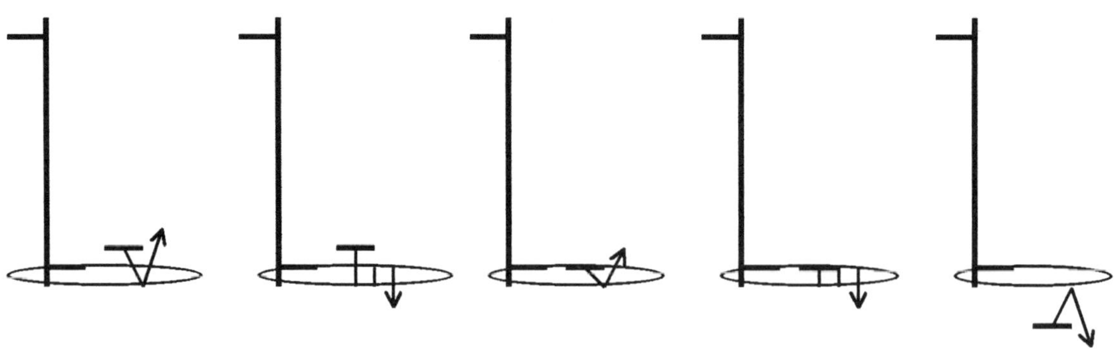

Actual chart examples follow that show first a daily and then a 5 minute bar chart for each stock. Visually tying both charts together helps you to recognize and act on these potential high probability trades.

Daily (Left) STARBUCKS CORP Bar MA (P=50)
1998
1999
SHORT SELL
62 60 58 56 54 52 50 48 46 44 42 40 38 36
28 30N 4 6 10 12 16 18 20 24 27 D 3 7 9 11 15 17 21 23 28 30 J 6 8 12 14 19 21 25 27 29F 3 5 9 11 16 18 22 24 26M 3 5 9

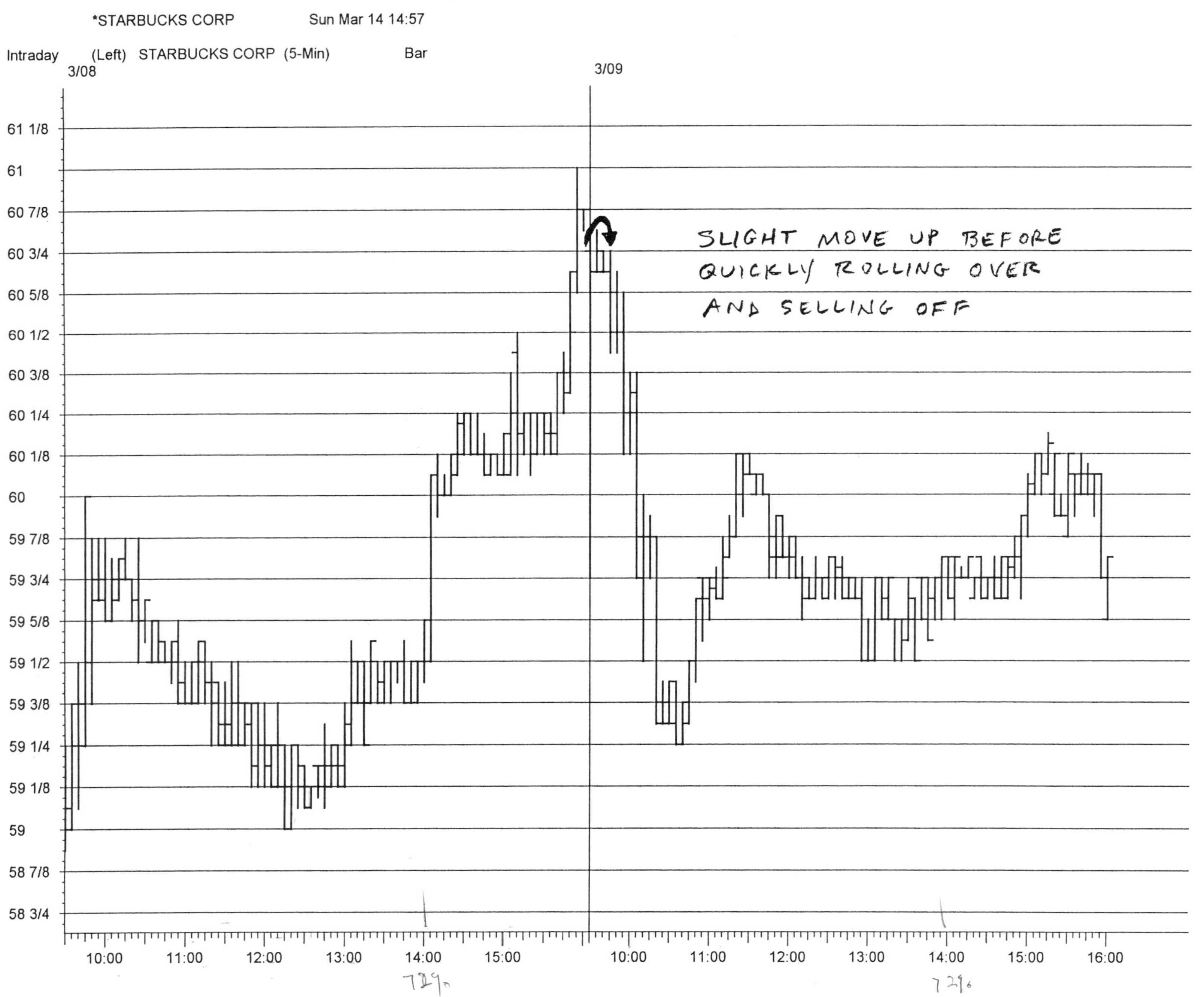

*STARBUCKS CORP
Sun Mar 14 14:57
Intraday
(Left) STARBUCKS CORP (5-Min)
Bar
3/08
3/09
61 1/8
61
60 7/8
60 3/4
60 5/8
60 1/2
60 3/8
60 1/4
60 1/8
60
59 7/8
59 3/4
59 5/8
59 1/2
59 3/8
59 1/4
59 1/8
59
58 7/8
58 3/4
10:00
11:00
12:00
13:00
14:00
15:00
10:00
11:00
12:00
13:00
14:00
15:00
16:00
SLIGHT MOVE UP BEFORE
QUICKLY ROLLING OVER
AND SELLING OFF

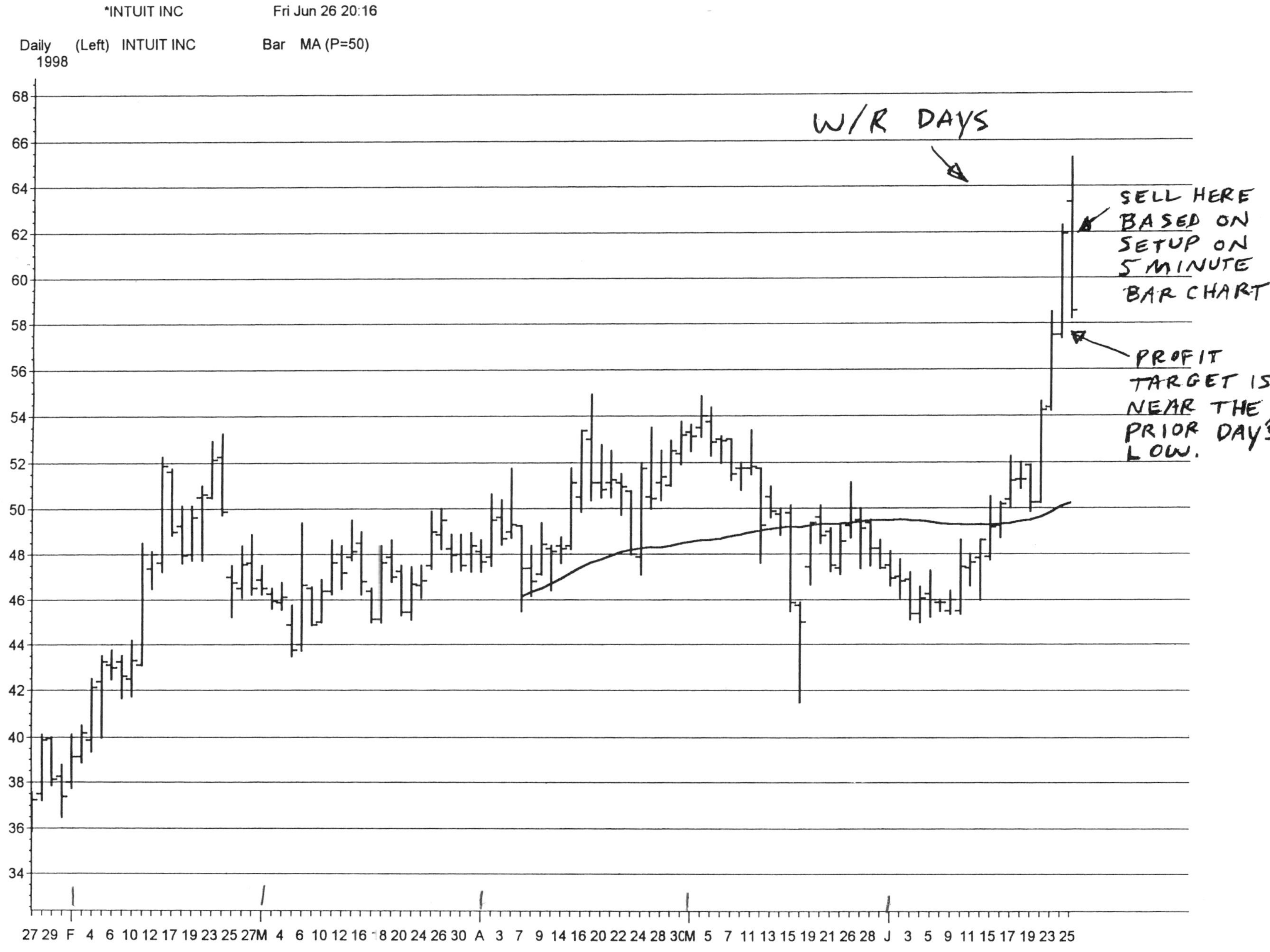
*INTUIT INC
Fri Jun 26 20:16
Daily 1998
(Left) INTUIT INC
Bar MA (P=50)
68 66 64 62 60 58 56 54 52 50 48 46 44 42 40 38 36 34
27 29 F 4 6 10 12 17 19 23 25 27M 4 6 10 12 16 8 20 24 26 30 A 3 7 9 14 16 20 22 24 28 30M 5 7 11 13 15 19 21 26 28 J 3 5 9 11 15 17 19 23 25
W/R DAYS
SELL HERE BASED ON SETUP ON 5 MINUTE BAR CHART
PROFIT TARGET IS NEAR THE PRIOR DAY'S LOW.

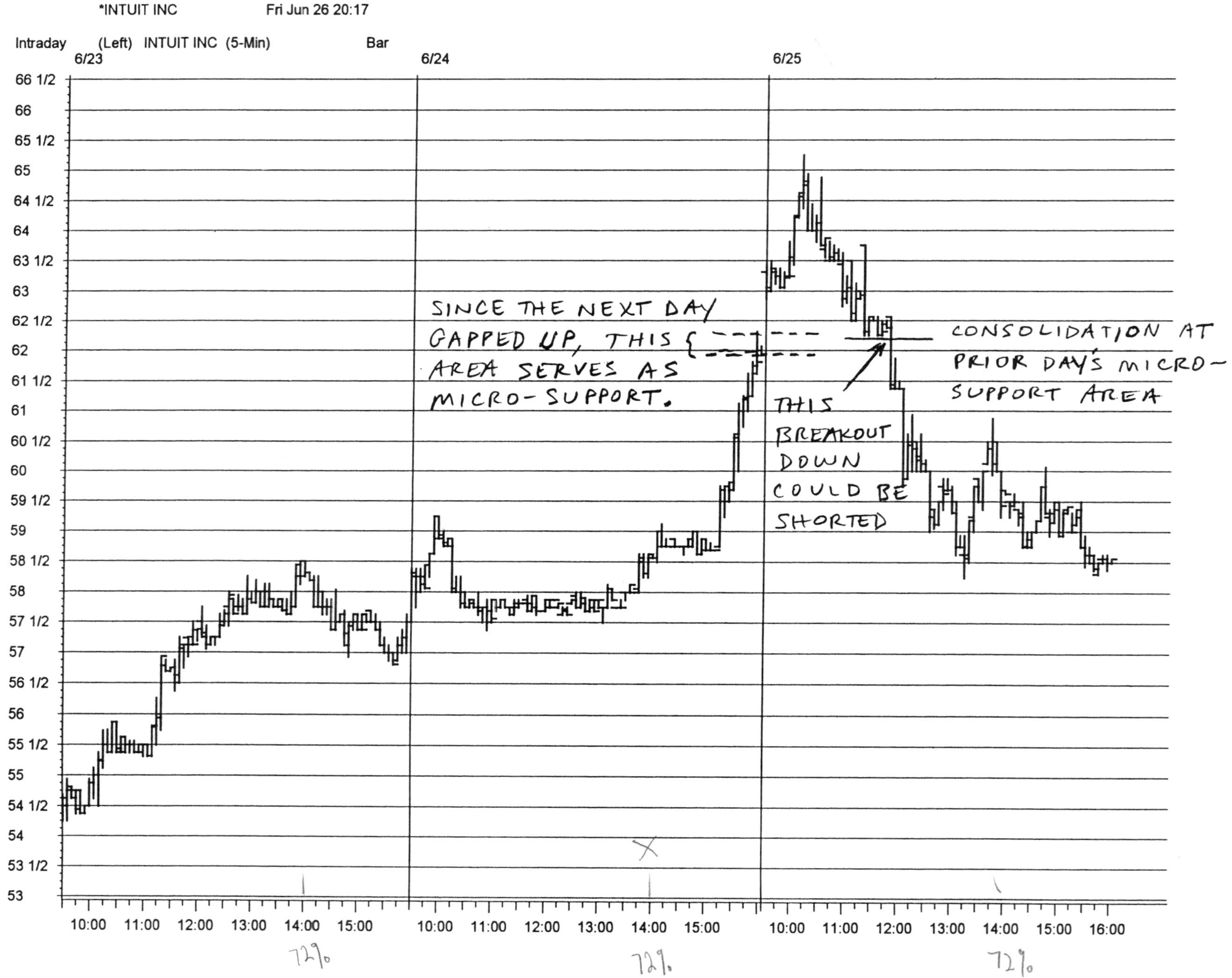
*INTUIT INC
Fri Jun 26 20:17
Intraday
(Left) INTUIT INC (5-Min)
Bar
6/23
6/24
6/25
66 1/2
66
65 1/2
65
64 1/2
64
63 1/2
63
62 1/2
62
61 1/2
61
60 1/2
60
59 1/2
59
58 1/2
58
57 1/2
57
56 1/2
56
55 1/2
55
54 1/2
54
53 1/2
53
10:00
11:00
12:00
13:00
14:00
15:00
16:00
SINCE THE NEXT DAY GAPPED UP, THIS AREA SERVES AS MICRO-SUPPORT.
CONSOLIDATION AT PRIOR DAY'S MICRO-SUPPORT AREA
THIS BREAKOUT DOWN COULD BE SHORTED
72%
72%
72%

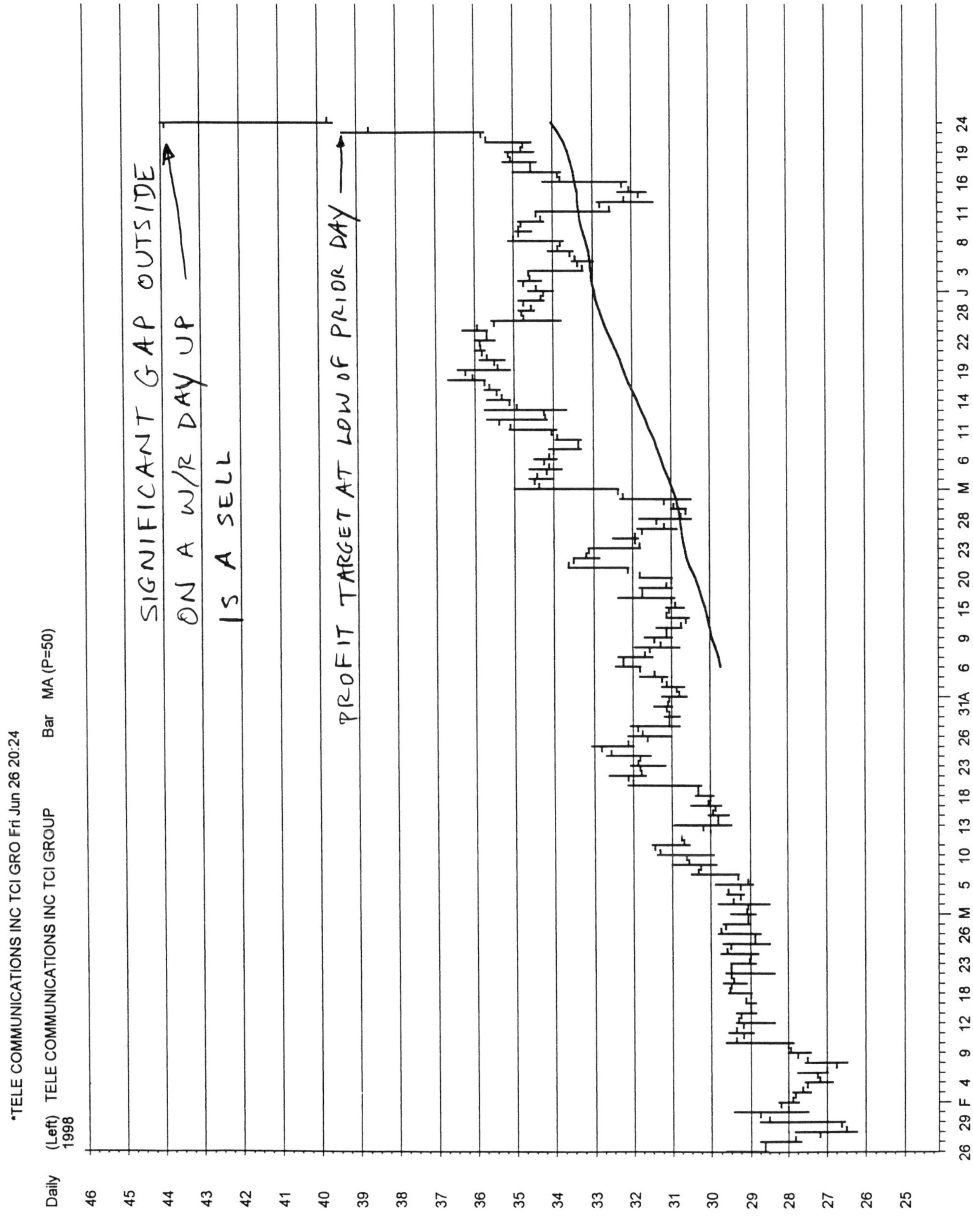

*TELE COMMUNICATIONS INC TCI GRO Fri Jun 26 20:24

Daily (Left) 1998 TELE COMMUNICATIONS INC TCI GROUP Bar MA (P=50)

46
45
44
43
42
41
40
39
38
37
36
35
34
33
32
31
30
29
28
27
26
25

26 29 F 4 9 12 18 23 26 M 5 10 13 18 23 26 31A 6 9 15 20 23 28 M 6 11 14 19 22 28 J 3 8 11 16 19 24

SIGNIFICANT GAP OUTSIDE
ON A W/R DAY UP
IS A SELL

PROFIT TARGET AT LOW OF PRIOR DAY

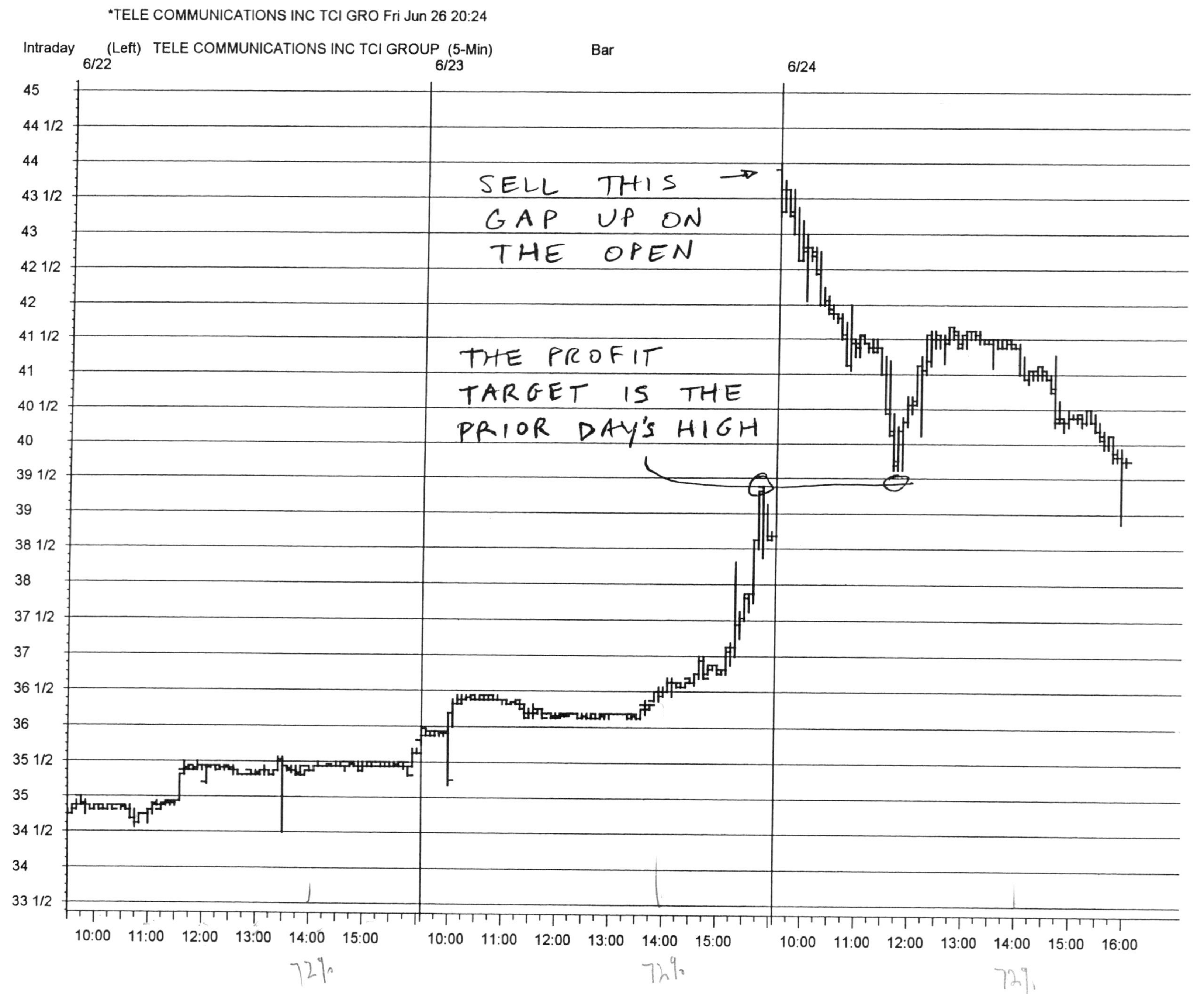
*TELE COMMUNICATIONS INC TCI GRO Fri Jun 26 20:24
Intraday (Left) TELE COMMUNICATIONS INC TCI GROUP (5-Min) Bar
6/22
6/23
6/24
45
44 1/2
44
43 1/2
43
42 1/2
42
41 1/2
41
40 1/2
40
39 1/2
39
38 1/2
38
37 1/2
37
36 1/2
36
35 1/2
35
34 1/2
34
33 1/2
10:00 11:00 12:00 13:00 14:00 15:00
10:00 11:00 12:00 13:00 14:00 15:00
10:00 11:00 12:00 13:00 14:00 15:00 16:00
SELL THIS GAP UP ON THE OPEN
THE PROFIT TARGET IS THE PRIOR DAY'S HIGH

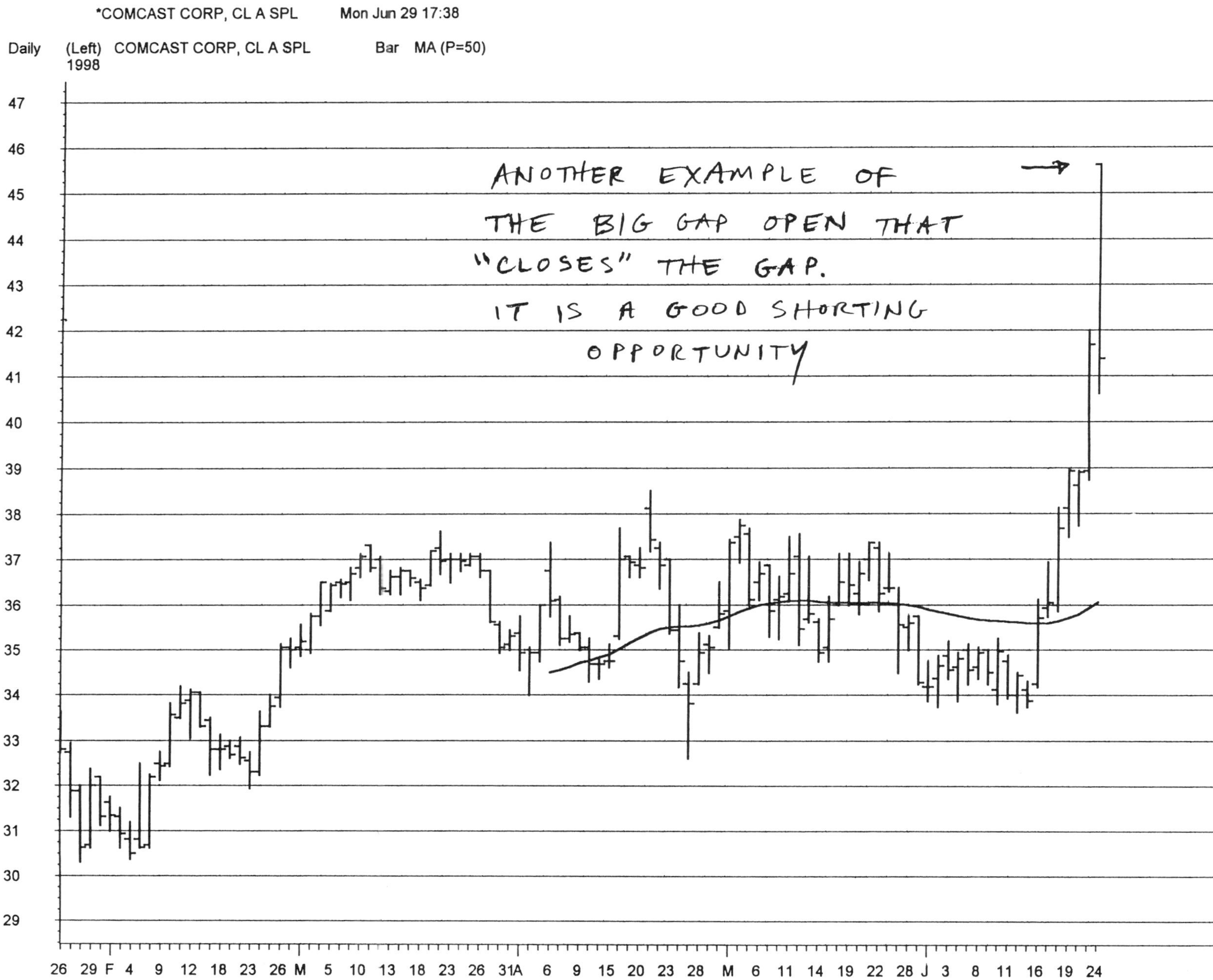
*COMCAST CORP, CL A SPL Mon Jun 29 17:38
Daily (Left) COMCAST CORP, CL A SPL Bar MA (P=50)
1998
47
46
45
44
43
42
41
40
39
38
37
36
35
34
33
32
31
30
29
26 29 F 4 9 12 18 23 26 M 5 10 13 18 23 26 31A 6 9 15 20 23 28 M 6 11 14 19 22 28 J 3 8 11 16 19 24
ANOTHER EXAMPLE OF
THE BIG GAP OPEN THAT
"CLOSES" THE GAP.
IT IS A GOOD SHORTING
OPPORTUNITY

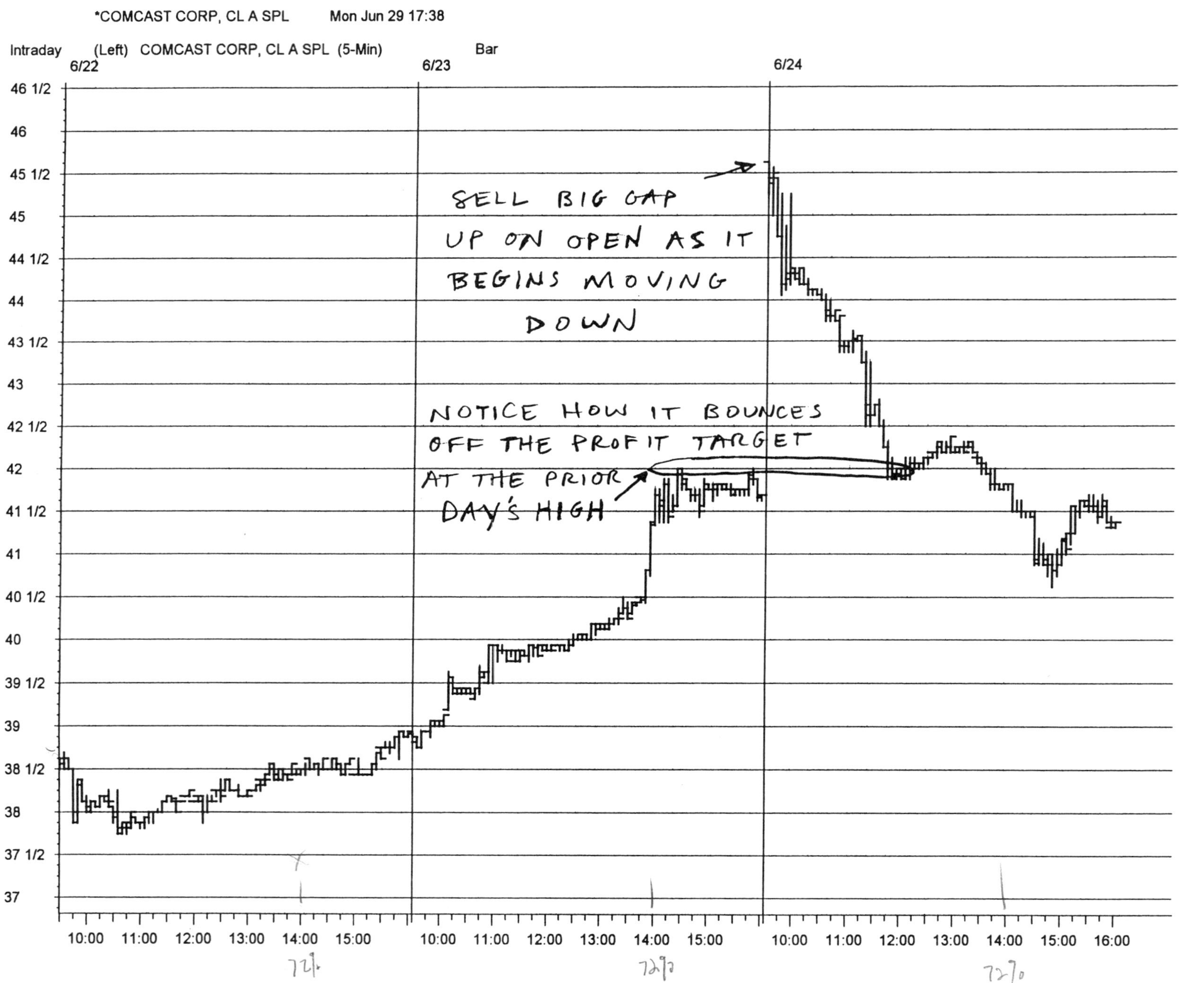
*COMCAST CORP, CL A SPL
Mon Jun 29 17:38
Intraday
(Left) COMCAST CORP, CL A SPL (5-Min)
Bar
6/22
6/23
6/24
46 1/2
46
45 1/2
45
44 1/2
44
43 1/2
43
42 1/2
42
41 1/2
41
40 1/2
40
39 1/2
39
38 1/2
38
37 1/2
37
10:00
11:00
12:00
13:00
14:00
15:00
16:00
SELL BIG GAP UP ON OPEN AS IT BEGINS MOVING DOWN
NOTICE HOW IT BOUNCES OFF THE PROFIT TARGET AT THE PRIOR DAY'S HIGH

*HBO & CO
Mon Jun 29 18:00
Daily
(Left) HBO & CO
1998
Bar MA (P=50)
← BUY POINT

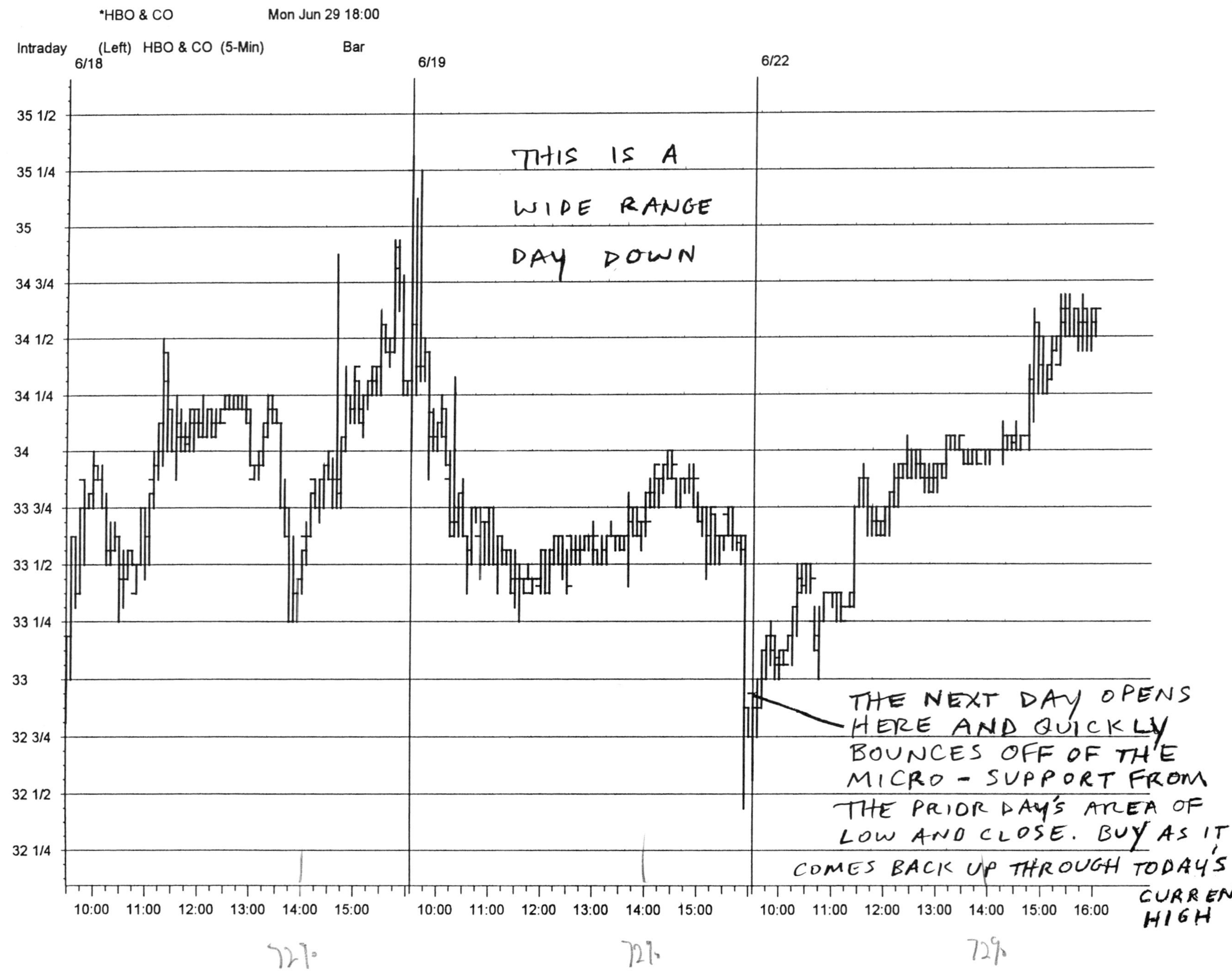
*HBO & CO
Mon Jun 29 18:00
Intraday
(Left) HBO & CO (5-Min)
Bar
6/18
6/19
6/22
35 1/2
35 1/4
35
34 3/4
34 1/2
34 1/4
34
33 3/4
33 1/2
33 1/4
33
32 3/4
32 1/2
32 1/4
10:00 11:00 12:00 13:00 14:00 15:00
10:00 11:00 12:00 13:00 14:00 15:00
10:00 11:00 12:00 13:00 14:00 15:00 16:00
THIS IS A WIDE RANGE DAY DOWN
THE NEXT DAY OPENS HERE AND QUICKLY BOUNCES OFF OF THE MICRO - SUPPORT FROM THE PRIOR DAY'S AREA OF LOW AND CLOSE. BUY AS IT COMES BACK UP THROUGH TODAY'S CURRENT HIGH

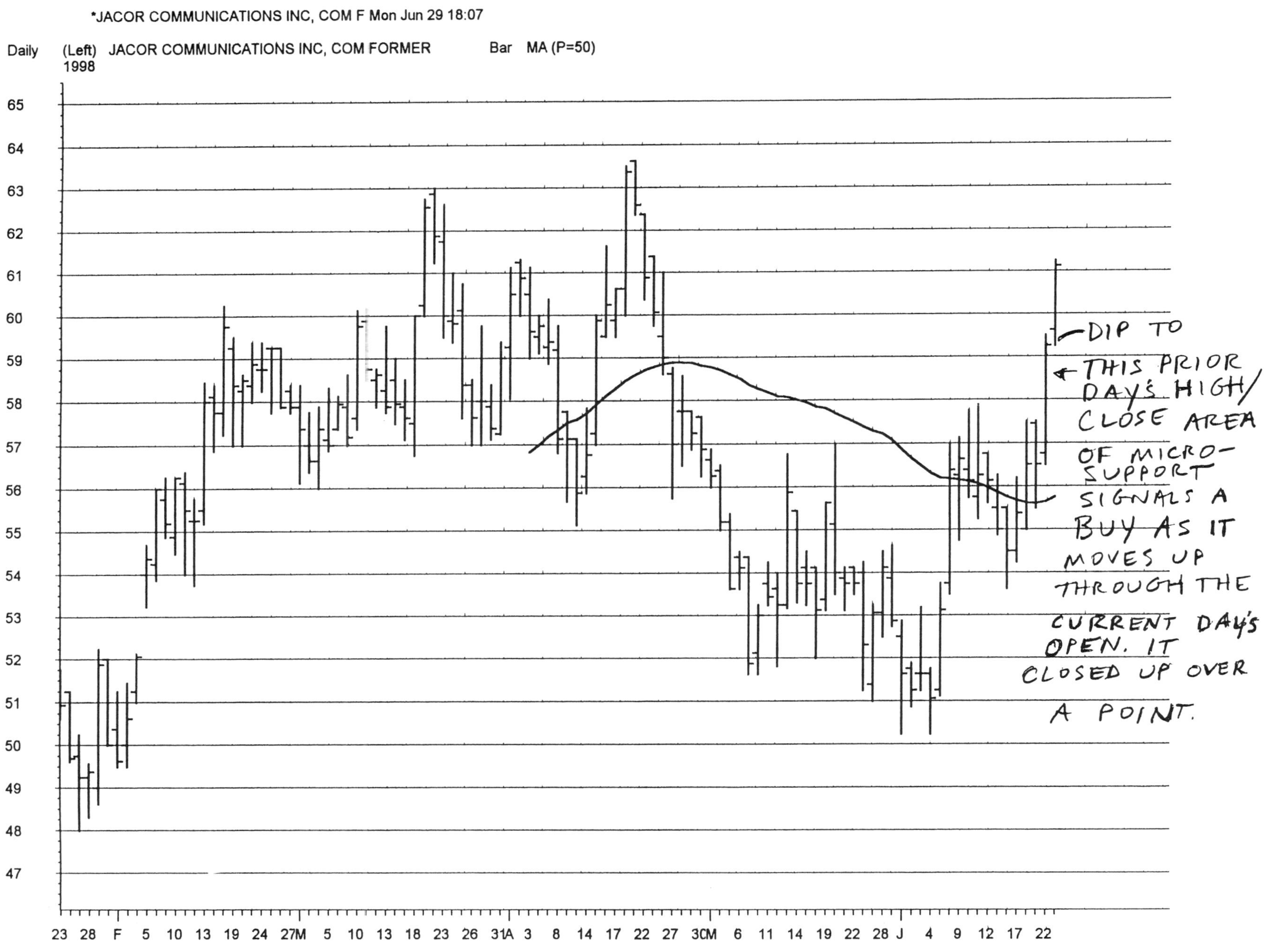
*JACOR COMMUNICATIONS INC, COM F Mon Jun 29 18:07
Daily (Left) JACOR COMMUNICATIONS INC, COM FORMER Bar MA (P=50)
1998
65
64
63
62
61
60
59
58
57
56
55
54
53
52
51
50
49
48
47
23 28 F 5 10 13 19 24 27M 5 10 13 18 23 26 31A 3 8 14 17 22 27 30M 6 11 14 19 22 28 J 4 9 12 17 22
DIP TO
THIS PRIOR DAY'S HIGH/CLOSE AREA OF MICRO-SUPPORT SIGNALS A BUY AS IT MOVES UP THROUGH THE CURRENT DAY'S OPEN. IT CLOSED UP OVER A POINT.

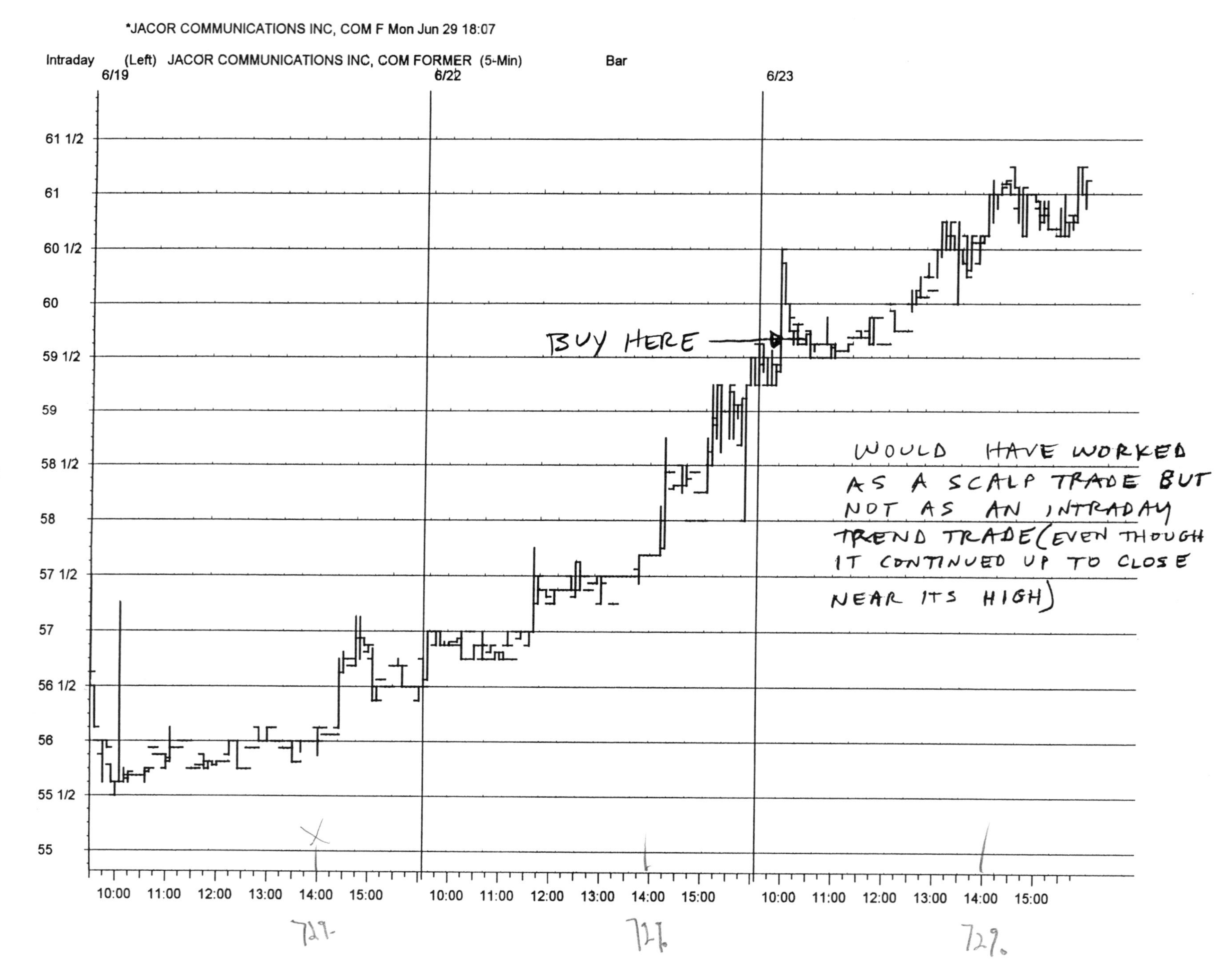
*JACOR COMMUNICATIONS INC, COM F Mon Jun 29 18:07
Intraday (Left) JACOR COMMUNICATIONS INC, COM FORMER (5-Min) Bar
6/19
6/22
6/23
61 1/2
61
60 1/2
60
59 1/2
59
58 1/2
58
57 1/2
57
56 1/2
56
55 1/2
55
10:00 11:00 12:00 13:00 14:00 15:00
10:00 11:00 12:00 13:00 14:00 15:00
10:00 11:00 12:00 13:00 14:00 15:00
BUY HERE
WOULD HAVE WORKED AS A SCALP TRADE BUT NOT AS AN INTRADAY TREND TRADE (EVEN THOUGH IT CONTINUED UP TO CLOSE NEAR ITS HIGH)

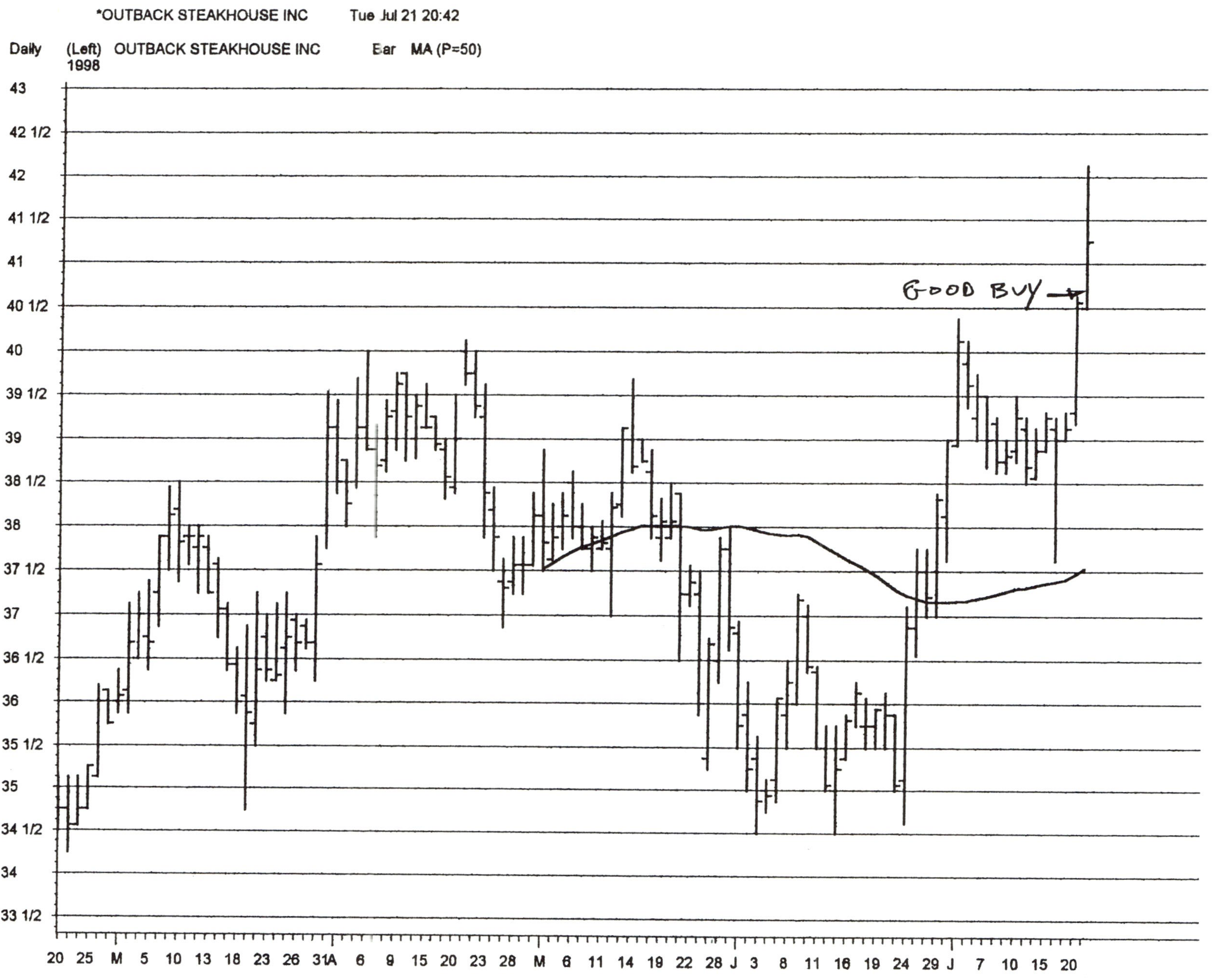
*OUTBACK STEAKHOUSE INC
Tue Jul 21 20:42
Daily
(Left) OUTBACK STEAKHOUSE INC
Bar
MA (P=50)
1998
43 42 1/2 42 41 1/2 41 40 1/2 40 39 1/2 39 38 1/2 38 37 1/2 37 36 1/2 36 35 1/2 35 34 1/2 34 33 1/2
20 25 M 5 10 13 18 23 26 31A 6 9 15 20 23 28 M 6 11 14 19 22 28 J 3 8 11 16 19 24 29 J 7 10 15 20
GOOD BUY

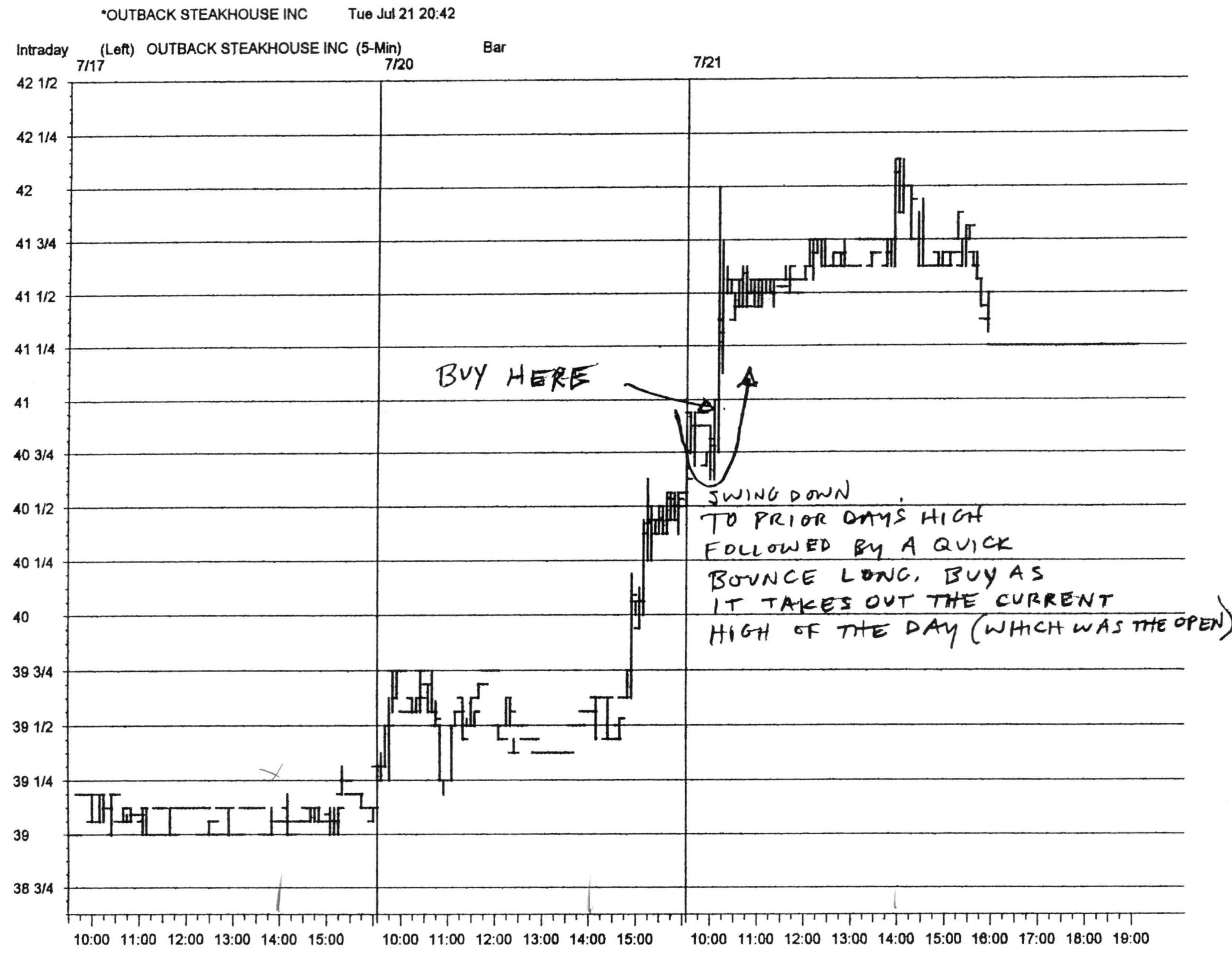
*OUTBACK STEAKHOUSE INC Tue Jul 21 20:42
Intraday (Left) OUTBACK STEAKHOUSE INC (5-Min) Bar
7/17
7/20
7/21
42 1/2
42 1/4
42
41 3/4
41 1/2
41 1/4
41
40 3/4
40 1/2
40 1/4
40
39 3/4
39 1/2
39 1/4
39
38 3/4
10:00 11:00 12:00 13:00 14:00 15:00
10:00 11:00 12:00 13:00 14:00 15:00
10:00 11:00 12:00 13:00 14:00 15:00 16:00 17:00 18:00 19:00
BUY HERE
SWING DOWN
TO PRIOR DAYS HIGH
FOLLOWED BY A QUICK
BOUNCE LONG. BUY AS
IT TAKES OUT THE CURRENT
HIGH OF THE DAY (WHICH WAS THE OPEN)

REVERSAL

SETUPS

<u>REVERSAL SETUPS</u>

"An enhancement: the dynamics behind the best reversal setups"

This section further explains the "reversal setups" from the book, *"Stock Patterns for Day Trading."* Since this price pattern setup using daily bar charts presents one of the strongest potential stock trades (both day trades and multi-day holds), I want to explain the nuances of a true reversal setup and provide a variety of actual examples. Entry points and exit points are covered. The specific factors that constitute a reversal setup, and the factors that negate an *apparent* reversal price setup are also elaborated upon in further detail.

What I describe as a reversal bar, or reversal setup, does not necessarily match the classic definition found in trading literature for a "reversal bar." It has certain characteristics which point to a stock that has expended its up or down price move and is now poised to trade in the opposite direction for one to several days.

I have excerpted 3 pages on the reversal setup pattern from the "1 to 3 Daily Bar Setups" section in the *"Stock Patterns"* book as a review. This is followed by comprehensive diagrams and descriptions of what constitutes a true reversal setup versus what factors negate an apparent reversal setup. Commentary will be provided to explain the subtleties of the pattern in each case. Since this price pattern is one that is best evaluated by "eyeballing" a stock's daily bar chart, numerous diagrams are drawn showing many slight variations along with specific commentary. Annotated chart examples follow, providing you a variety of actual stock reversal setup examples.

As with many trading methods, you often have several, well-defined and specific rules. But your own judgment must also enter into the evaluation to some degree. This is the "art" of trading. I bclicvc this section will help you to better understand and recognize the reversal setups…and trade them with greater success.

REVERSAL BAR SETUP

This 3 bar pattern when completed resembles this:

The setup consists of only the first two bars. The key here is

1) The close of bar 1 must be near its low
2) Bar 2's high must not be much above the low of bar 1
3) Bar 2 must close at or near its high (and preferably have opened near its high as well)
4) Bar 1's high should be 1+ points above the close (or high) of bar 2 to provide a decent profit -- the expectation is for day 3 to attempt to trade up to day 1's high

Bar 2 thus sets up as a potential reversal bar, and you look for a trade on day 3. If day 3 opens at or near the close of day 2 and begins moving up, this may be a good buy at anytime during the trading session of day 3. At this point the 5 minute intraday bar chart can play an additional role if you see consolidation and then a breakout to the upside. This way you have 2 time frames working for you at once (daily and intraday). Buy the breakout. The wider the range of bar 1, the better the trade.

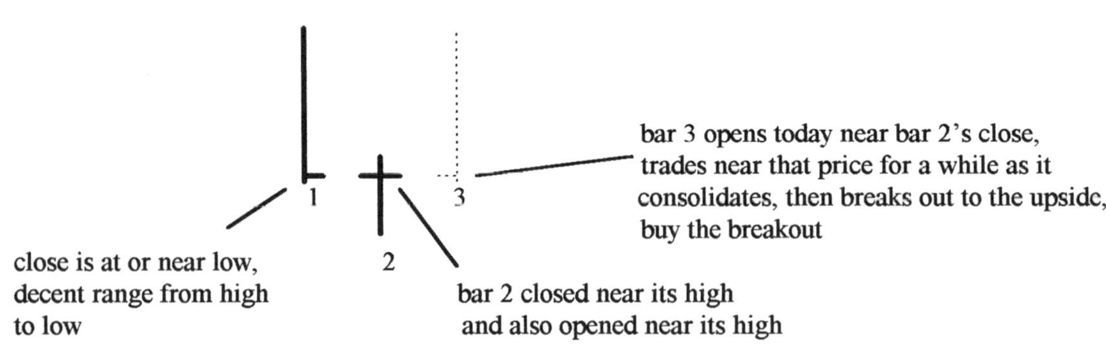

This setup can also have the following look to bar #2 (the reversal bar):

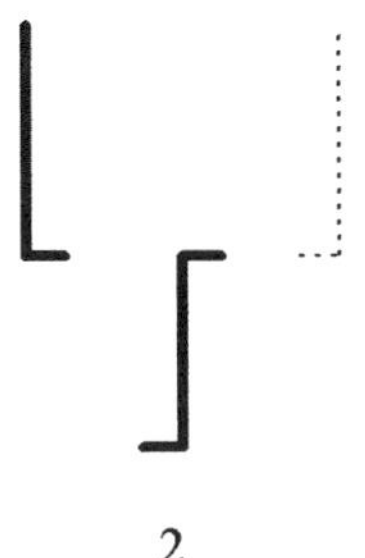

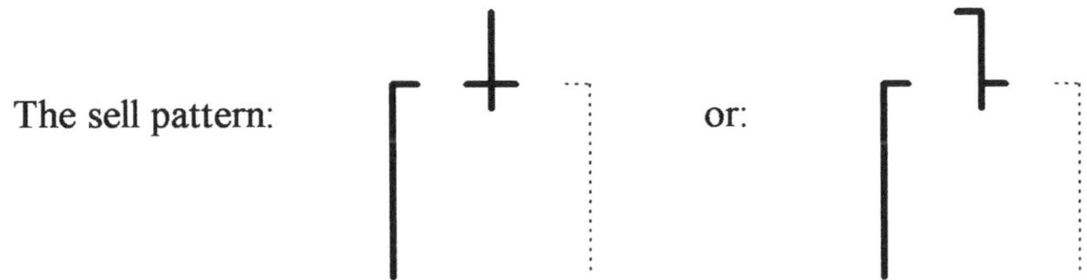

DELAYED REVERSAL SETUP

This is a variation on the 1 bar reversal. It is a 4 bar pattern with 3 bars setting up the trade for the fourth day. Day 1 must close at or near the bottom of that day's range. Day 2 opens at or near the close of day 1 and continues the prior day's sell off. Day 2 must also close at or near the low of that day's range. Day 3 must open at or near the close of day 2 and retrace back up to (or very near) the high of day 2. Also, day 3 must close at or near its high of the day. If the stock opens on day 4 near the close of day 3 and begins to move up, buy it. The wider the range of bar 1, the better the trade.

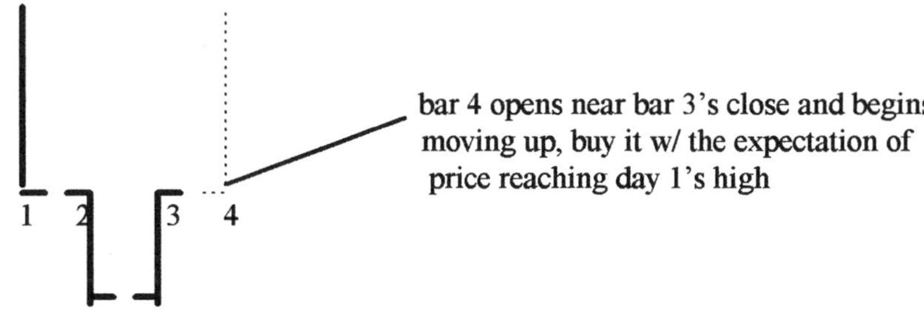

the inverse

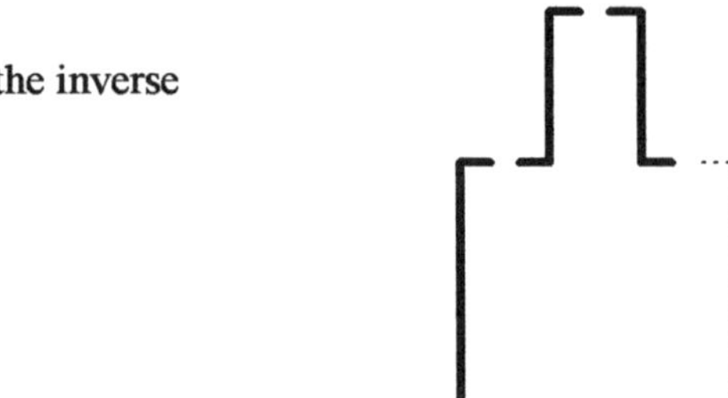

So, how do you find these reversal setup of bars? By trading and reviewing charts daily you will learn to pick out possible setups and earmark those stocks in your mind. A daily analysis worksheet is provided later in the manual. When one of those particular stocks comes across the ticker, you go to that stock's screen and automatically know what you are looking for. If the setup is there, and you're getting a breakout, consider taking the trade. The sell setup is an inverted reversal pattern. In a buy setup the expectation is that the stock will move up to or near the high of bar 1. In the inverted reversal sell setup you would expect the stock to sell off down to or near the low of bar 1.

<u>**THE FOLLOWING POINTS ARE COVERED**</u>:

(for a reversal setup long)

1. How far can the reversal bar extend up into the prior day's range?

2. Where should the close of the reversal bar be in relation to the high or low of the reversal bar's range?

3. How big should the range be from high to low for the day preceding the reversal bar, and where should the close of that day be?

4. Where should the open be on the bar preceding the reversal bar day?

5. How far should the low of the reversal bar extend downward for the best setup?

6. What about multiple day runs up (or down) followed by a reversal bar setup pointing to a trade in the opposite direction?

7. Where to enter the trade on a reversal setup.

8. The intraday dynamics of why the reversal setup works.

9. A quick review of all of the components of the reversal setup pattern.

10. The "delayed reversal setup"

11. <u>**REVERSAL SETUP - ENHANCEMENTS**</u>

***Throughout this section, most reversal setups are shown as the long (buy side) examples. The sell setups for a reversal setup short (including the price dynamics) are the exact same, simply the <u>inverse</u> of what is drawn and described.

1. The reversal bar must not have its high extending very far above the prior day's low and close.

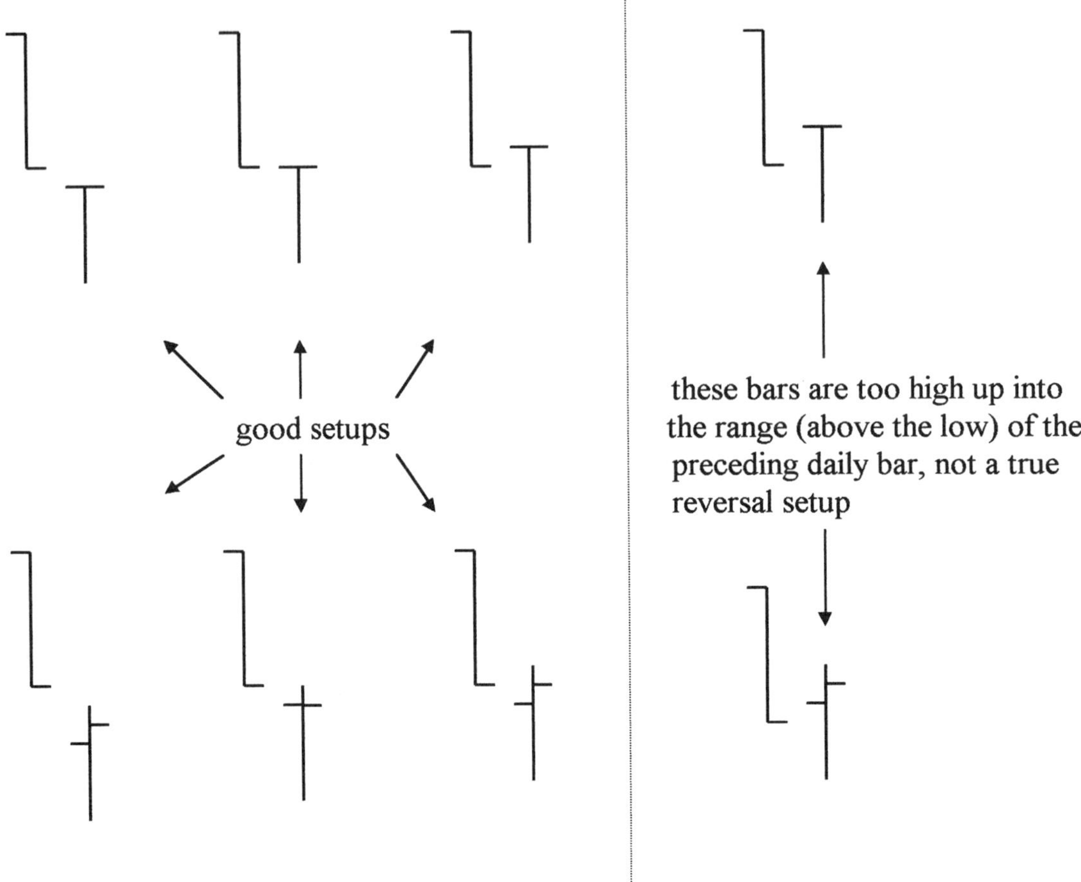

2. The close of the reversal bar must be at or very near the high of its range.

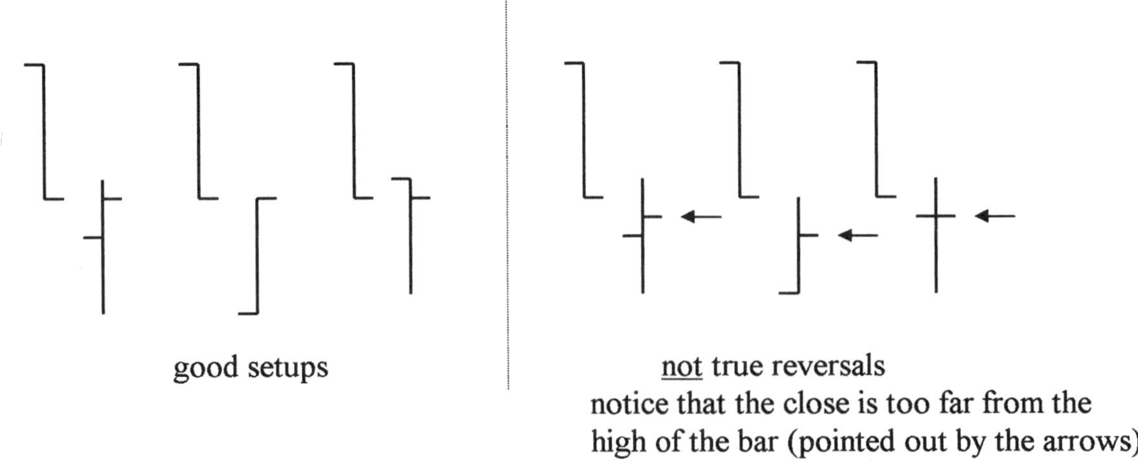

The nearer the close is to the high of the reversal bar, the stronger the potential setup. *The close should be at least in the top 25% of that bars range to even be considered!

3. The day preceding the reversal bar must be at least 1 point or more from high to low <u>and</u> have closed roughly within 15% of its low.

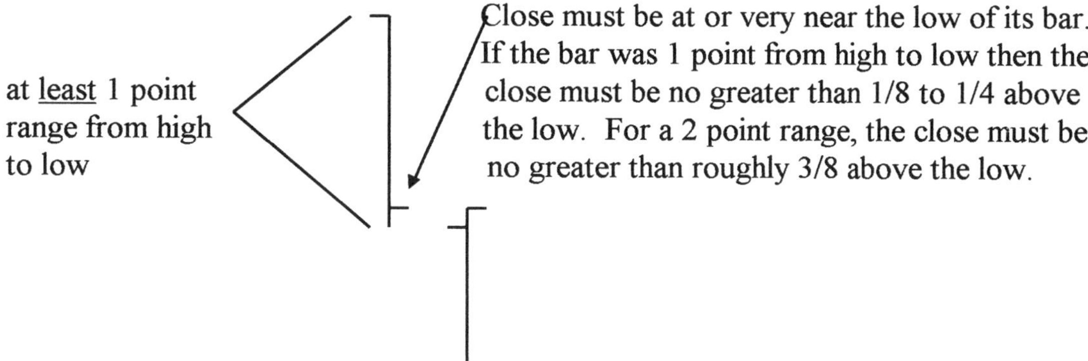

4. The open of the day preceding the reversal bar day must be at or very near its high.

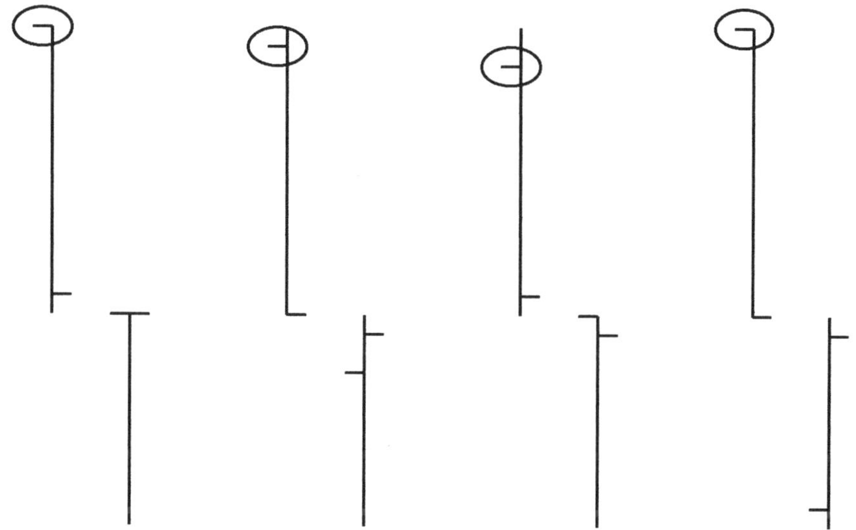

These circled "opens" (above) are all near enough to the high of the bar.

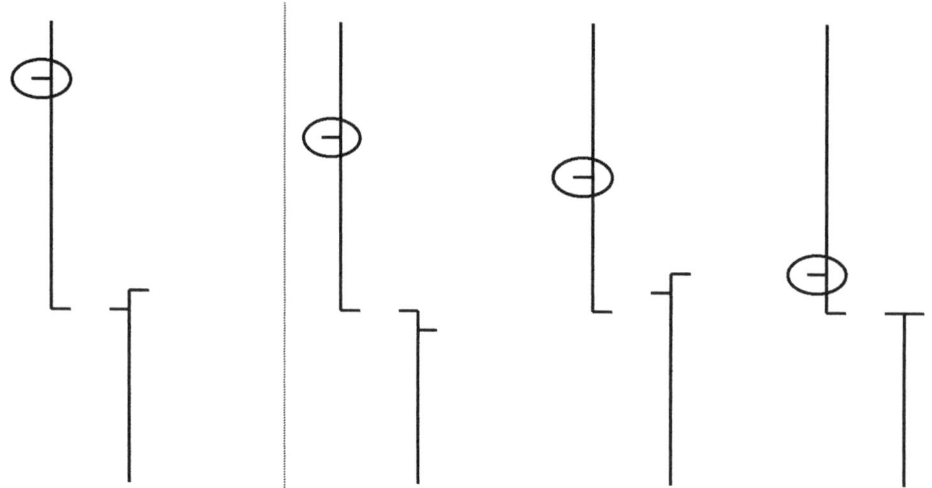

This circled "open" is borderline to being too far from the bar's high --but-- if the rest of the components of the setup are strong, it may be worth considering... especially if that bar's range from high to low is significant i.e. 2 points +

These circled "opens" are definitely too far from the high of the bar.

The ideal bar preceding the reversal bar opens at its high and closes at its low with a range from high to low of 1 1/2 points or more. The further you depart from the "ideal," the more the odds decrease for a follow-through to trade the next day after the reversal bar is in place.

5. The further down the reversal bar's low extends (for the buy setup), the stronger the pattern...too long though, and it's not as effective. It needs some symmetry.

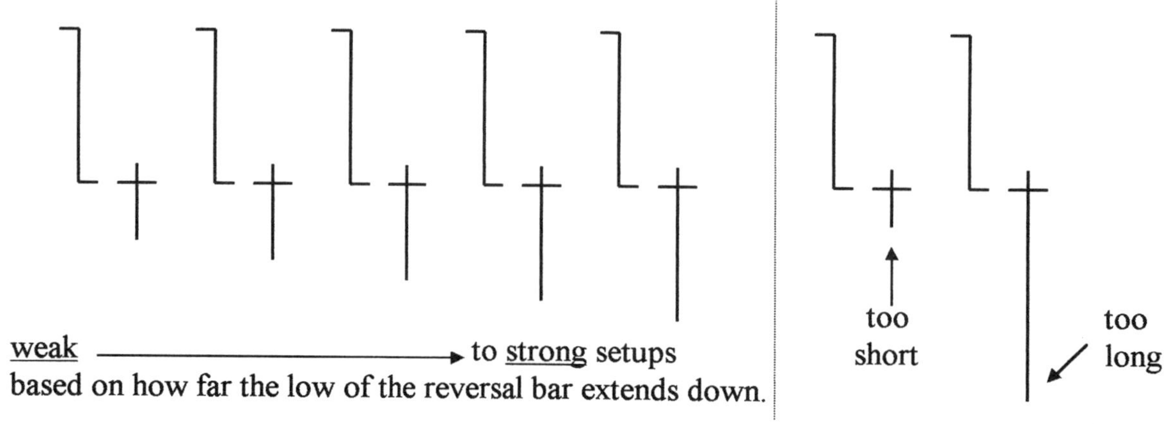

6. A strong 2 + day run-up, followed by a reversal setup, enhances the follow-through potential back in the other direction (sometimes for a multi-day hold). This is a "rubber band" effect with the stock moving too far, too fast, in one direction and is due for a pull back in price.

The Sell Setup

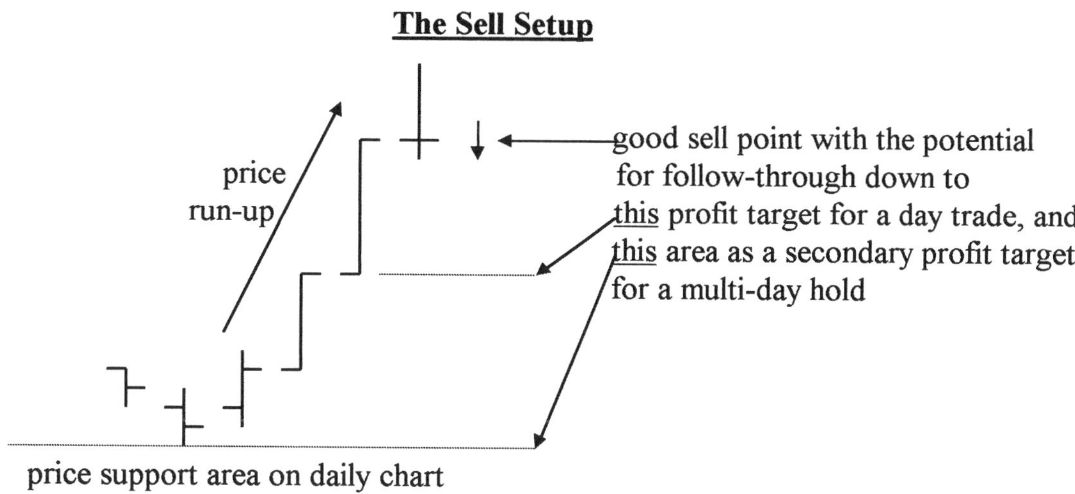

The Buy Setup

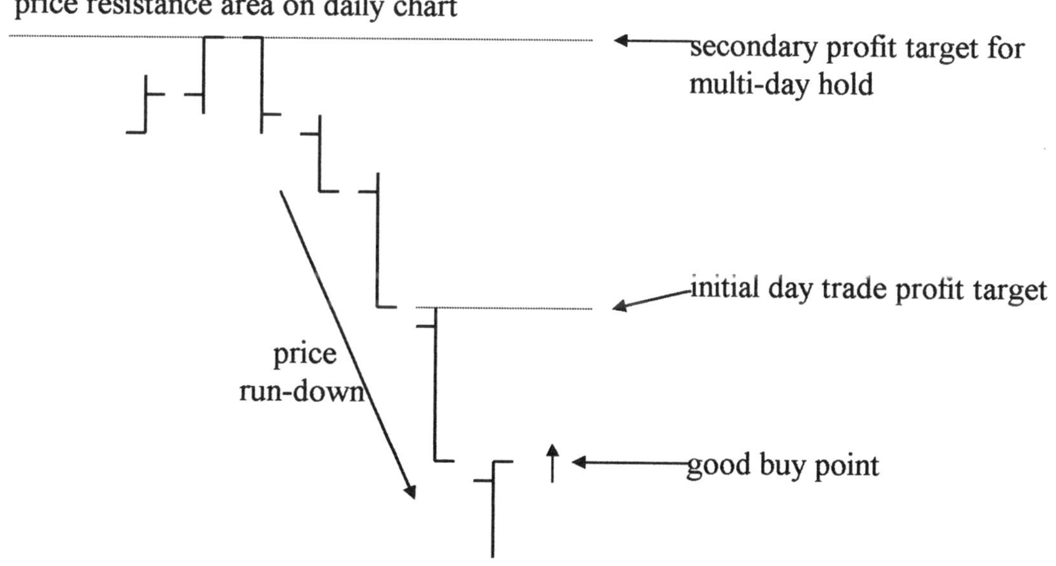

* Always be careful with any multi-day holds since they can gap against you overnight. These setups offer excellent day trade potential. Overnight holds are not recommended due to their risk. This example simply depicts likely price targets.

7. The entry point for a reversal setup trade (the reversal bar long, buy scenario).

   Where the stock opens on the day following the reversal bar determines when and where to consider initiating a long position. This open (for the buy setup) must be evaluated in relation to the close of the prior reversal bar's day. If the stock opens anywhere from 1/8 below the reversal bar's close up to 3/8 above the close, then it may be deemed tradable.

   Once the stock opens in this tradable area, if it begins to move up, immediately buy it. If you cannot get your buy order filled before the stock moves up beyond 3/8 above the reversal bar's close, then pass up the trade. It is better to miss the trade than to get filled at a price that is too far into the initial move off of the open. Also, make sure that the intraday trend of the market indices are moving up in your favor to increase the odds of a successful trade with follow-through potential.

   If the stock opens above or below the "tradable range" described above then it negates the trade.

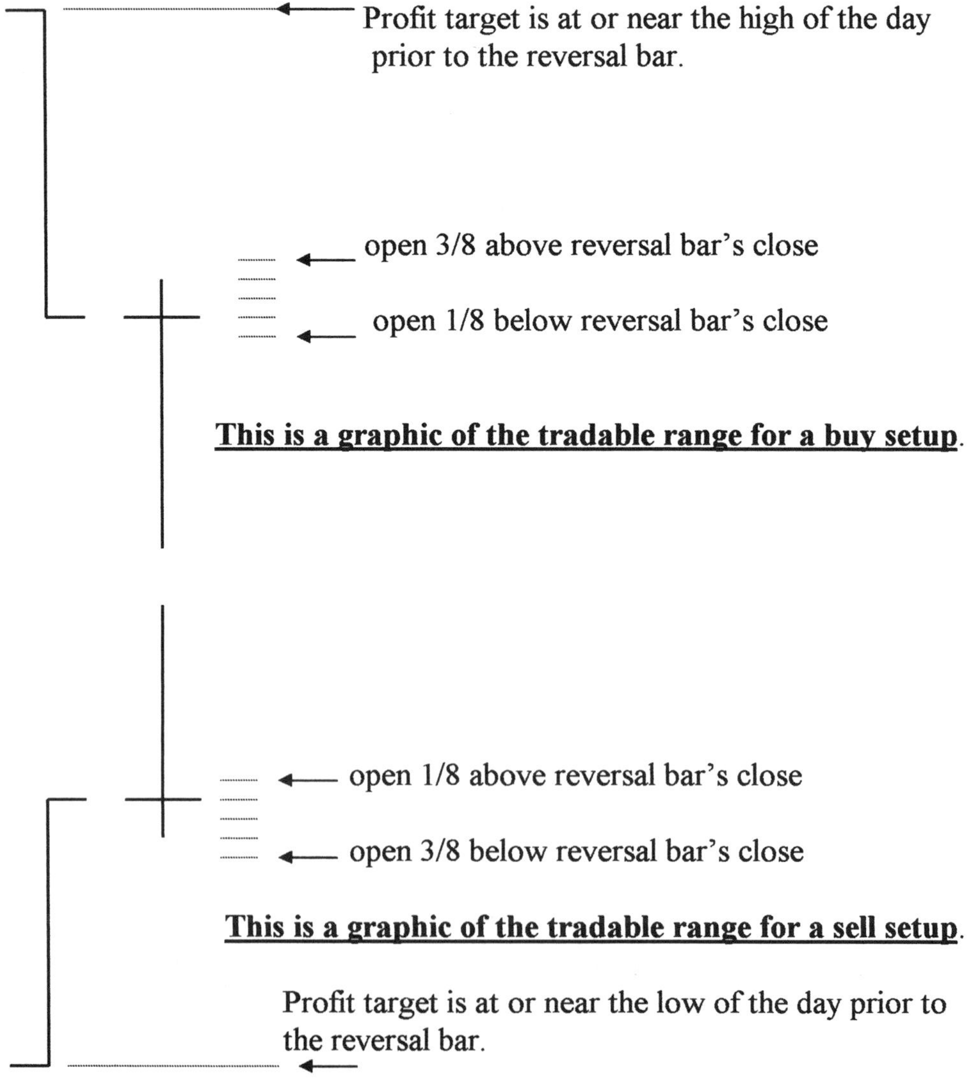

8. The intraday dynamics of why the reversal setup works: For a buy setup, the selling has been expended during the course of the first day and a half whereupon the buyers take over sometime during the reversal day. Once the selling is done and the buyers take over, the stock's price is driven from its low back up to or very near its high of the day where it closes, creating the reversal bar.

   Therefore, the "reversal setup" is a 2 bar setup. The reversal bar and the day preceding it. A glimpse into the intraday action of the price activity of a reversal setup using a 5 minute intraday bar chart demonstrates the buying and selling (supply and demand) dynamics showing why this pattern is so significant.

   Here is an example of how a 5 minute chart might look:

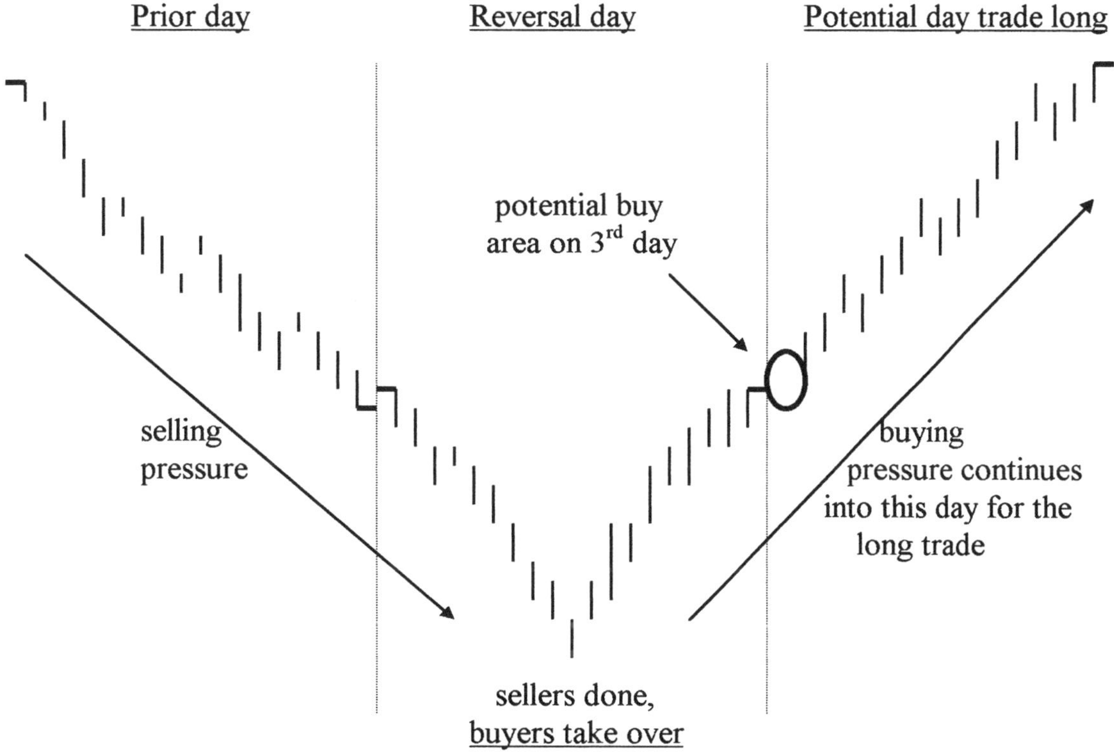

If you compress the 5 minute chart into daily bars, you then see the rationale behind the "reversal setup" as shown below with a completed 3rd day using daily bars:

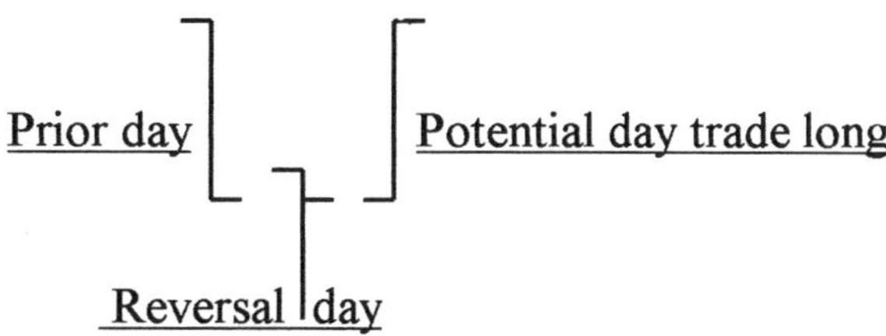

Here is another example of how a 5 minute intraday chart might look for a reversal setup:

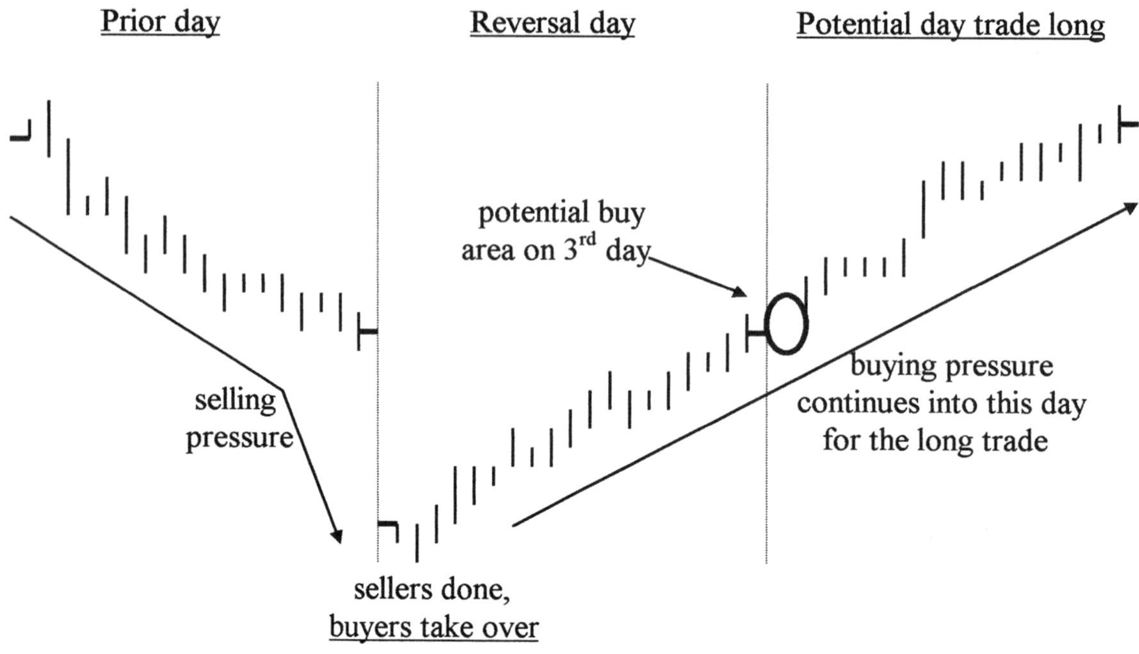

If you compress the above 5 minute chart into daily bars, you again see the rationale for the "reversal setup" as shown below with the completed 3rd day using daily bars:

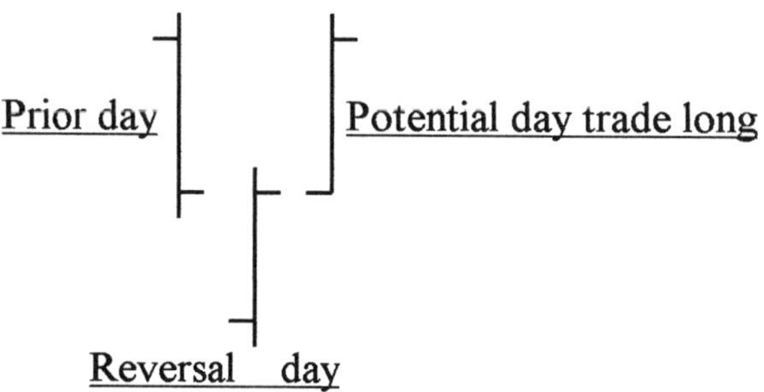

The price dynamics for both the 5 minute intraday chart and daily bar chart which form the reversal setup are the same for both buy and sell setups. They are simply the inverse of each other as you view them on stock charts.

9. A quick review of all of the components of the reversal setup pattern

For a buy setup:

- The day prior to the reversal bar must have a range from high to low of 1+ points
- The open of that prior day must be at or very near the high of that day
- The close of that prior day must be at or very near the low of that day
- The reversal day's high must not extend very much at all above the prior day's low
- The close of the reversal day must be at or very near the high of that day
- The further down the low of the reversal bar extends, the better (within reason)
- The profit target is at or near the high of the day prior to the reversal bar

(buy setup diagrammed)

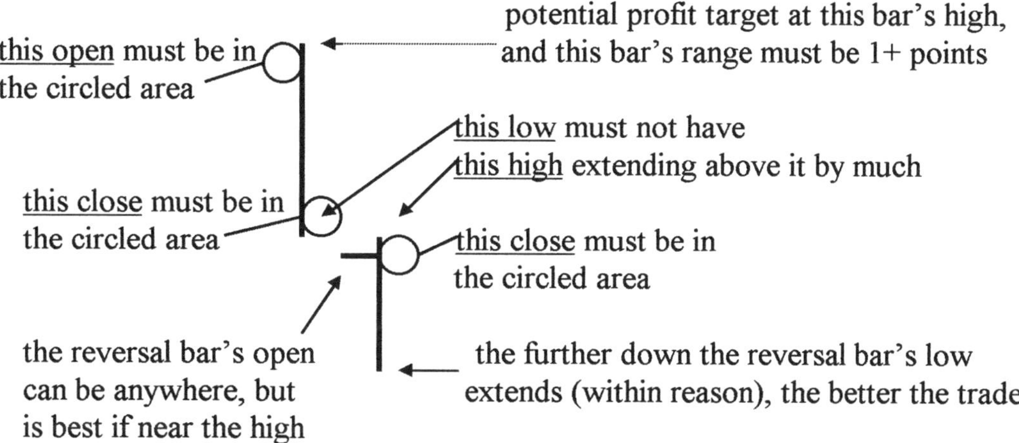

For a sell setup:

- The day prior to the reversal bar must have a range from high to low of 1+ points
- The open of that prior day must be at or very near the low of that day
- The close of that prior day must be at or very near the high of that day
- The reversal day's low must not extend very much at all below the prior day's high
- The close of the reversal day must be at or very near the low of that day
- The further up the high of the reversal bar extends, the better (within reason)
- The profit target is at or near the low of the day prior to the reversal bar

(sell setup diagrammed)

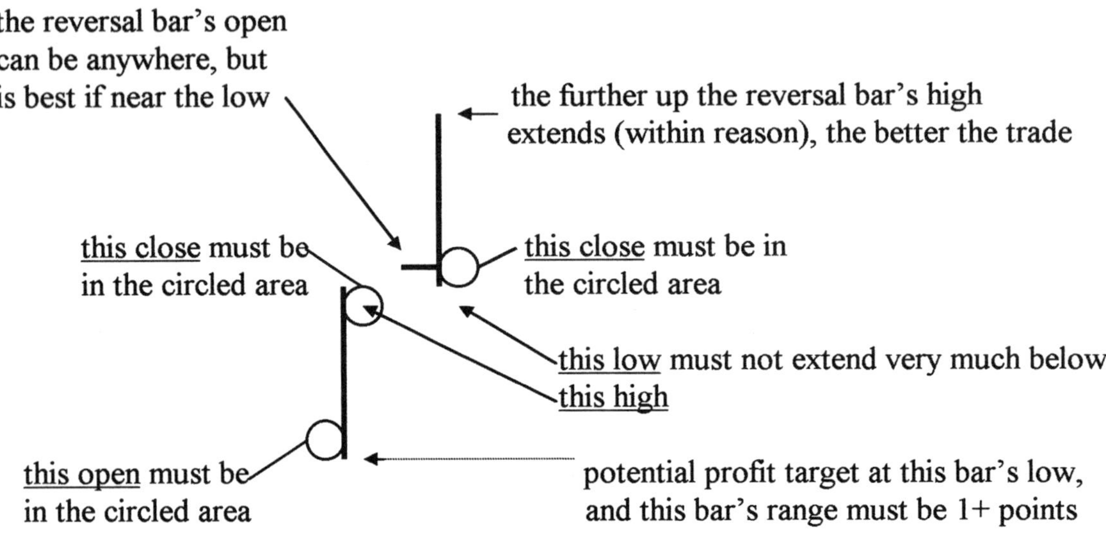

10. The "delayed reversal setup"

The delayed reversal setup is actually a 3 day setup with the 4th day being the potential day trade. Although the delayed reversal provides good trade opportunities, it occurs much less often than the regular reversal pattern. Therefore, I will only briefly cover its key components with the diagram provided below. It is an example of a buy setup. As usual, the sell setup is simply its inverse.

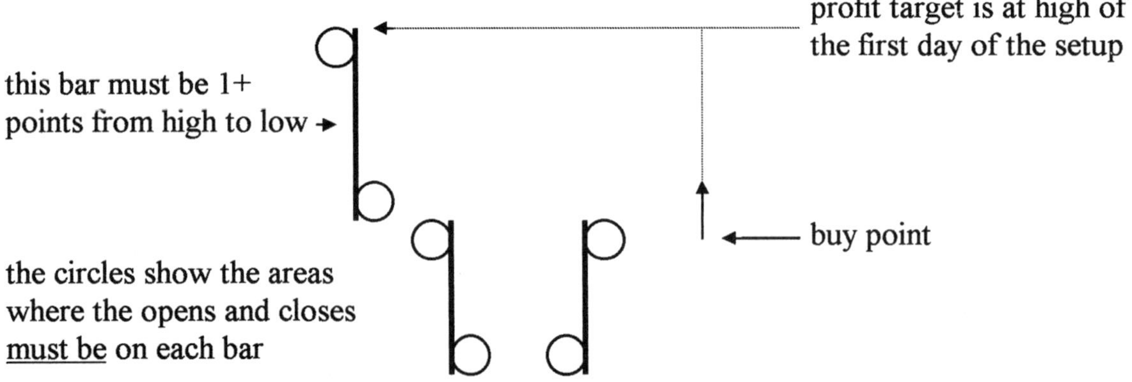

The key to this pattern is that it must have a symmetrical, balanced look if it were to be completed on the trade-entry day.

11. **REVERSAL SETUP - ENHANCEMENTS**

The reversal setups can be used as stand-alone patterns for high-probability day trades, or they may be enhanced by incorporating other factors when evaluating the setup on the daily bar chart. These factors include:

- Historical price support and resistance as seen on the daily chart
- The 50 and 200 day simple moving averages
- Trendlines
- Pullbacks in an established daily uptrend, or rallies in an established downtrend

When you have one or more of these factors lining up with the reversal setup, the odds of a successful trade with strong follow-through are significantly enhanced.

HISTORICAL PRICE SUPPORT OR RESISTANCE:

If a reversal bar bounces off of a price support level on the daily bar chart, strength is added to the setup. The more significant the support level, the better.

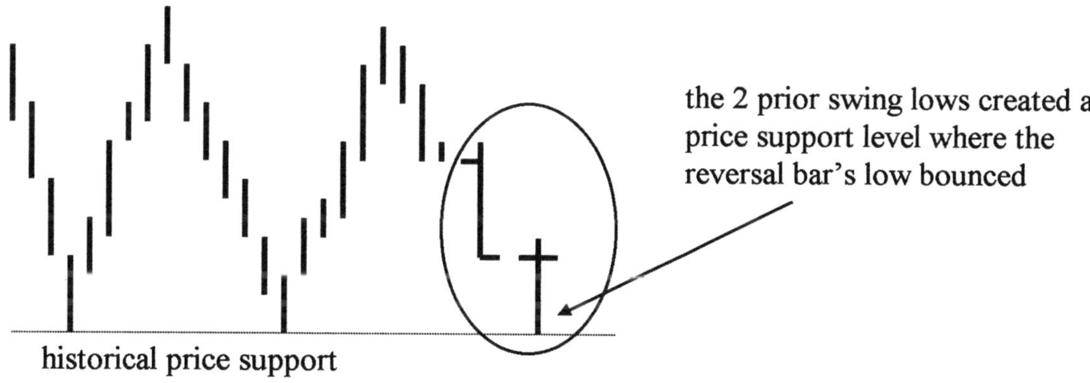

The same is true as a prior resistance level is penetrated to the upside. That level often becomes support. If price trades back down to that same level and puts in a reversal setup, then the odds of a successful long trade are enhanced.

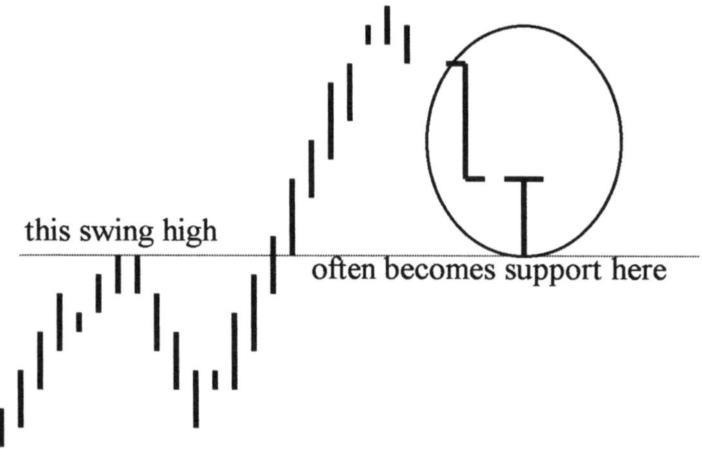

A reversal setup short whose reversal bar's high was halted by historical price resistance reinforces the success of a good short play. This is simply the inverse of a reversal buy setup off of support; the underlying concept is the same.

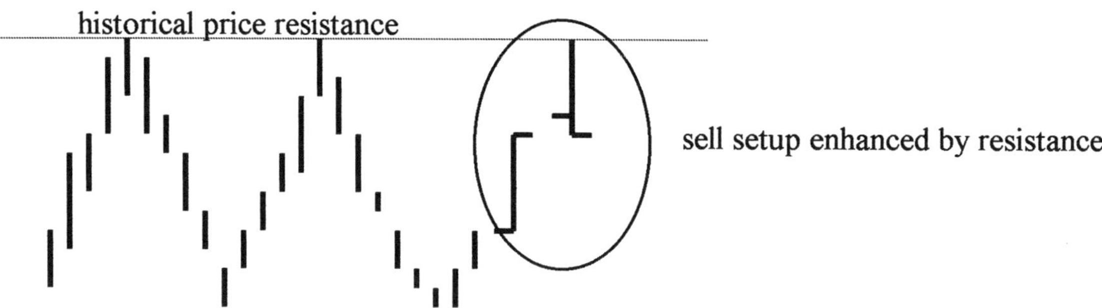

Prior support that has been penetrated to the downside often becomes resistance. This is another point which strengthens the odds of a sell with a reversal setup short.

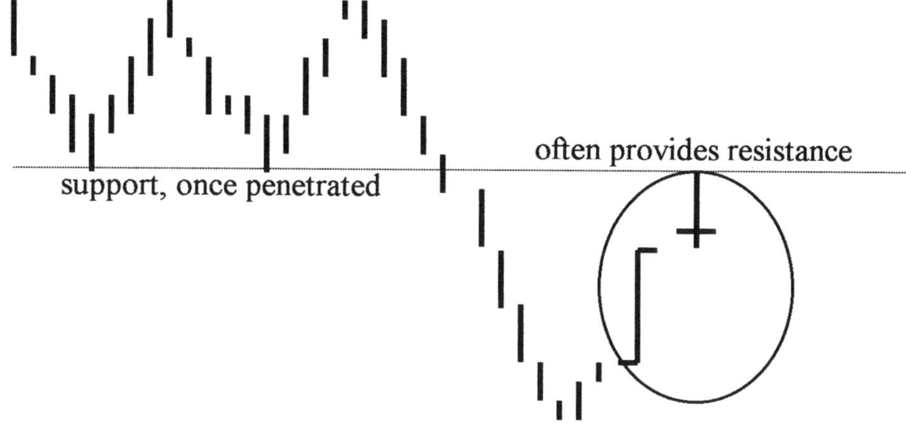

50 AND 200 DAY SIMPLE MOVING AVERAGES:

In the same way that price support and resistance levels tend to halt a stock's move, so do the 50 and 200 day moving averages. They serve as support and resistance to price. If a reversal setup long appears to be "bouncing" off one of these averages, a long trade is enhanced. The inverse is also true. If a stock trades up to one of these averages and is halted, and a reversal setup short is formed, the odds of a successful short trade are reinforced.

(a buy setup)

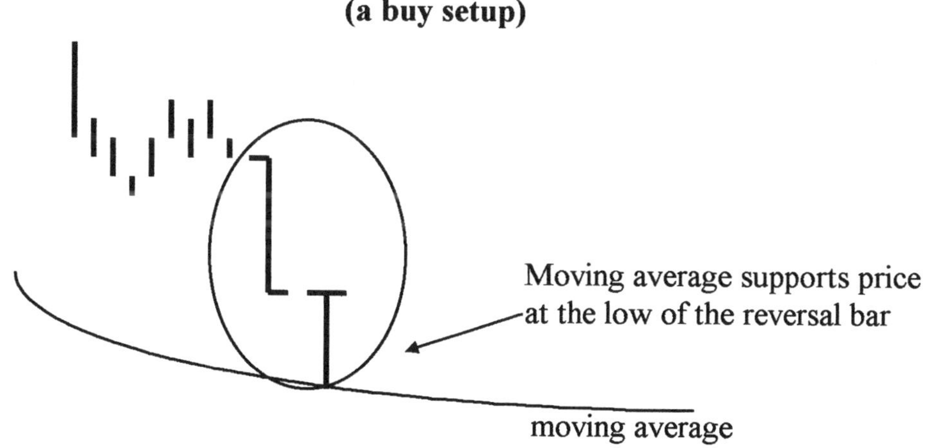

(a sell setup)

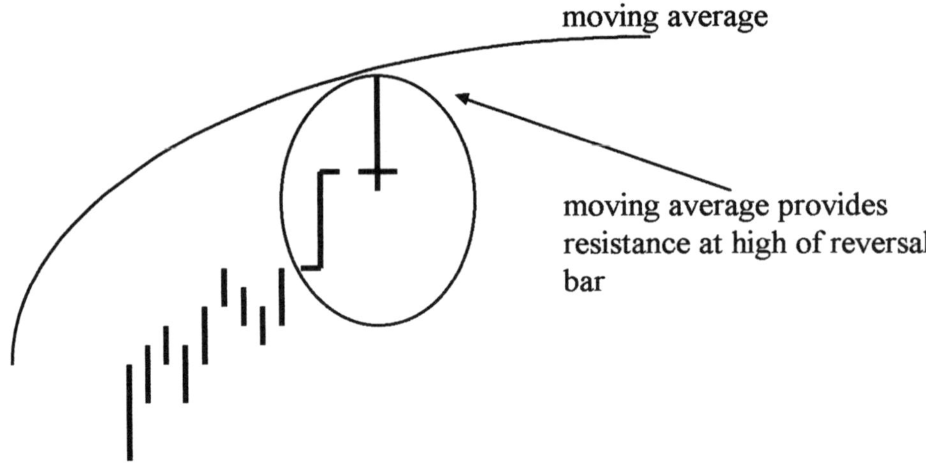

TRENDLINES:

Trendlines can also provide support or resistance to price. When a reversal setup reacts off of a trendline, the odds of a winning trade are increased.

(a buy setup)

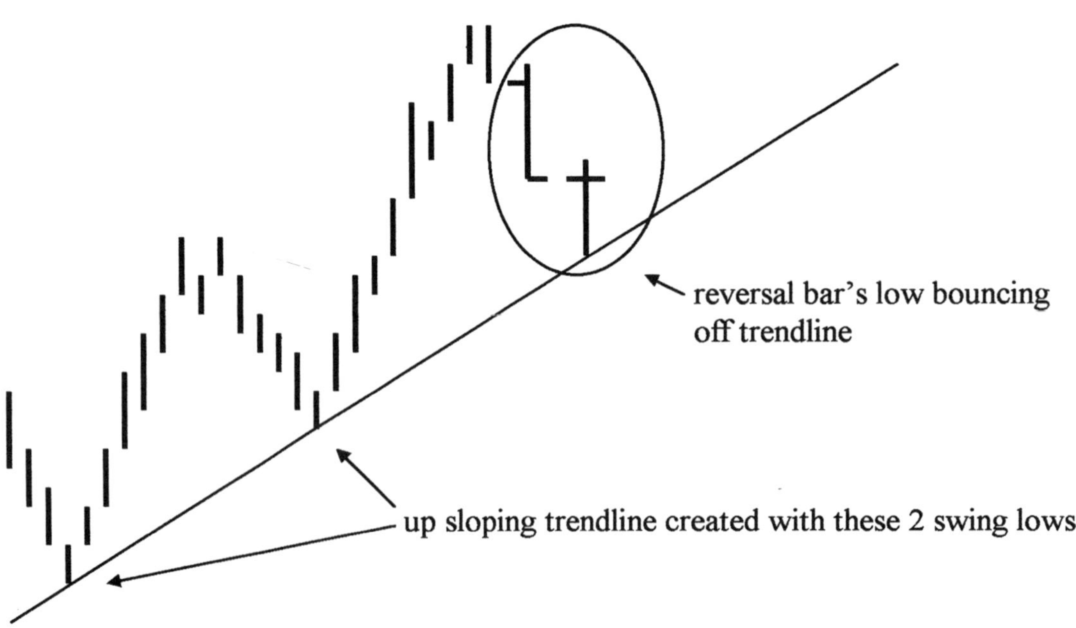

(a sell setup)

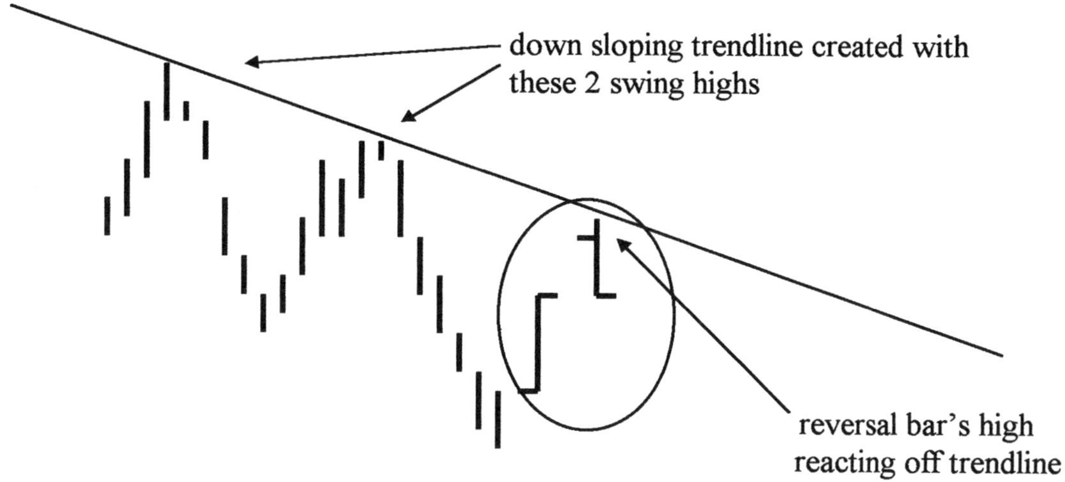

PULLBACKS IN AN UPTREND, RALLIES IN A DOWNTREND:

If an established trend is in place, a reaction against that trend followed by a reversal setup enhances the odds of a successful trade back in the direction of the trend.

(a buy setup)

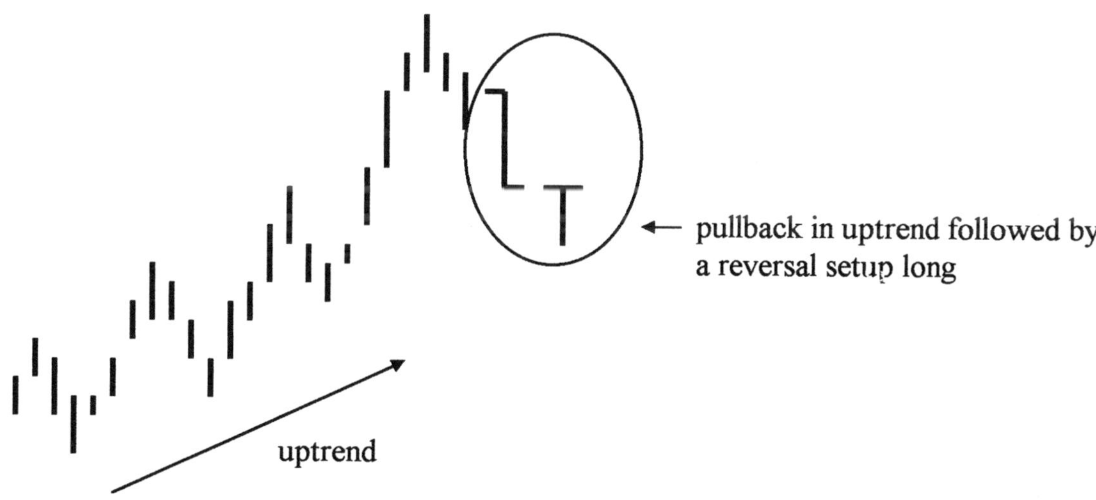

(a sell setup)

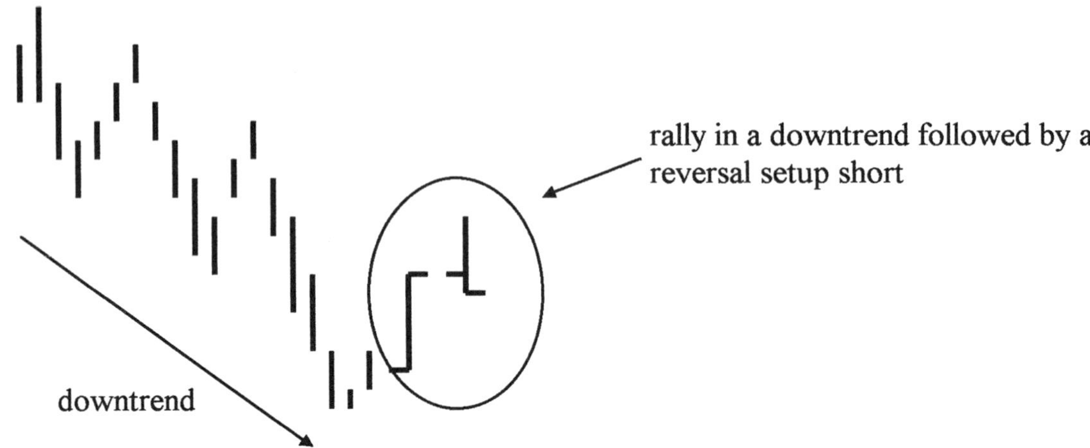

We have now covered the 4 main "Reversal Setup - Enhancements": 1) Historical price support and resistance 2) The 50 and 200 day moving averages 3) Trendlines and 4) Pullbacks in an uptrend/rallies in a downtrend. Although the concepts are relatively simple, it is the combination with the reversal setup pattern and all of its nuances which isolate some of the most powerful trade candidates.

Most of the diagrams of the enhancements showed the high or low of the reversal bar reacting off of a significant point on the daily chart. Although these are how the ideal setups may appear, it does not have to be this specific. A reversal bar long may have a low that has actually penetrated below a price support level or moving average. These are also playable as long as the reversal bar's close is back above the price support or moving average. For example:

The above setups are also acceptable even though the reversal bar penetrated through a support or resistance area. The reversal bar's close must be back on the correct side of the support or resistance, and the complete reversal setup pattern must be in place.

The more "enhancement" factors reinforcing a reversal bar setup, the better the potential trade. The diagram below shows how this might look.

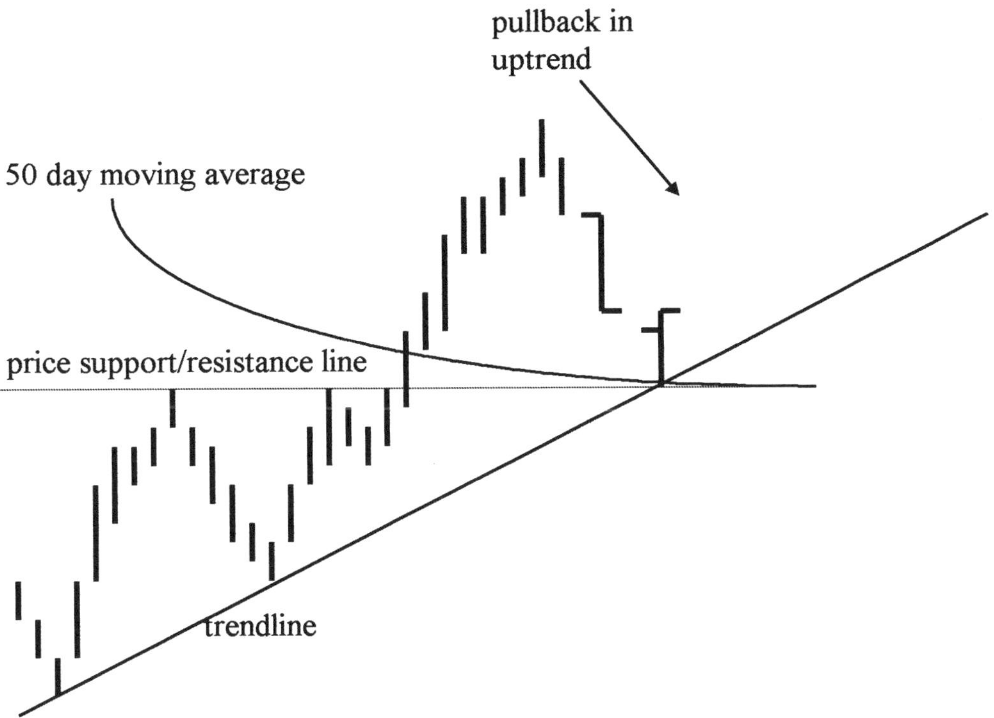

In the above diagram everything lines up perfectly.

- There was a pullback in an established uptrend
- The reversal bar found support at the:
    1. price support/resistance line
    2. 50 day moving average
    3. upsloping trendline
- A good reversal setup pattern formed

If this stock opened in the tradable range the next day and started to make a move long, it is one of the strongest buy candidates you will ever find. Make sure the market indices are also beginning to trend up to confirm the trade.

Obviously these factors don't line up for a trade like this every day, but they happen more often than one might think. The reversal setup and its enhancements are patterns that you should train your eye to look for. With time, these trades can be recognized and acted upon easily and quickly.

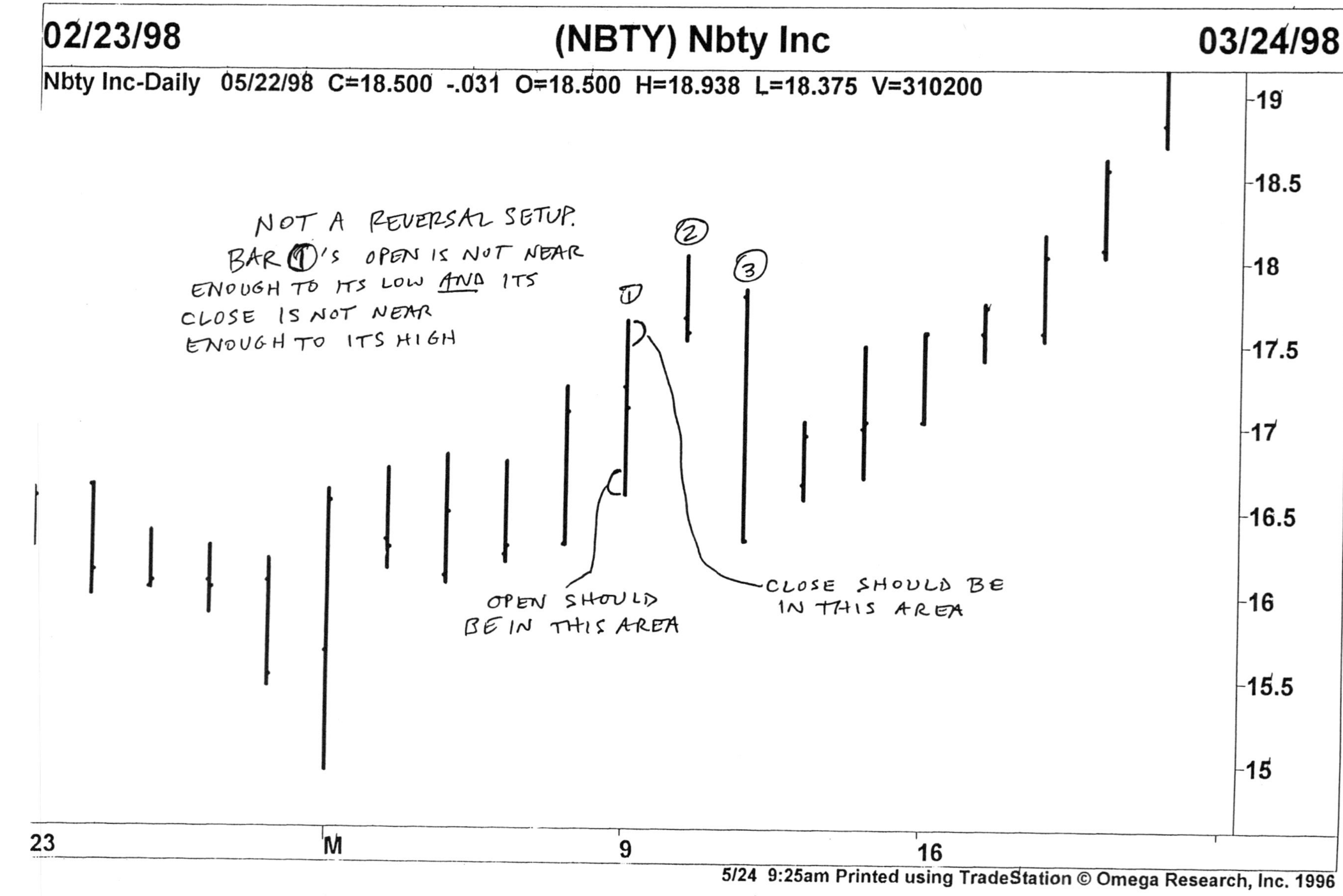

02/23/98
(NBTY) Nbty Inc
03/24/98
Nbty Inc-Daily 05/22/98 C=18.500 -.031 O=18.500 H=18.938 L=18.375 V=310200
NOT A REVERSAL SETUP.
BAR ①'S OPEN IS NOT NEAR ENOUGH TO ITS LOW AND ITS CLOSE IS NOT NEAR ENOUGH TO ITS HIGH
①
②
③
OPEN SHOULD BE IN THIS AREA
CLOSE SHOULD BE IN THIS AREA
19
18.5
18
17.5
17
16.5
16
15.5
15
23
M
9
16
5/24 9:25am Printed using TradeStation © Omega Research, Inc. 1996

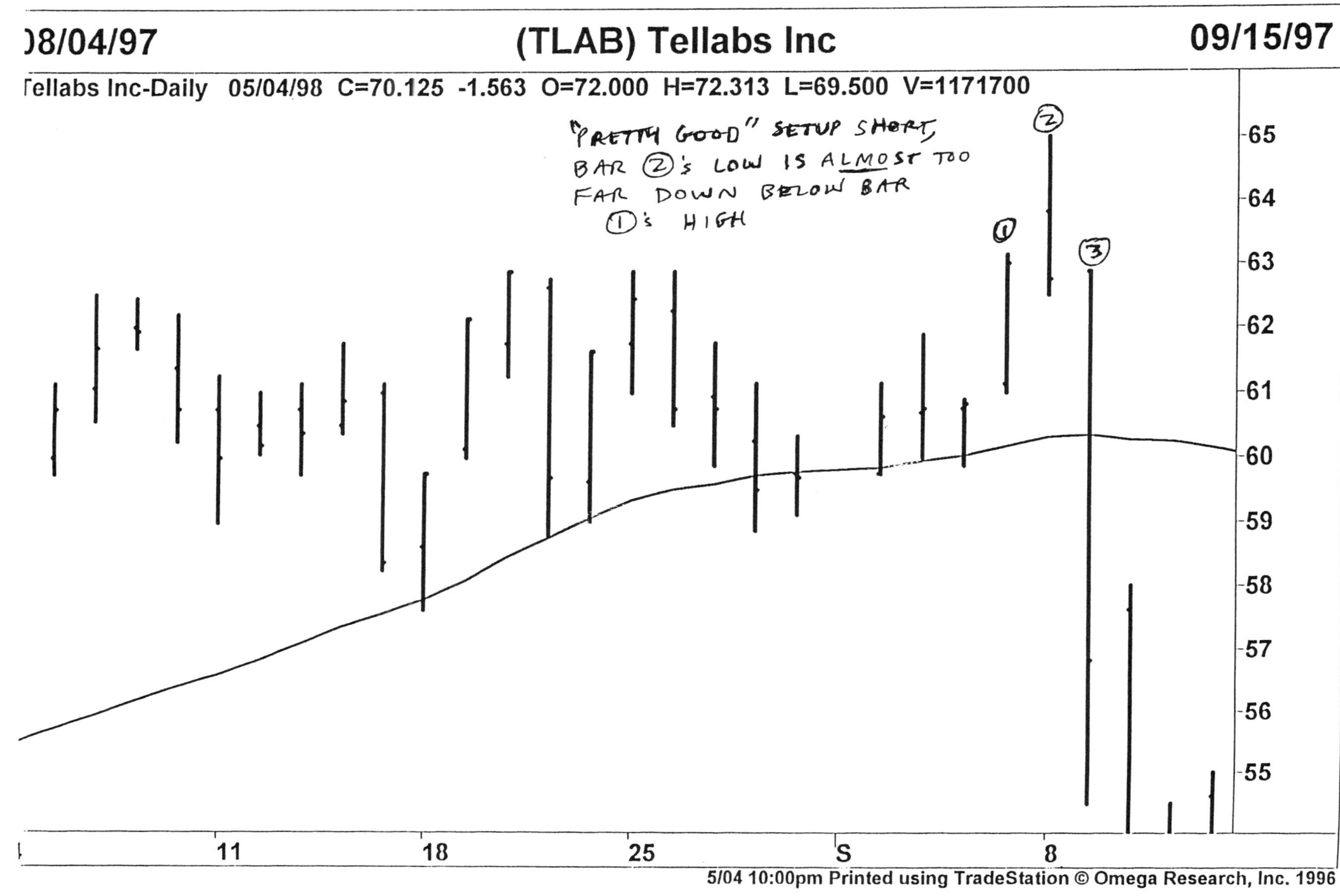

)8/04/97
(TLAB) Tellabs Inc
09/15/97
Tellabs Inc-Daily 05/04/98 C=70.125 -1.563 O=72.000 H=72.313 L=69.500 V=1171700
"PRETTY GOOD" SETUP SHORT,
BAR 2's LOW IS ALMOST TOO
FAR DOWN BELOW BAR
1's HIGH
1
2
3
65
64
63
62
61
60
59
58
57
56
55
11
18
25
S
8
5/04 10:00pm Printed using TradeStation © Omega Research, Inc. 1996

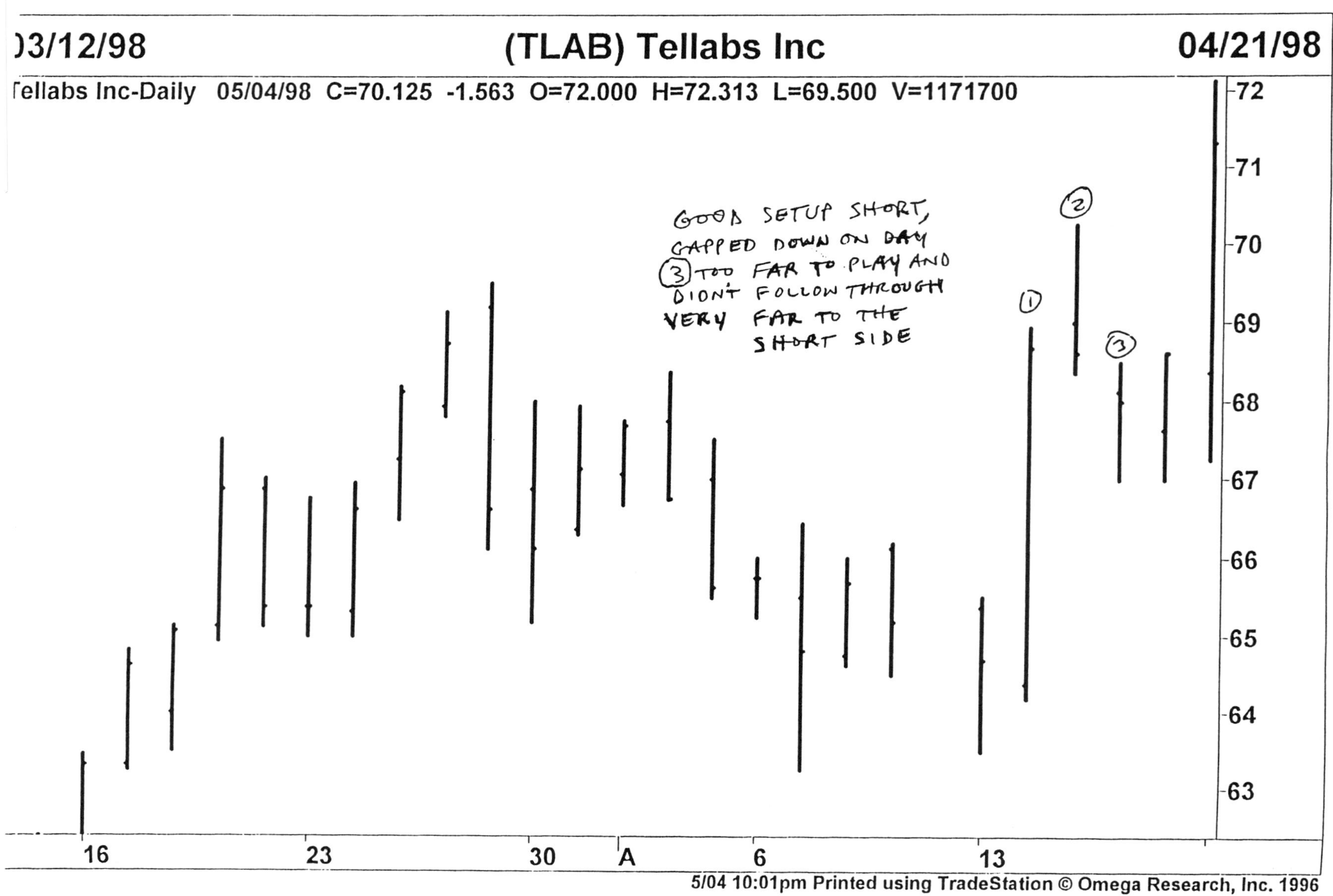
03/12/98
(TLAB) Tellabs Inc
04/21/98
Tellabs Inc-Daily 05/04/98 C=70.125 -1.563 O=72.000 H=72.313 L=69.500 V=1171700
GOOD SETUP SHORT, GAPPED DOWN ON DAY 3 TOO FAR TO PLAY AND DIDN'T FOLLOW THROUGH VERY FAR TO THE SHORT SIDE
1
2
3
72
71
70
69
68
67
66
65
64
63
16
23
30
A
6
13
5/04 10:01pm Printed using TradeStation © Omega Research, Inc. 1996

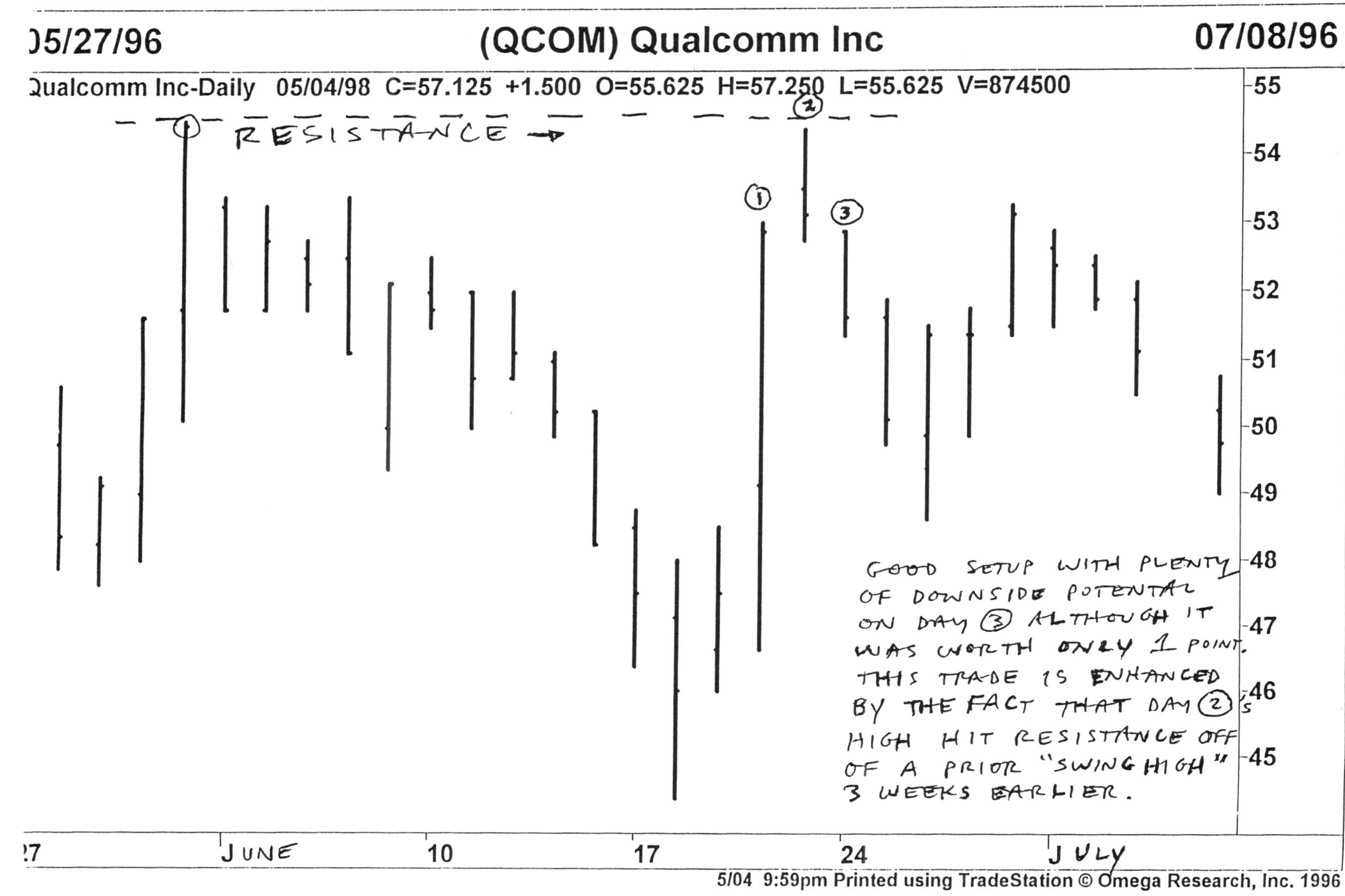
05/27/96
(QCOM) Qualcomm Inc
07/08/96
Qualcomm Inc-Daily 05/04/98 C=57.125 +1.500 O=55.625 H=57.250 L=55.625 V=874500
RESISTANCE
55
54
53
52
51
50
49
48
47
46
45
GOOD SETUP WITH PLENTY OF DOWNSIDE POTENTIAL ON DAY 3 ALTHOUGH IT WAS WORTH ONLY 1 POINT. THIS TRADE IS ENHANCED BY THE FACT THAT DAY 2's HIGH HIT RESISTANCE OFF OF A PRIOR "SWING HIGH" 3 WEEKS EARLIER.
27
JUNE
10
17
24
JULY
5/04 9:59pm Printed using TradeStation © Omega Research, Inc. 1996

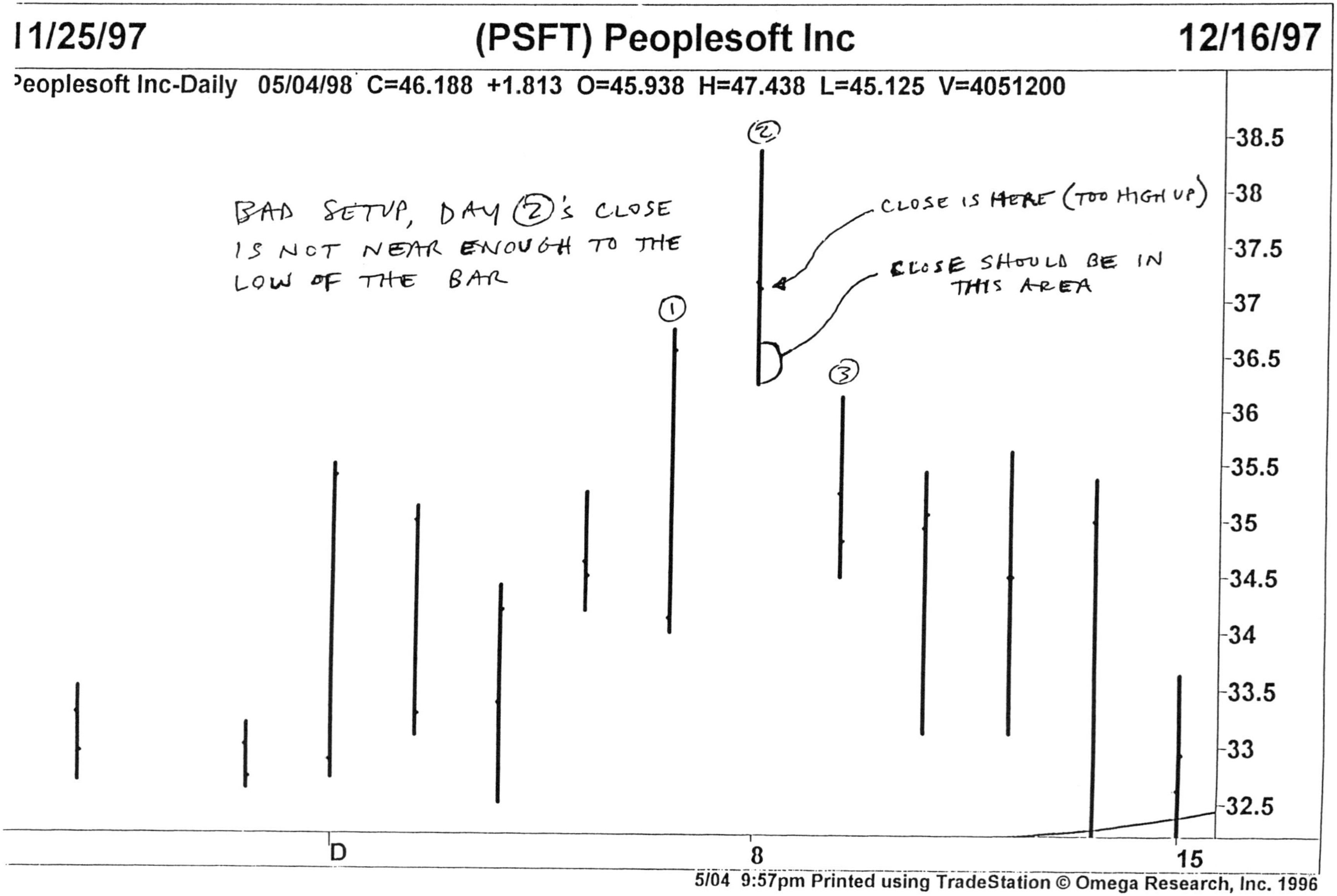

11/25/97 (PSFT) Peoplesoft Inc 12/16/97

Peoplesoft Inc-Daily 05/04/98 C=46.188 +1.813 O=45.938 H=47.438 L=45.125 V=4051200

BAD SETUP, DAY (2)'S CLOSE IS NOT NEAR ENOUGH TO THE LOW OF THE BAR

(1) (2) (3)

CLOSE IS HERE (TOO HIGH UP)

CLOSE SHOULD BE IN THIS AREA

38.5
38
37.5
37
36.5
36
35.5
35
34.5
34
33.5
33
32.5

D 8 15

5/04 9:57pm Printed using TradeStation © Omega Research, Inc. 1996

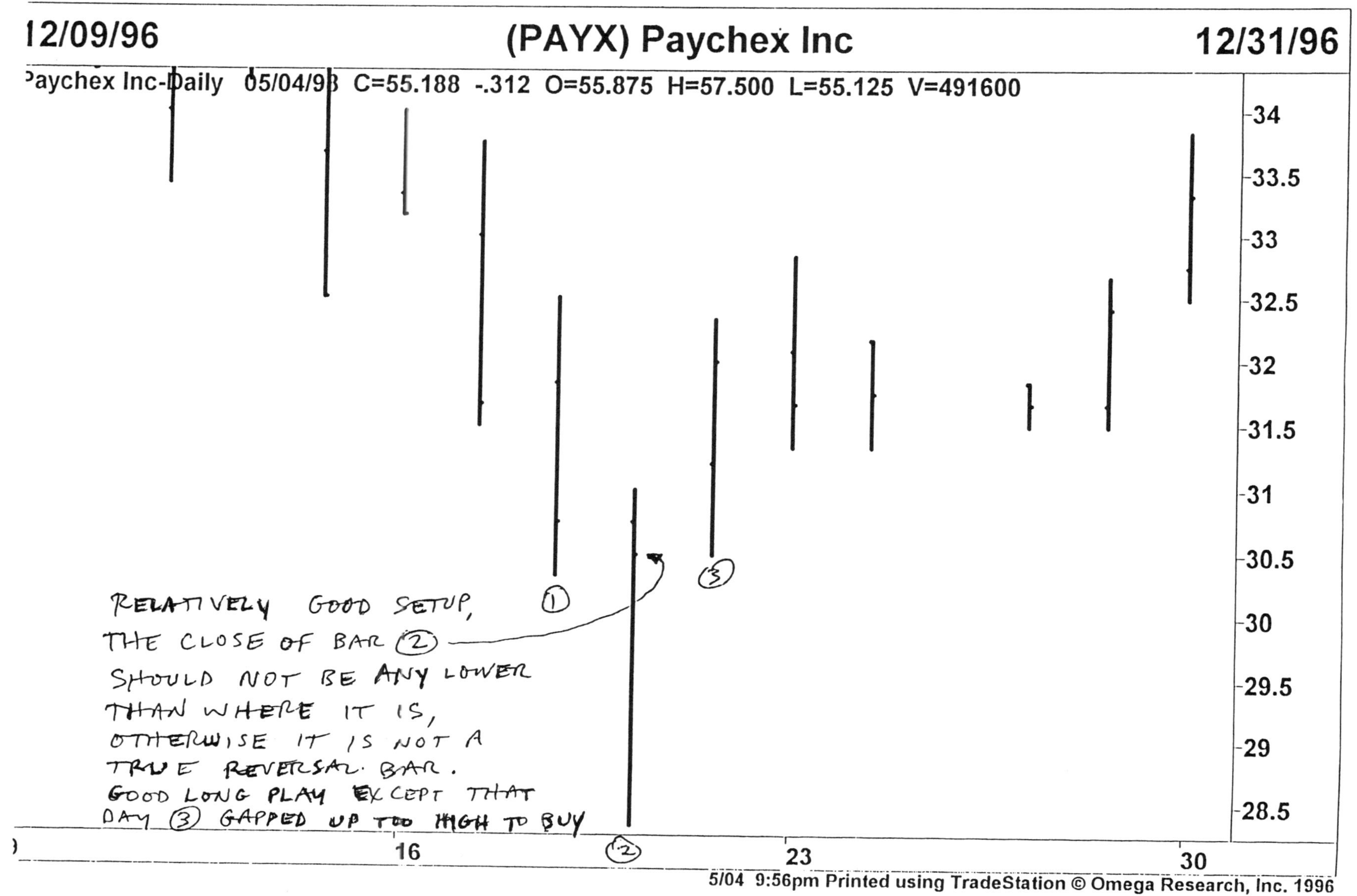

12/09/96
(PAYX) Paychex Inc
12/31/96
Paychex Inc-Daily 05/04/98 C=55.188 -.312 O=55.875 H=57.500 L=55.125 V=491600
34
33.5
33
32.5
32
31.5
31
30.5
30
29.5
29
28.5
16
23
30
1
2
3
RELATIVELY GOOD SETUP,
THE CLOSE OF BAR 2
SHOULD NOT BE ANY LOWER
THAN WHERE IT IS,
OTHERWISE IT IS NOT A
TRUE REVERSAL BAR.
GOOD LONG PLAY EXCEPT THAT
DAY 3 GAPPED UP TOO HIGH TO BUY
5/04 9:56pm Printed using TradeStation © Omega Research, Inc. 1996

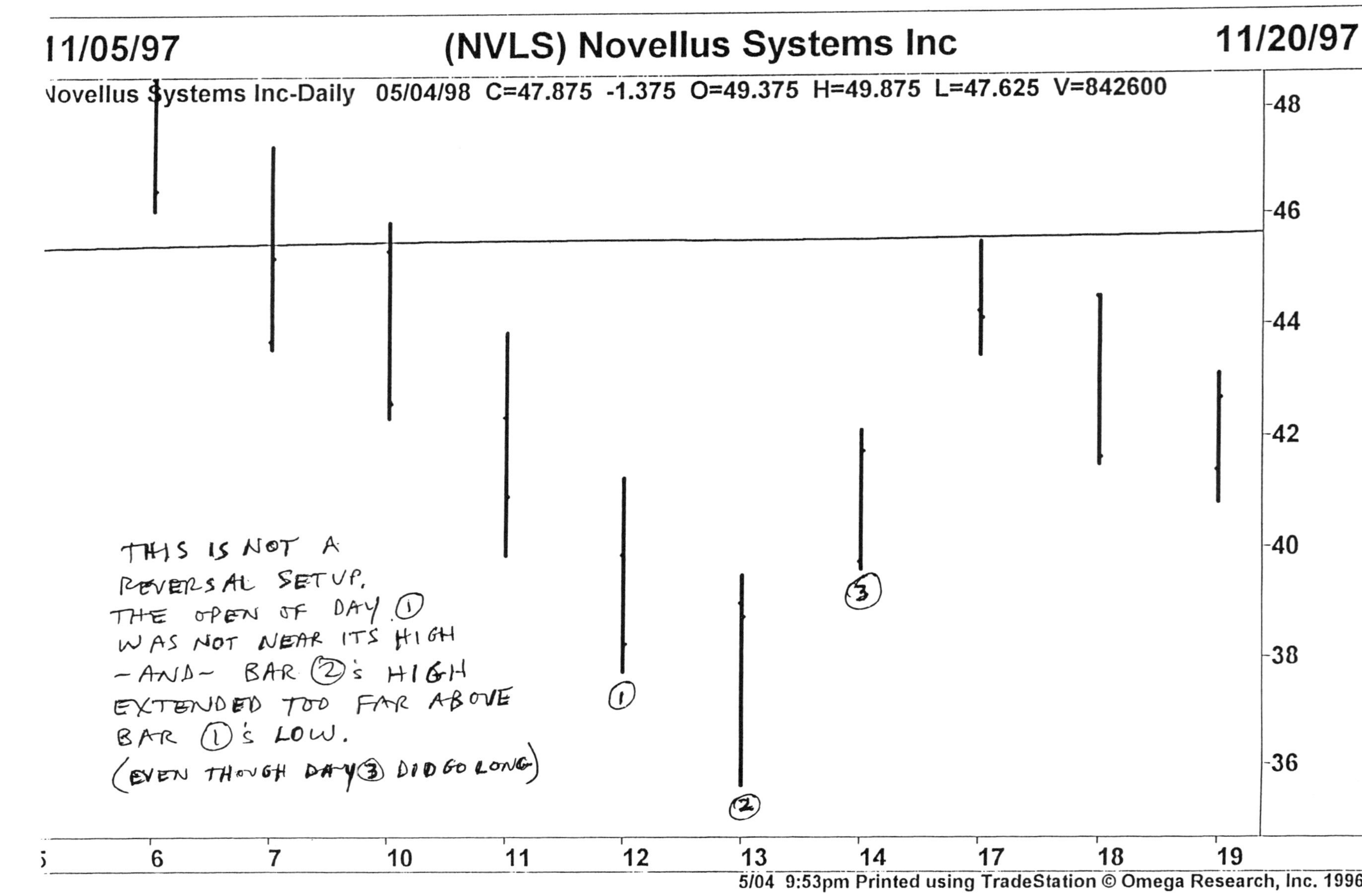

11/05/97
(NVLS) Novellus Systems Inc
11/20/97
Novellus Systems Inc-Daily 05/04/98 C=47.875 -1.375 O=49.375 H=49.875 L=47.625 V=842600
48
46
44
42
40
38
36
6
7
10
11
12
13
14
17
18
19
1
2
3
THIS IS NOT A
REVERSAL SETUP.
THE OPEN OF DAY 1
WAS NOT NEAR ITS HIGH
-AND- BAR 2's HIGH
EXTENDED TOO FAR ABOVE
BAR 1's LOW.
(EVEN THOUGH DAY 3 DID GO LONG)
5/04 9:53pm Printed using TradeStation © Omega Research, Inc. 1996

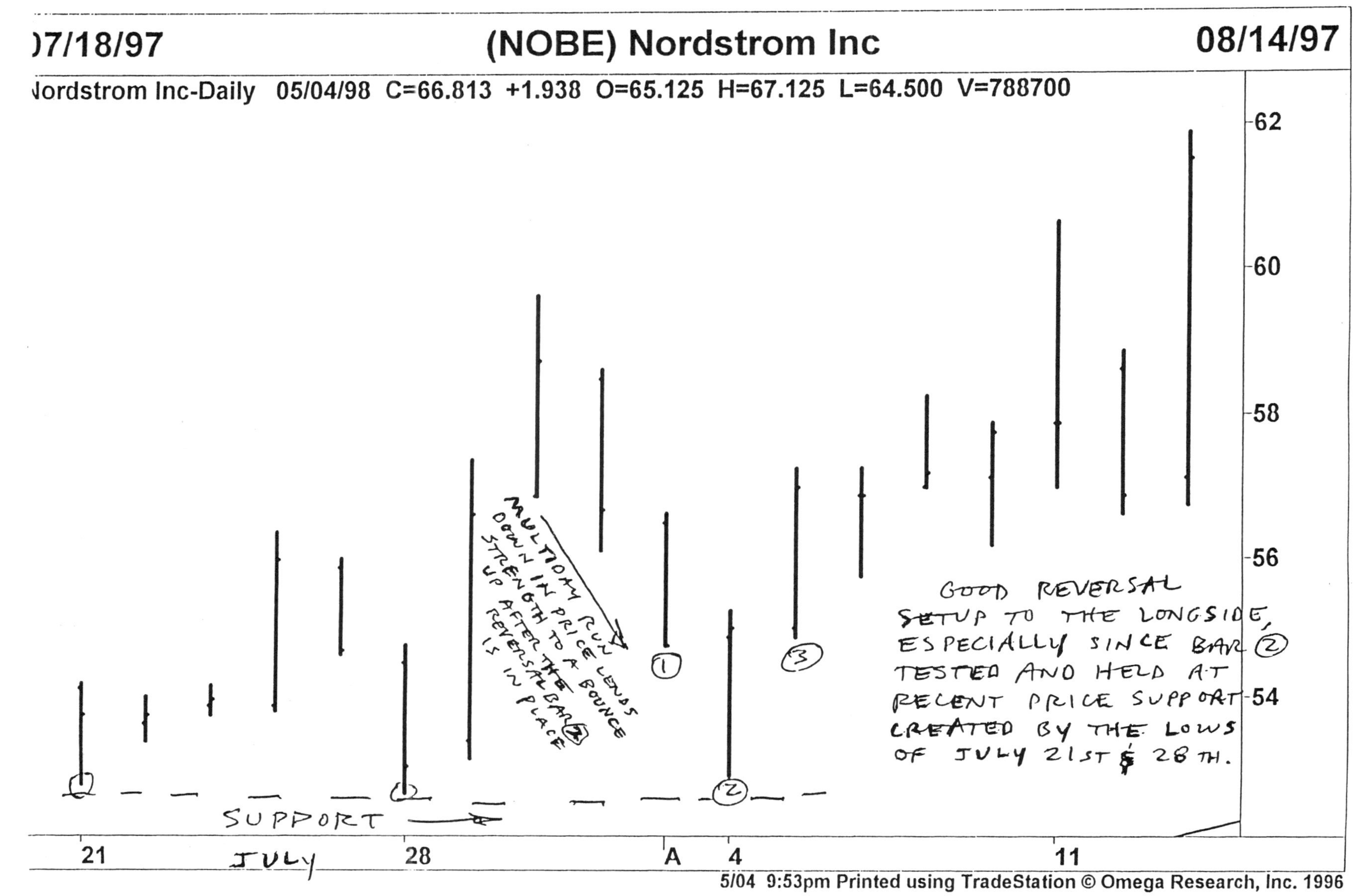

)7/18/97
(NOBE) Nordstrom Inc
08/14/97
Nordstrom Inc-Daily 05/04/98 C=66.813 +1.938 O=65.125 H=67.125 L=64.500 V=788700
62
60
58
56
54
21
JULY
28
A
4
11
SUPPORT
MULTIDAY RUN DOWN IN PRICE LENDS STRENGTH TO A BOUNCE UP AFTER THE REVERSAL BAR 2 IS IN PLACE
GOOD REVERSAL SETUP TO THE LONGSIDE, ESPECIALLY SINCE BAR 2 TESTED AND HELD AT RECENT PRICE SUPPORT CREATED BY THE LOWS OF JULY 21ST & 28TH.
5/04 9:53pm Printed using TradeStation © Omega Research, Inc. 1996

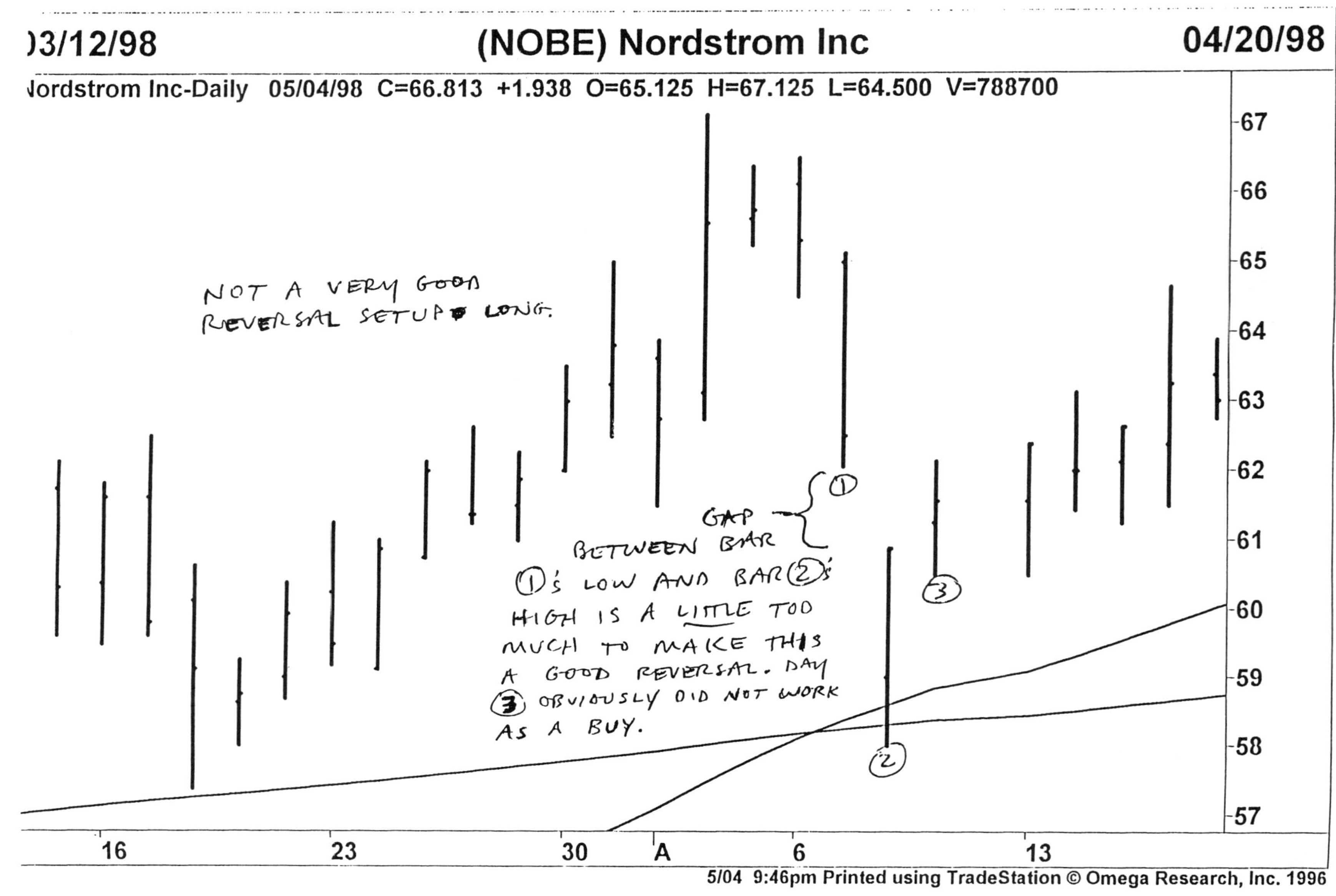

)3/12/98
(NOBE) Nordstrom Inc
04/20/98
Jordstrom Inc-Daily 05/04/98 C=66.813 +1.938 O=65.125 H=67.125 L=64.500 V=788700
67
66
65
64
63
62
61
60
59
58
57
16
23
30
A
6
13
5/04 9:46pm Printed using TradeStation © Omega Research, Inc. 1996
NOT A VERY GOOD REVERSAL SETUP LONG.
GAP BETWEEN BAR 1's LOW AND BAR 2's HIGH IS A LITTLE TOO MUCH TO MAKE THIS A GOOD REVERSAL. DAY 3 OBVIOUSLY DID NOT WORK AS A BUY.
1
2
3

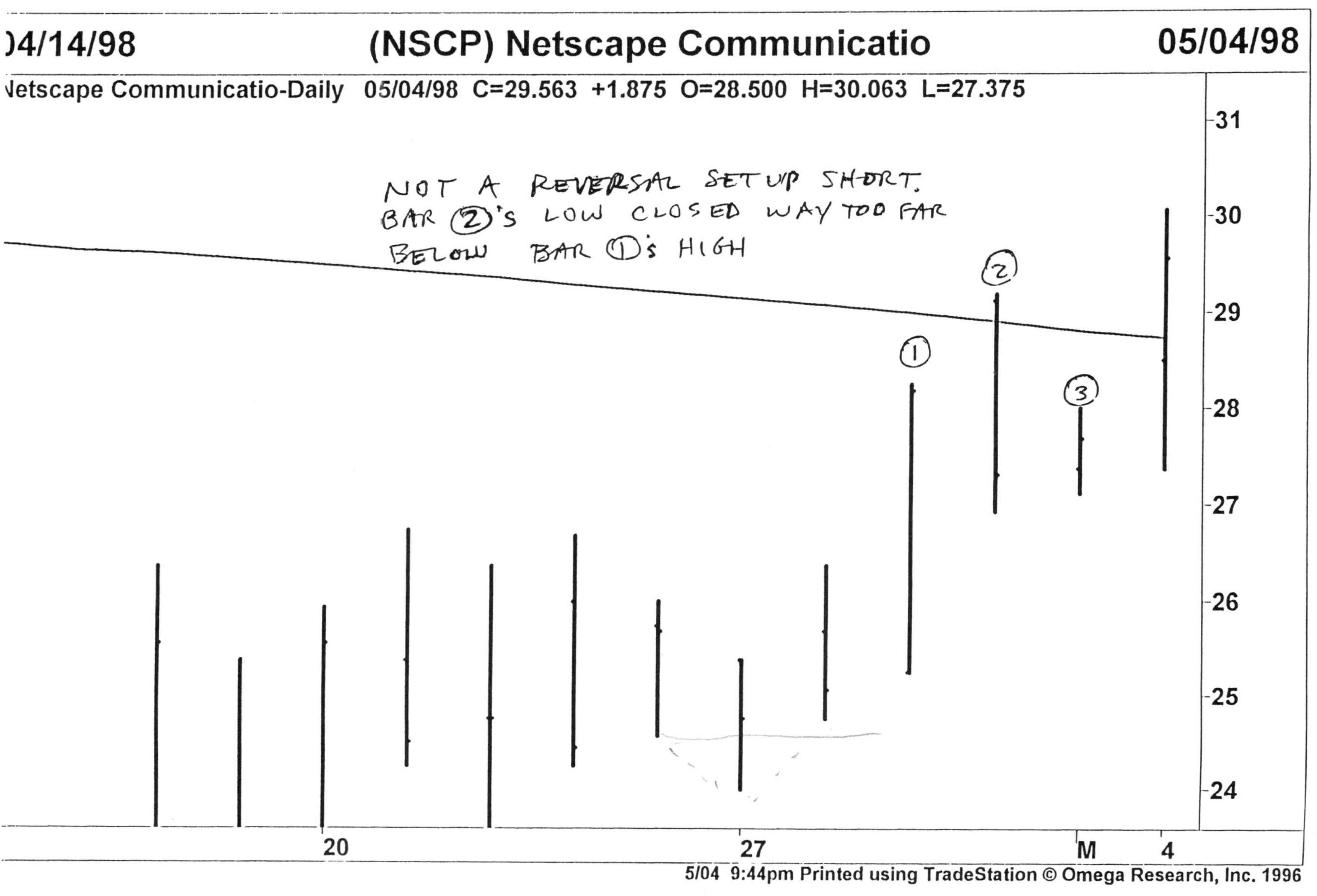

4/14/98
(NSCP) Netscape Communicatio
05/04/98
etscape Communicatio-Daily 05/04/98 C=29.563 +1.875 O=28.500 H=30.063 L=27.375
NOT A REVERSAL SET UP SHORT.
BAR 2's LOW CLOSED WAY TOO FAR
BELOW BAR 1's HIGH
1
2
3
31
30
29
28
27
26
25
24
20
27
M
4
5/04 9:44pm Printed using TradeStation © Omega Research, Inc. 1996

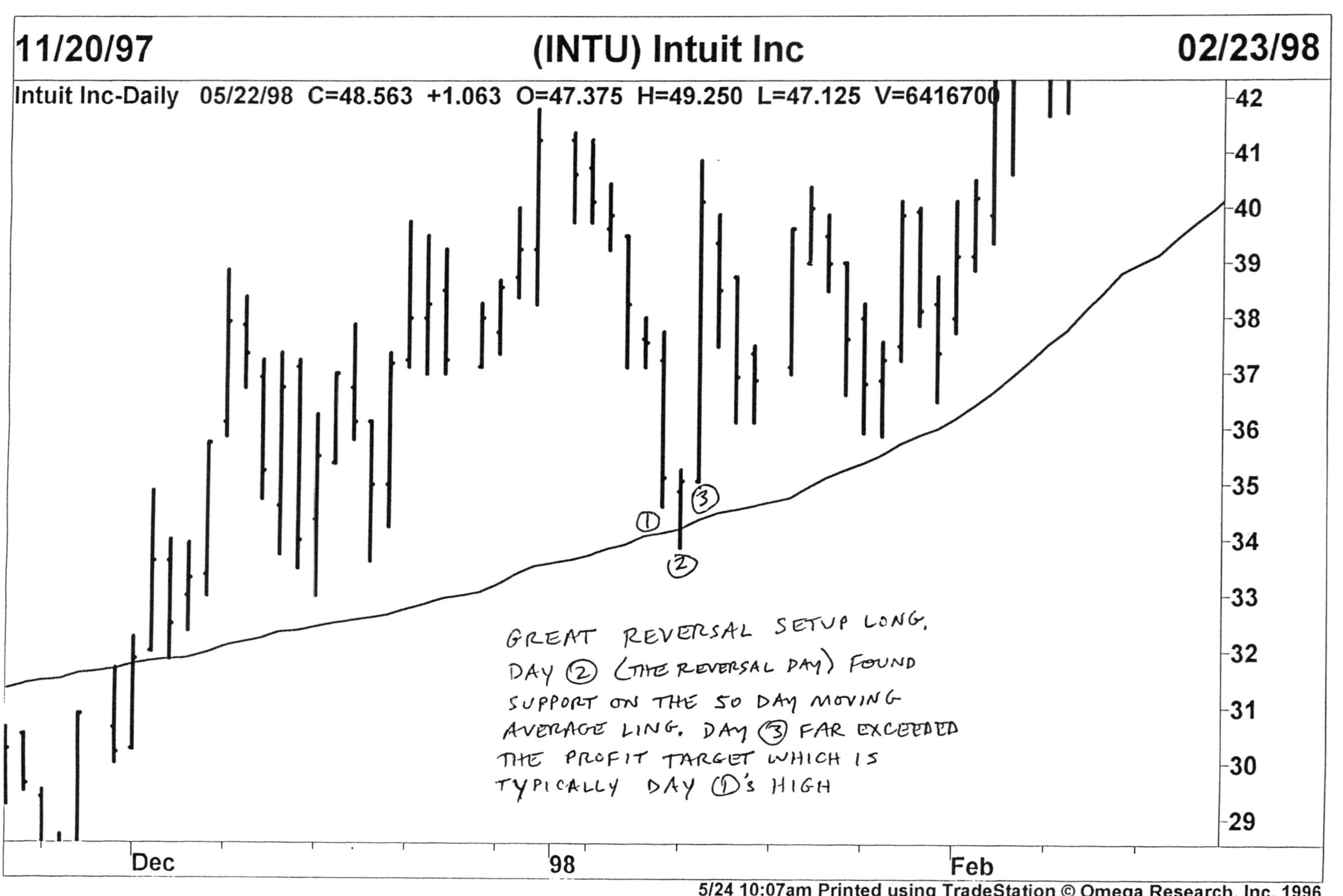
11/20/97
(INTU) Intuit Inc
02/23/98
Intuit Inc-Daily 05/22/98 C=48.563 +1.063 O=47.375 H=49.250 L=47.125 V=6416700
42
41
40
39
38
37
36
35
34
33
32
31
30
29
Dec
98
Feb
1
2
3
GREAT REVERSAL SETUP LONG.
DAY 2 (THE REVERSAL DAY) FOUND
SUPPORT ON THE 50 DAY MOVING
AVERAGE LINE. DAY 3 FAR EXCEEDED
THE PROFIT TARGET WHICH IS
TYPICALLY DAY 1's HIGH
5/24 10:07am Printed using TradeStation © Omega Research, Inc. 1996

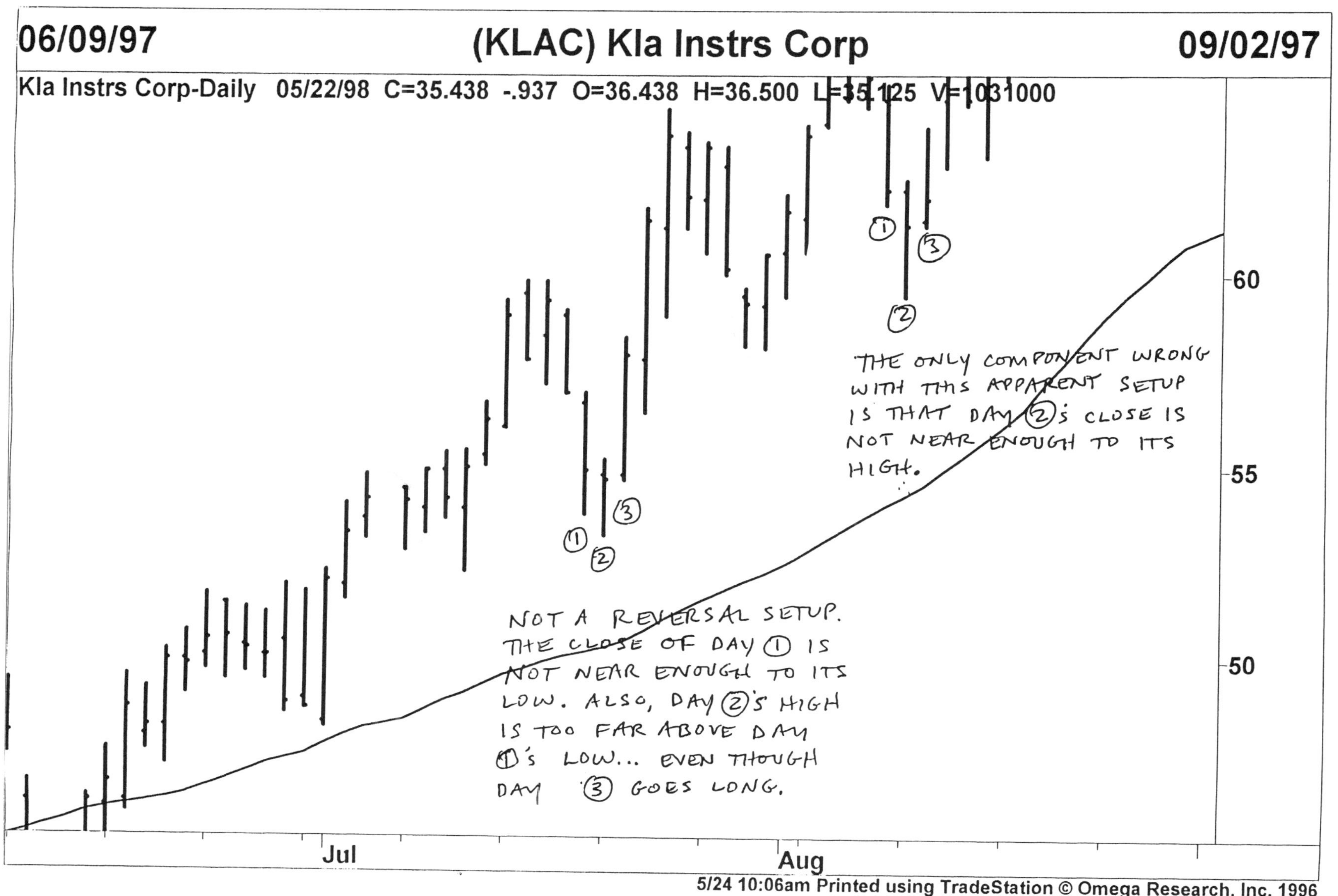
06/09/97
(KLAC) Kla Instrs Corp
09/02/97
Kla Instrs Corp-Daily 05/22/98 C=35.438 -.937 O=36.438 H=36.500 L=35.125 V=1031000
60
55
50
Jul
Aug
5/24 10:06am Printed using TradeStation © Omega Research, Inc. 1996
① ② ③
NOT A REVERSAL SETUP. THE CLOSE OF DAY ① IS NOT NEAR ENOUGH TO ITS LOW. ALSO, DAY ②'S HIGH IS TOO FAR ABOVE DAY ①'S LOW... EVEN THOUGH DAY ③ GOES LONG.
① ② ③
THE ONLY COMPONENT WRONG WITH THIS APPARENT SETUP IS THAT DAY ②'S CLOSE IS NOT NEAR ENOUGH TO ITS HIGH.

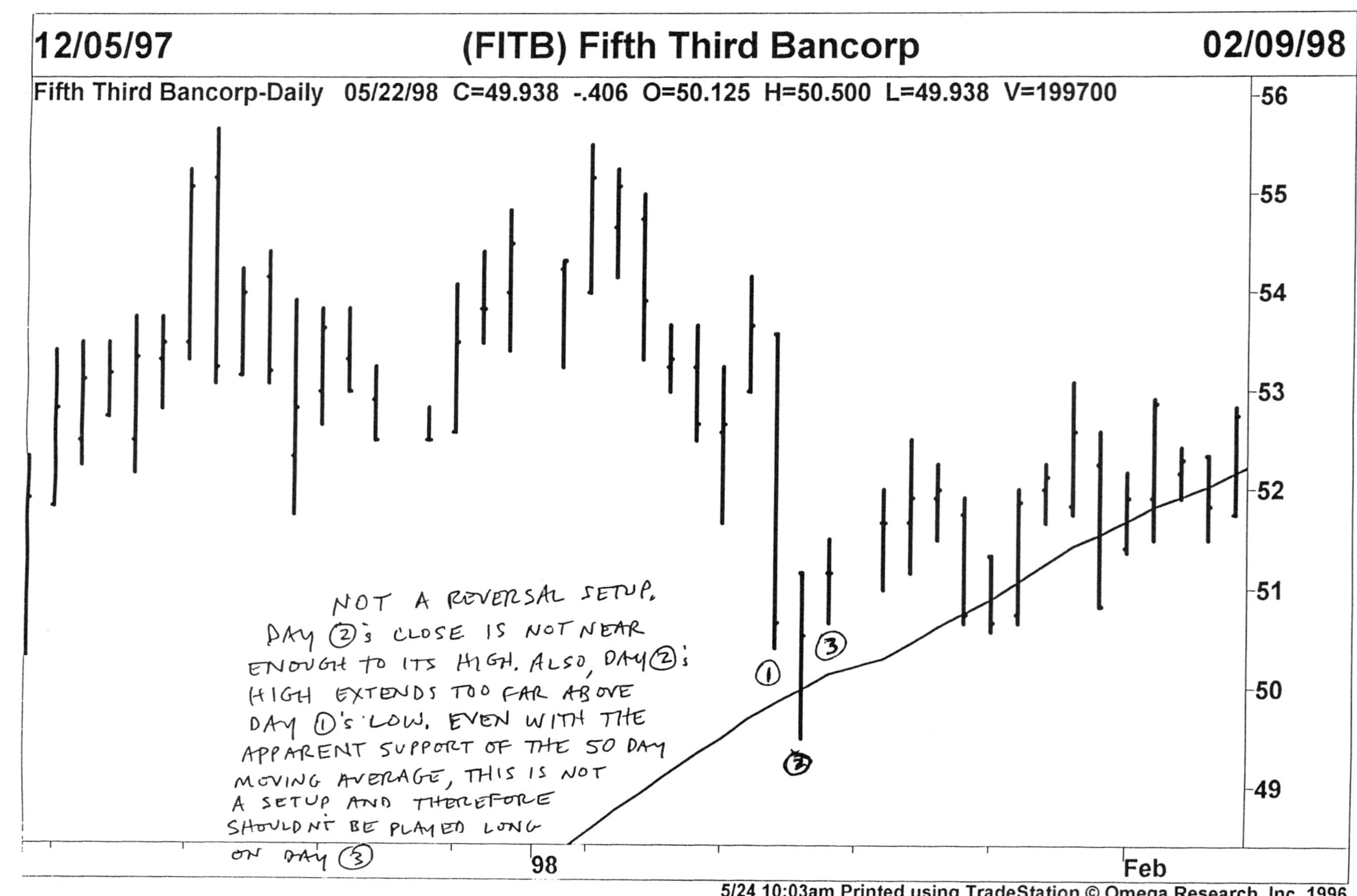

12/05/97
(FITB) Fifth Third Bancorp
02/09/98
Fifth Third Bancorp-Daily 05/22/98 C=49.938 -.406 O=50.125 H=50.500 L=49.938 V=199700
56
55
54
53
52
51
50
49
98
Feb
5/24 10:03am Printed using TradeStation © Omega Research, Inc. 1996
1
2
3
NOT A REVERSAL SETUP. DAY 2's CLOSE IS NOT NEAR ENOUGH TO ITS HIGH. ALSO, DAY 2's HIGH EXTENDS TOO FAR ABOVE DAY 1's LOW. EVEN WITH THE APPARENT SUPPORT OF THE 50 DAY MOVING AVERAGE, THIS IS NOT A SETUP AND THEREFORE SHOULDN'T BE PLAYED LONG ON DAY 3

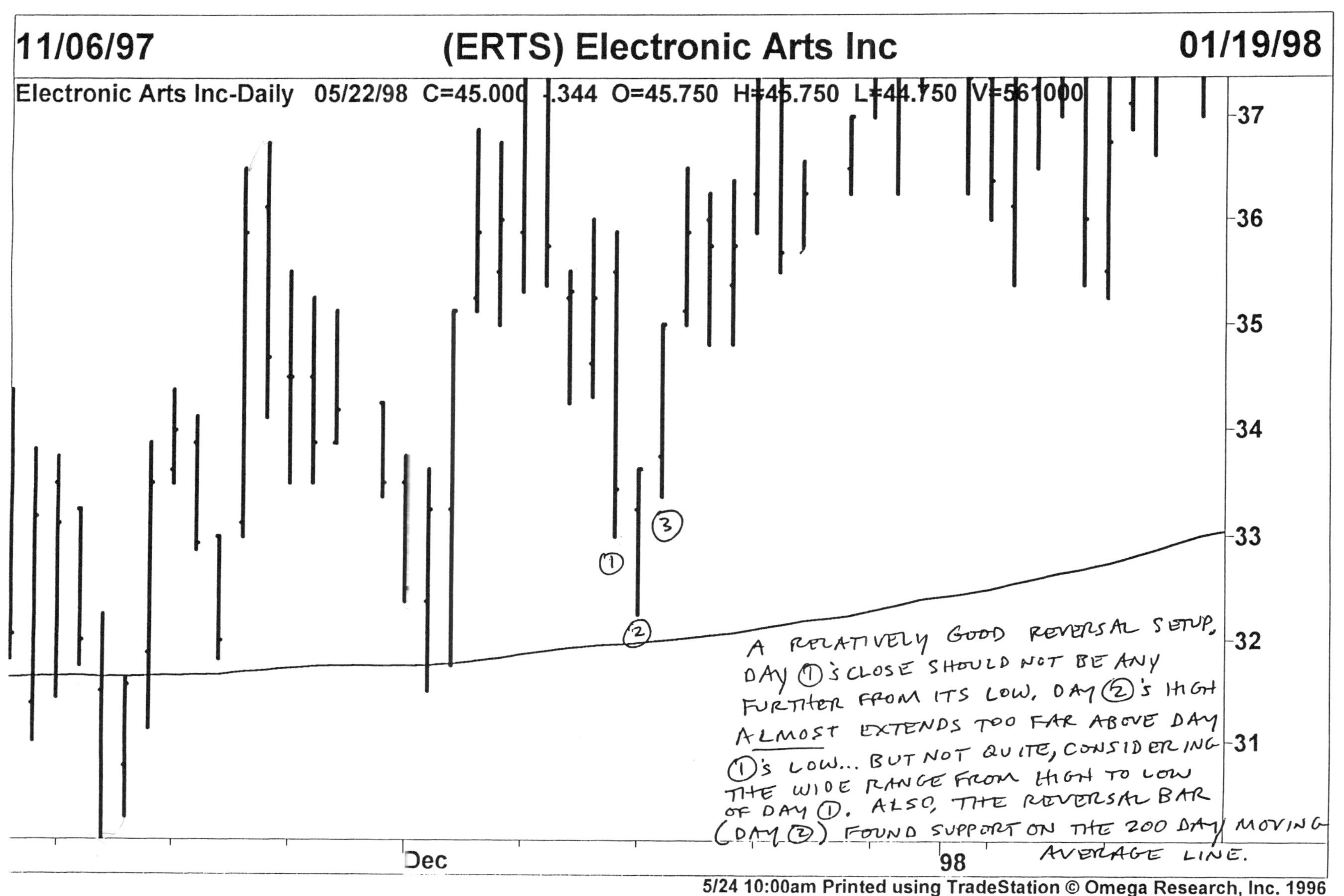
11/06/97
(ERTS) Electronic Arts Inc
01/19/98
Electronic Arts Inc-Daily 05/22/98 C=45.000 -.344 O=45.750 H=45.750 L=44.750 V=561000
37
36
35
34
33
32
31
Dec
98
5/24 10:00am Printed using TradeStation © Omega Research, Inc. 1996
1
2
3
A RELATIVELY GOOD REVERSAL SETUP, DAY 1's CLOSE SHOULD NOT BE ANY FURTHER FROM ITS LOW. DAY 2's HIGH ALMOST EXTENDS TOO FAR ABOVE DAY 1's LOW... BUT NOT QUITE, CONSIDERING THE WIDE RANGE FROM HIGH TO LOW OF DAY 1. ALSO, THE REVERSAL BAR (DAY 2) FOUND SUPPORT ON THE 200 DAY MOVING AVERAGE LINE.

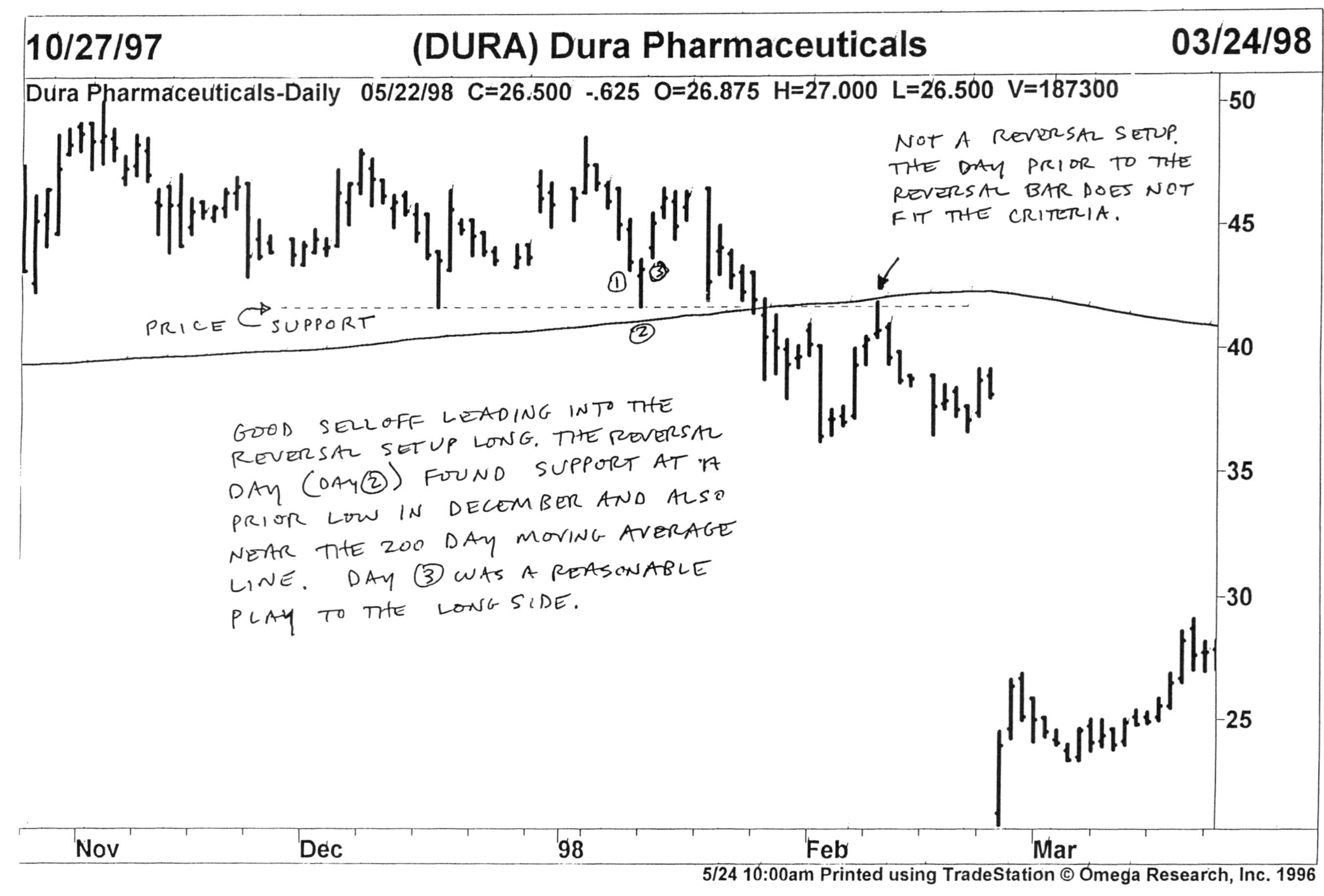
10/27/97
(DURA) Dura Pharmaceuticals
03/24/98
Dura Pharmaceuticals-Daily 05/22/98 C=26.500 -.625 O=26.875 H=27.000 L=26.500 V=187300
50
45
40
35
30
25
Nov
Dec
98
Feb
Mar
NOT A REVERSAL SETUP. THE DAY PRIOR TO THE REVERSAL BAR DOES NOT FIT THE CRITERIA.
PRICE SUPPORT
①
②
③
GOOD SELLOFF LEADING INTO THE REVERSAL SETUP LONG. THE REVERSAL DAY (DAY②) FOUND SUPPORT AT THE PRIOR LOW IN DECEMBER AND ALSO NEAR THE 200 DAY MOVING AVERAGE LINE. DAY ③ WAS A REASONABLE PLAY TO THE LONG SIDE.
5/24 10:00am Printed using TradeStation © Omega Research, Inc. 1996

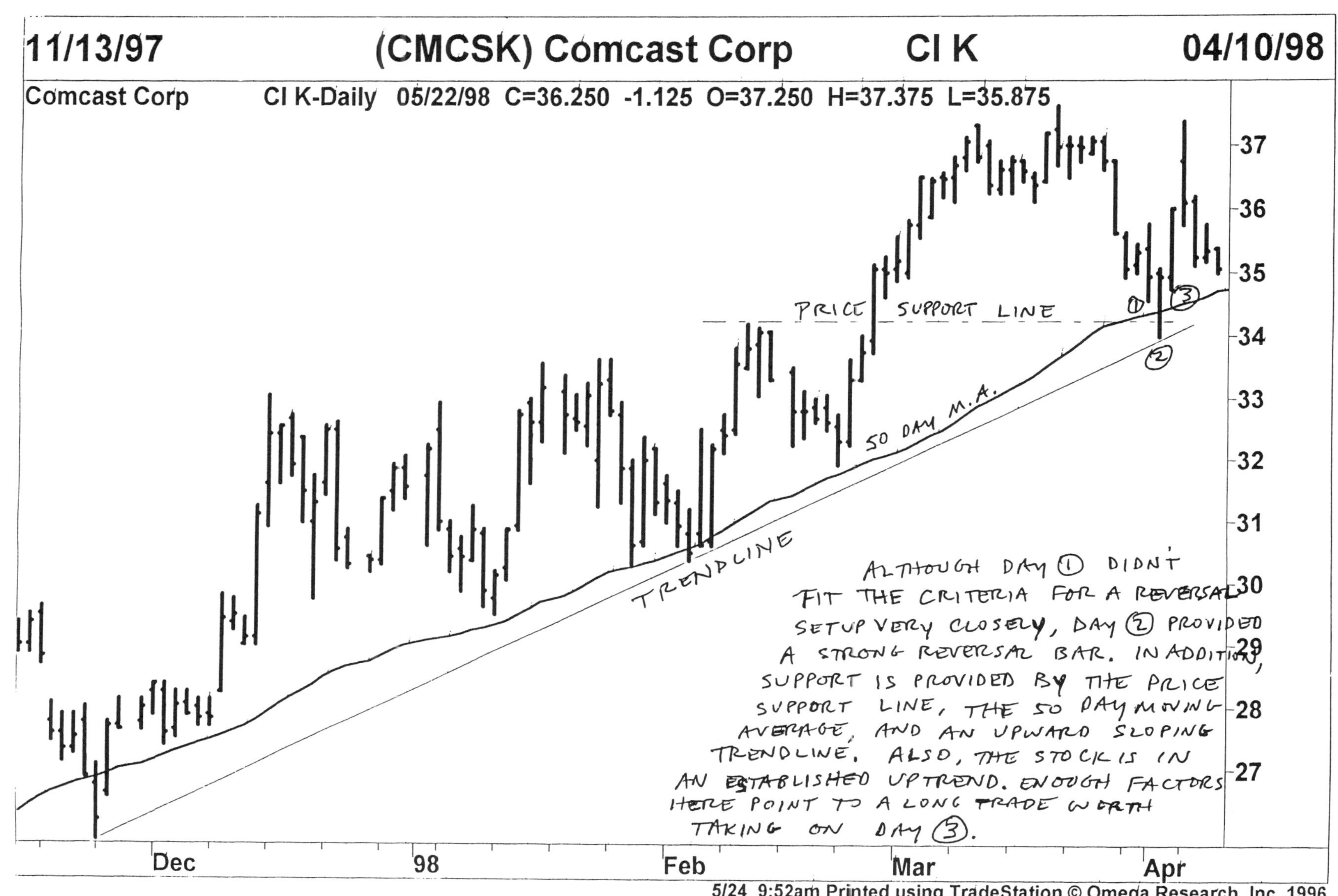
11/13/97
(CMCSK) Comcast Corp
Cl K
04/10/98
Comcast Corp
Cl K-Daily 05/22/98 C=36.250 -1.125 O=37.250 H=37.375 L=35.875
37
36
35
34
33
32
31
30
29
28
27
Dec
98
Feb
Mar
Apr
PRICE SUPPORT LINE
50 DAY M.A.
TRENDLINE
1
2
3
ALTHOUGH DAY 1 DIDN'T FIT THE CRITERIA FOR A REVERSAL SETUP VERY CLOSELY, DAY 2 PROVIDED A STRONG REVERSAL BAR. IN ADDITION, SUPPORT IS PROVIDED BY THE PRICE SUPPORT LINE, THE 50 DAY MOVING AVERAGE, AND AN UPWARD SLOPING TRENDLINE. ALSO, THE STOCK IS IN AN ESTABLISHED UPTREND. ENOUGH FACTORS HERE POINT TO A LONG TRADE WORTH TAKING ON DAY 3.
5/24 9:52am Printed using TradeStation © Omega Research, Inc. 1996

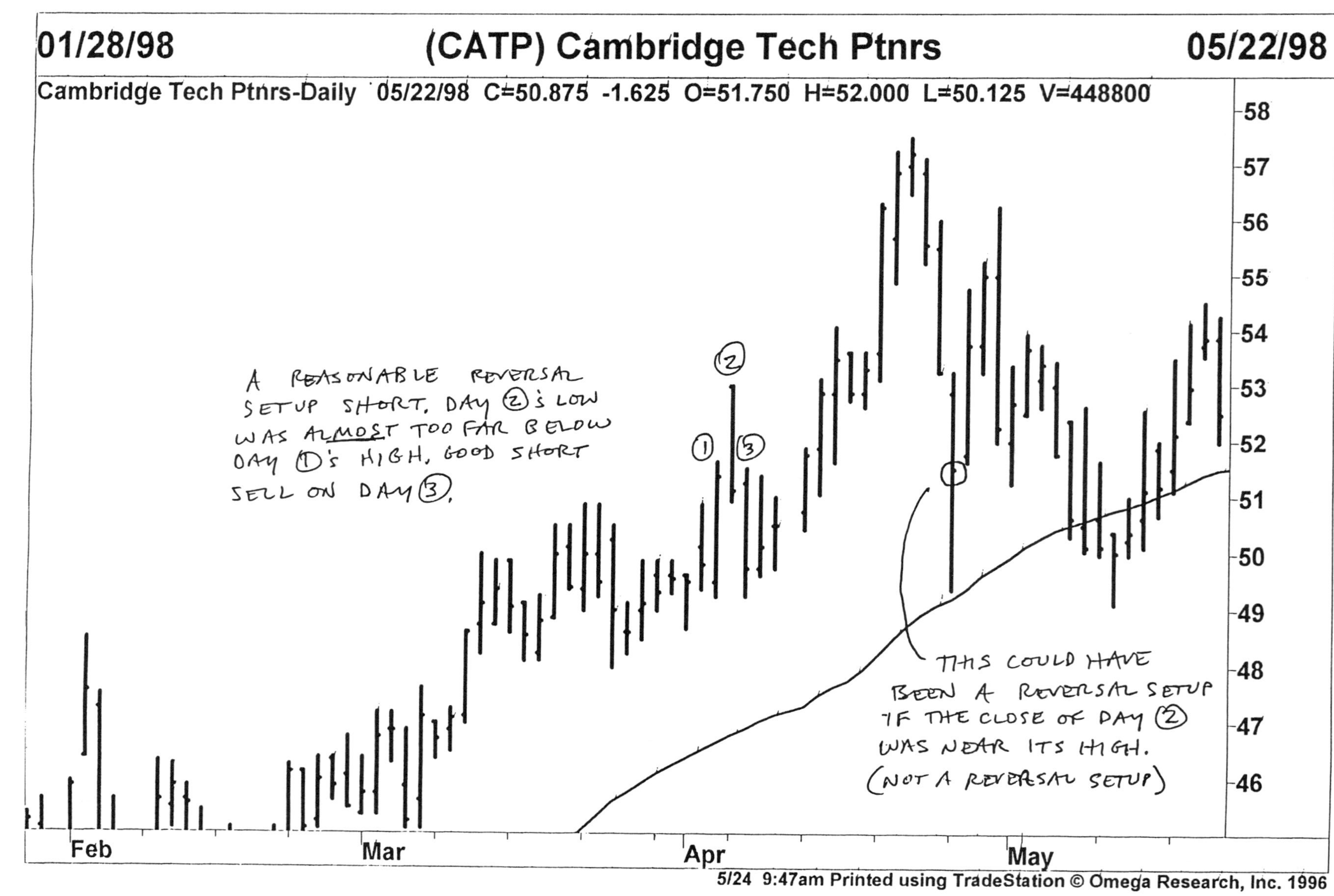
01/28/98
(CATP) Cambridge Tech Ptnrs
05/22/98
Cambridge Tech Ptnrs-Daily 05/22/98 C=50.875 -1.625 O=51.750 H=52.000 L=50.125 V=448800
58
57
56
55
54
53
52
51
50
49
48
47
46
Feb
Mar
Apr
May
A REASONABLE REVERSAL SETUP SHORT. DAY 2's LOW WAS ALMOST TOO FAR BELOW DAY 1's HIGH, GOOD SHORT SELL ON DAY 3.
1
2
3
THIS COULD HAVE BEEN A REVERSAL SETUP IF THE CLOSE OF DAY 2 WAS NEAR ITS HIGH. (NOT A REVERSAL SETUP)
5/24 9:47am Printed using TradeStation © Omega Research, Inc. 1996

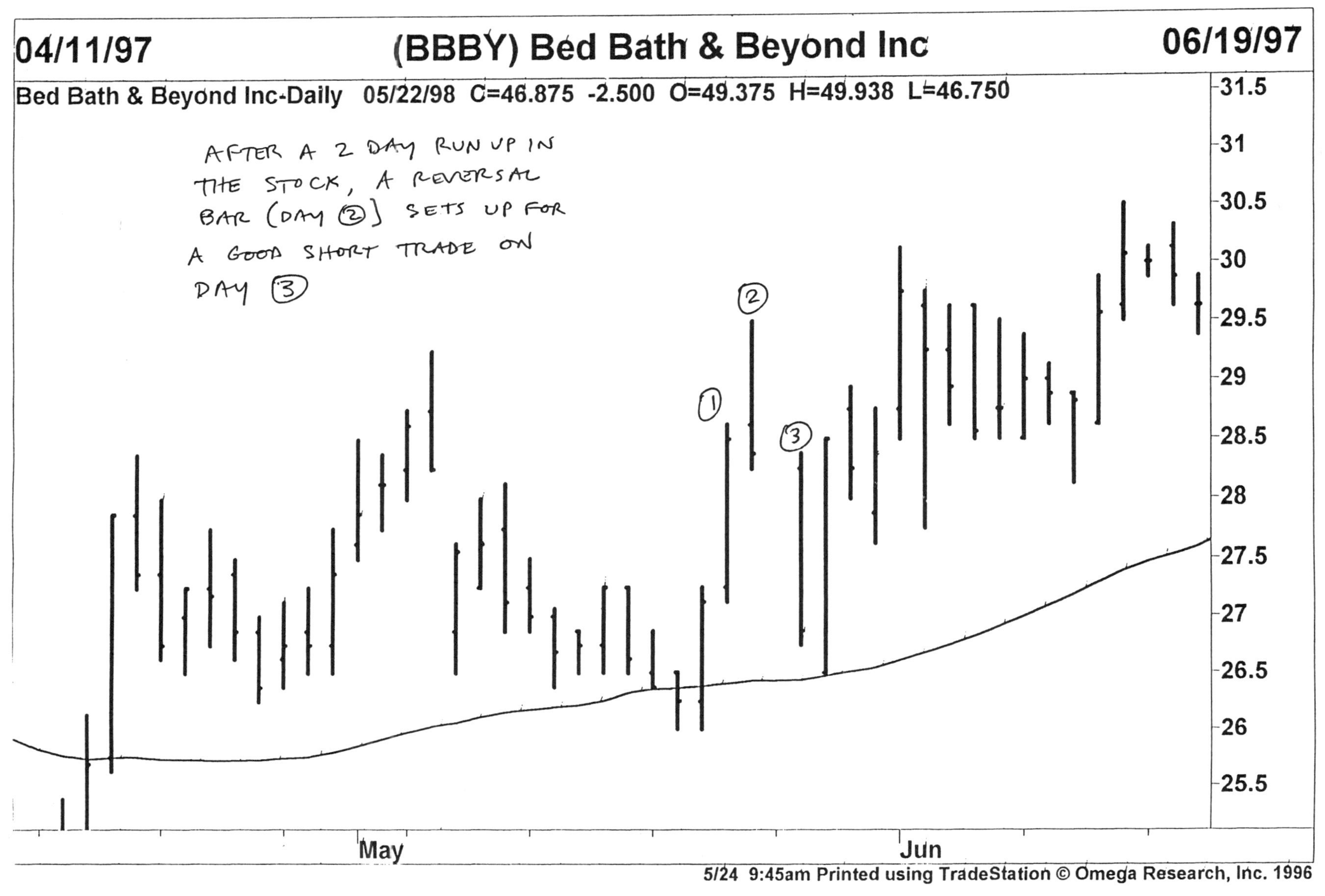
04/11/97
(BBBY) Bed Bath & Beyond Inc
06/19/97
Bed Bath & Beyond Inc-Daily 05/22/98 C=46.875 -2.500 O=49.375 H=49.938 L=46.750
AFTER A 2 DAY RUN UP IN THE STOCK, A REVERSAL BAR (DAY ②) SETS UP FOR A GOOD SHORT TRADE ON DAY ③
1
2
3
31.5
31
30.5
30
29.5
29
28.5
28
27.5
27
26.5
26
25.5
May
Jun
5/24 9:45am Printed using TradeStation © Omega Research, Inc. 1996

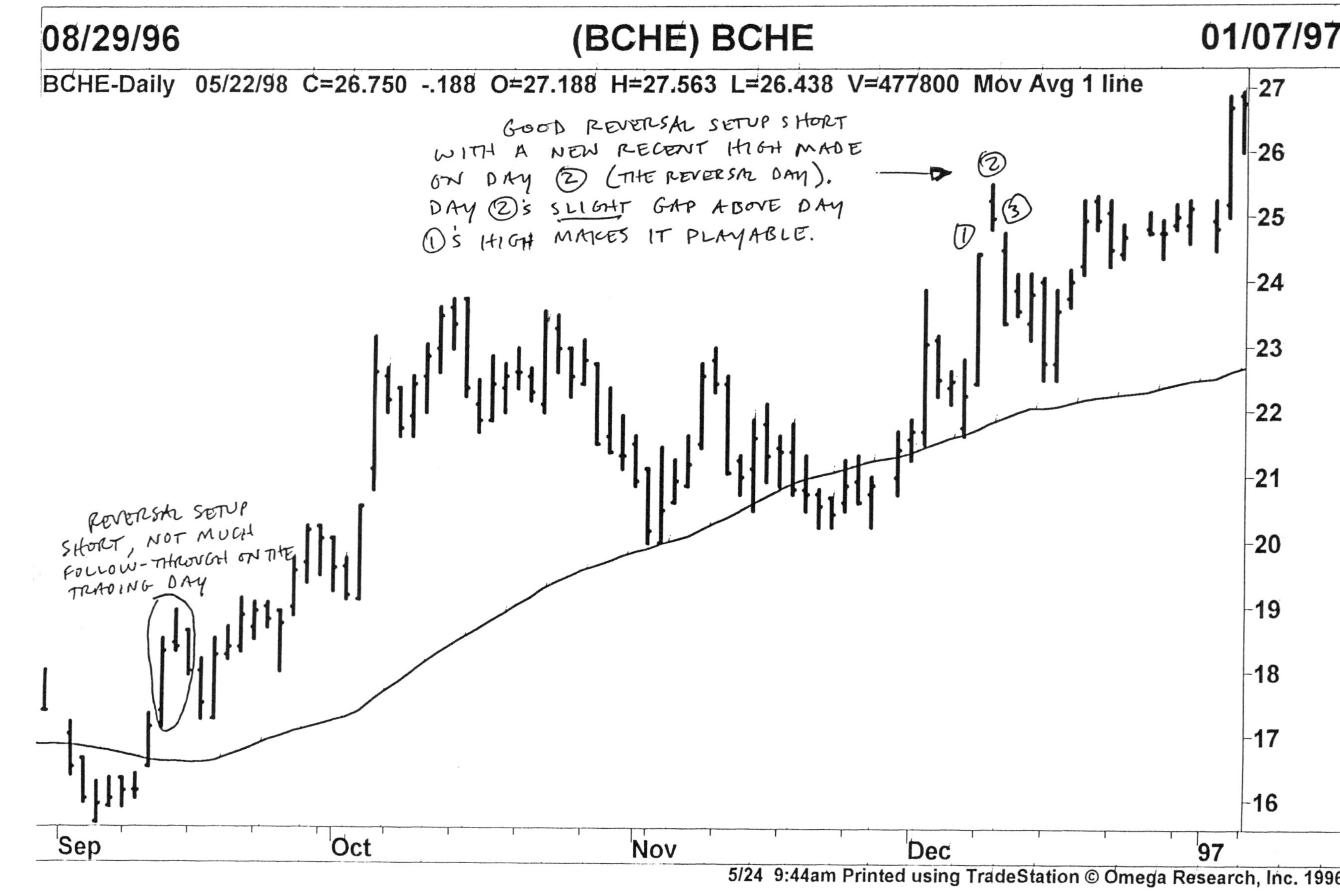

08/29/96
(BCHE) BCHE
01/07/97
BCHE-Daily 05/22/98 C=26.750 -.188 O=27.188 H=27.563 L=26.438 V=477800 Mov Avg 1 line
GOOD REVERSAL SETUP SHORT WITH A NEW RECENT HIGH MADE ON DAY ② (THE REVERSAL DAY). DAY ②'S SLIGHT GAP ABOVE DAY ①'S HIGH MAKES IT PLAYABLE.
①
②
③
REVERSAL SETUP SHORT, NOT MUCH FOLLOW-THROUGH ON THE TRADING DAY
27
26
25
24
23
22
21
20
19
18
17
16
Sep
Oct
Nov
Dec
97
5/24 9:44am Printed using TradeStation © Omega Research, Inc. 1996

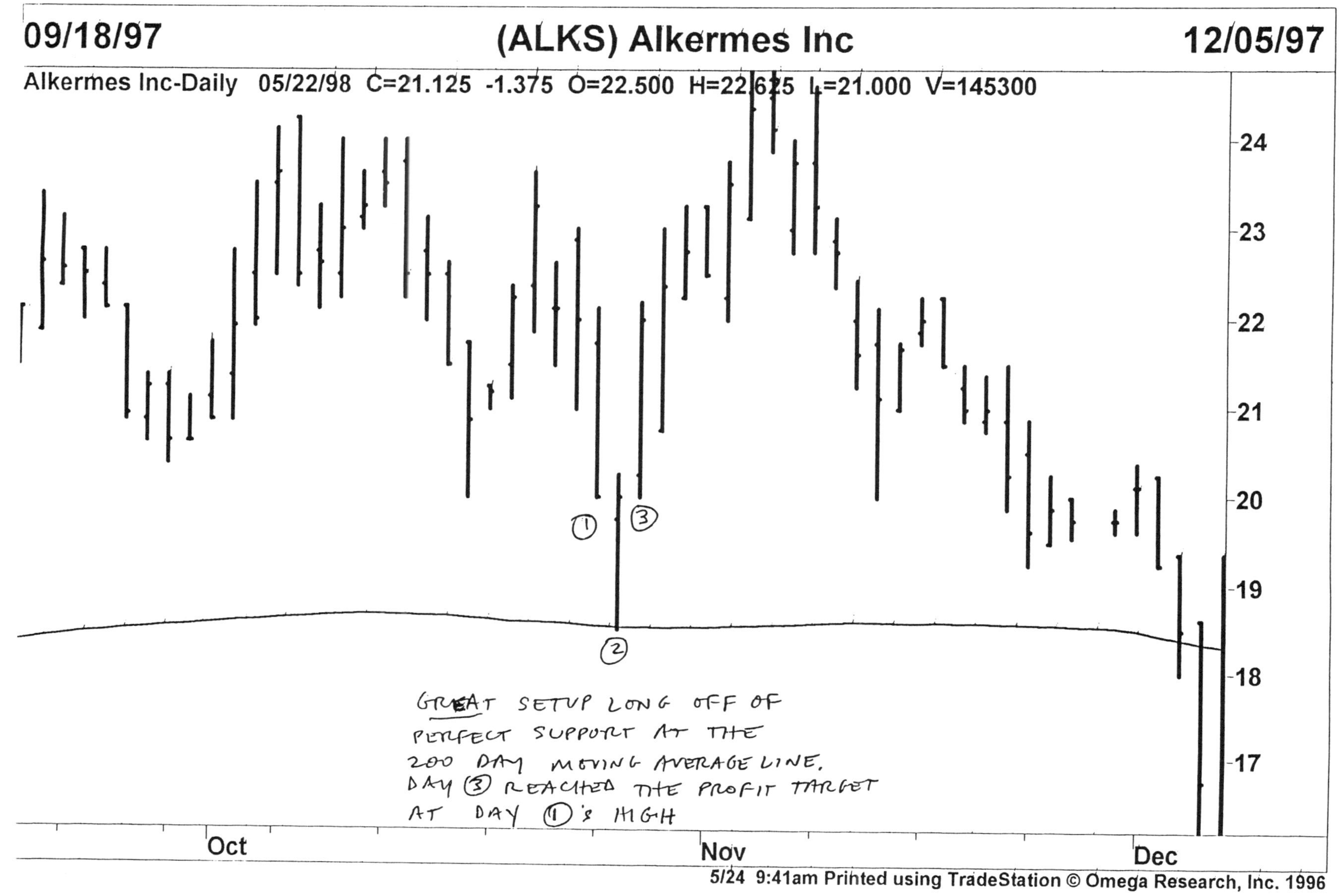

09/18/97
(ALKS) Alkermes Inc
12/05/97
Alkermes Inc-Daily 05/22/98 C=21.125 -1.375 O=22.500 H=22.625 L=21.000 V=145300
24
23
22
21
20
19
18
17
1
2
3
GREAT SETUP LONG OFF OF
PERFECT SUPPORT AT THE
200 DAY MOVING AVERAGE LINE.
DAY 3 REACHED THE PROFIT TARGET
AT DAY 1's HIGH
Oct
Nov
Dec
5/24 9:41am Printed using TradeStation © Omega Research, Inc. 1996

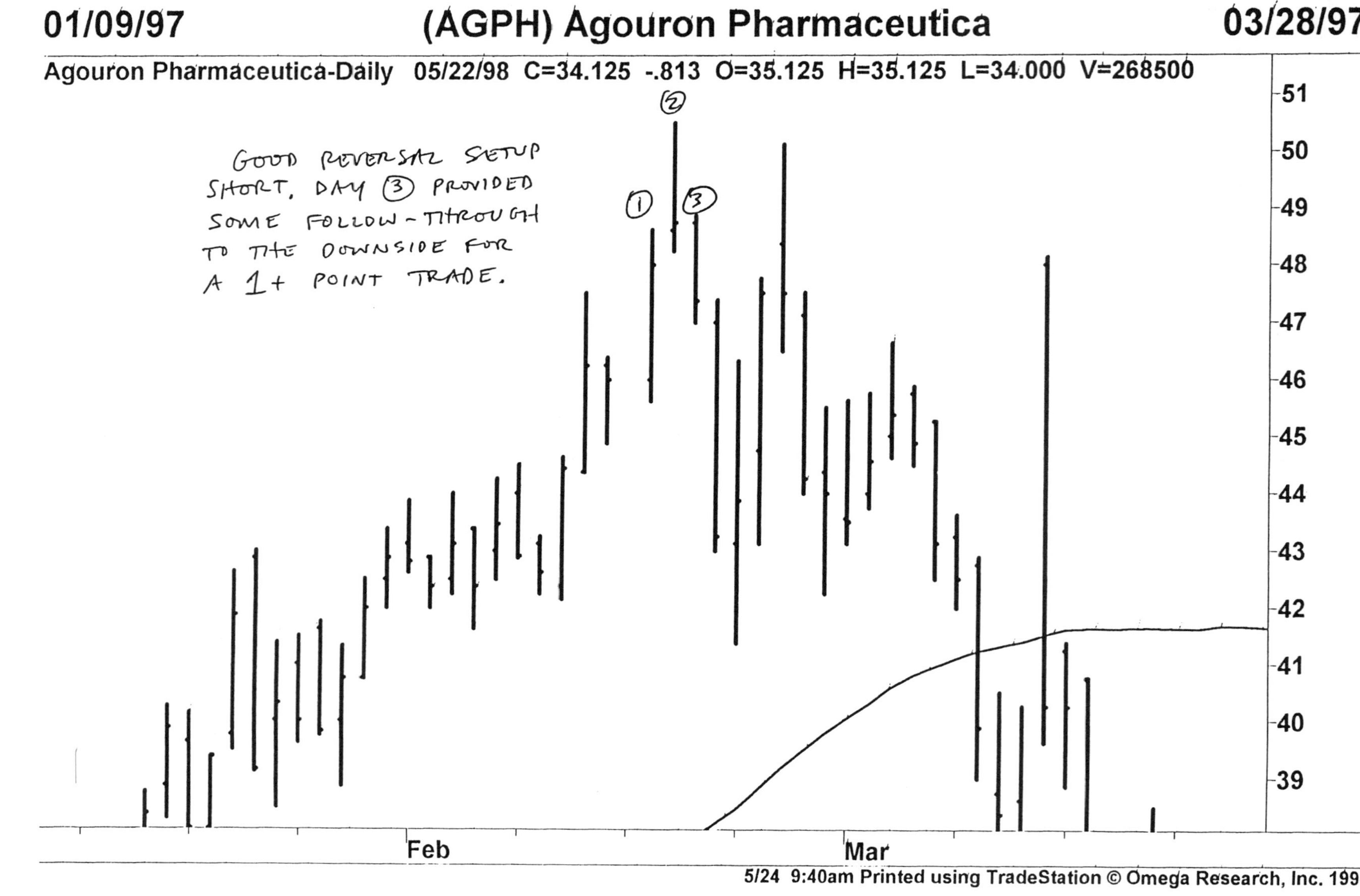
01/09/97
(AGPH) Agouron Pharmaceutica
03/28/97
Agouron Pharmaceutica-Daily 05/22/98 C=34.125 -.813 O=35.125 H=35.125 L=34.000 V=268500
GOOD REVERSAL SETUP SHORT, DAY (3) PROVIDED SOME FOLLOW-THROUGH TO THE DOWNSIDE FOR A 1+ POINT TRADE.
(1)
(2)
(3)
51
50
49
48
47
46
45
44
43
42
41
40
39
Feb
Mar
5/24 9:40am Printed using TradeStation © Omega Research, Inc. 1996

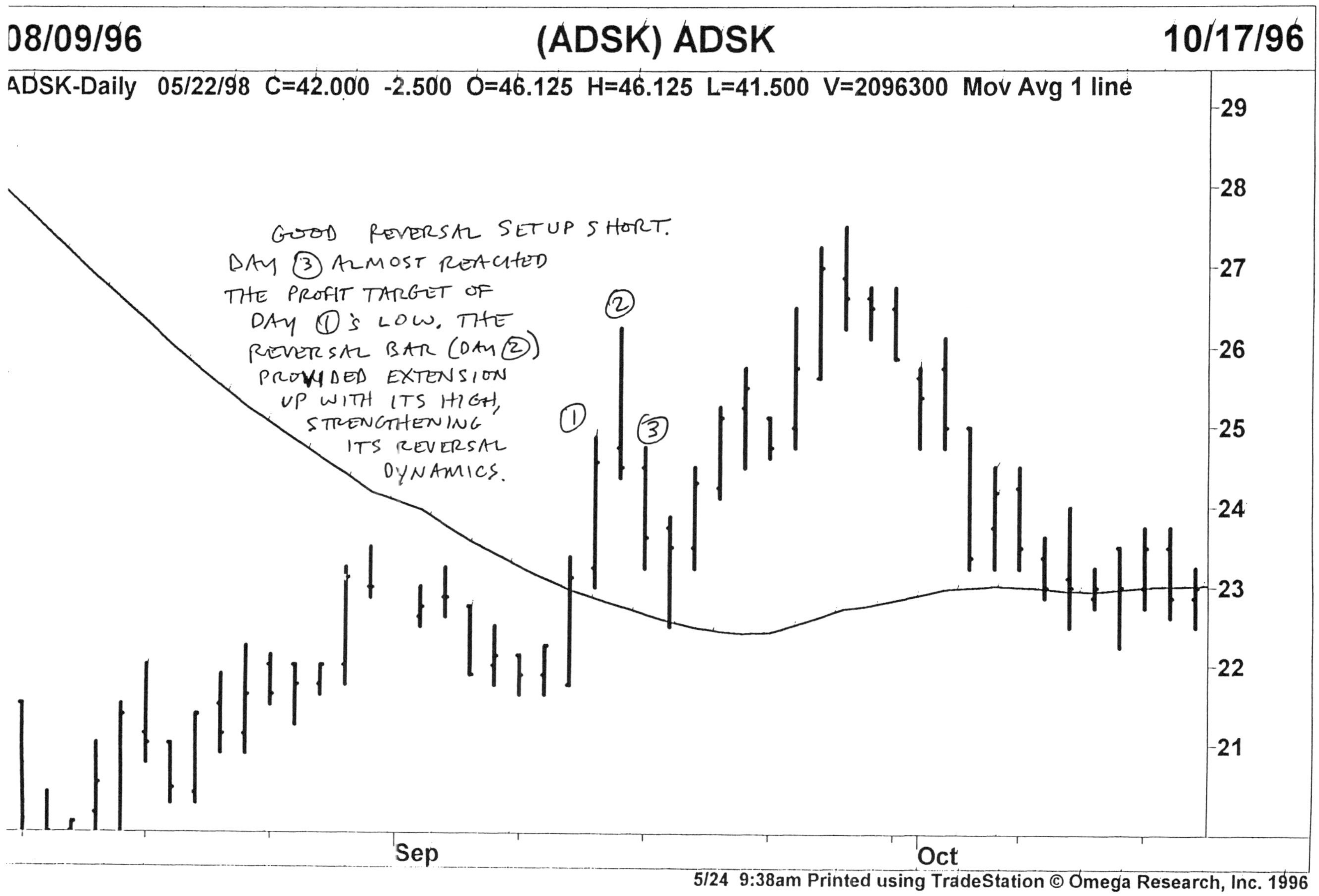
08/09/96
(ADSK) ADSK
10/17/96
ADSK-Daily 05/22/98 C=42.000 -2.500 O=46.125 H=46.125 L=41.500 V=2096300 Mov Avg 1 line
29
28
27
26
25
24
23
22
21
Sep
Oct
GOOD REVERSAL SETUP SHORT.
DAY (3) ALMOST REACHED
THE PROFIT TARGET OF
DAY (1)'s LOW, THE
REVERSAL BAR (DAY (2))
PROVIDED EXTENSION
UP WITH ITS HIGH,
STRENGTHENING
ITS REVERSAL
DYNAMICS.
(1)
(2)
(3)
5/24 9:38am Printed using TradeStation © Omega Research, Inc. 1996

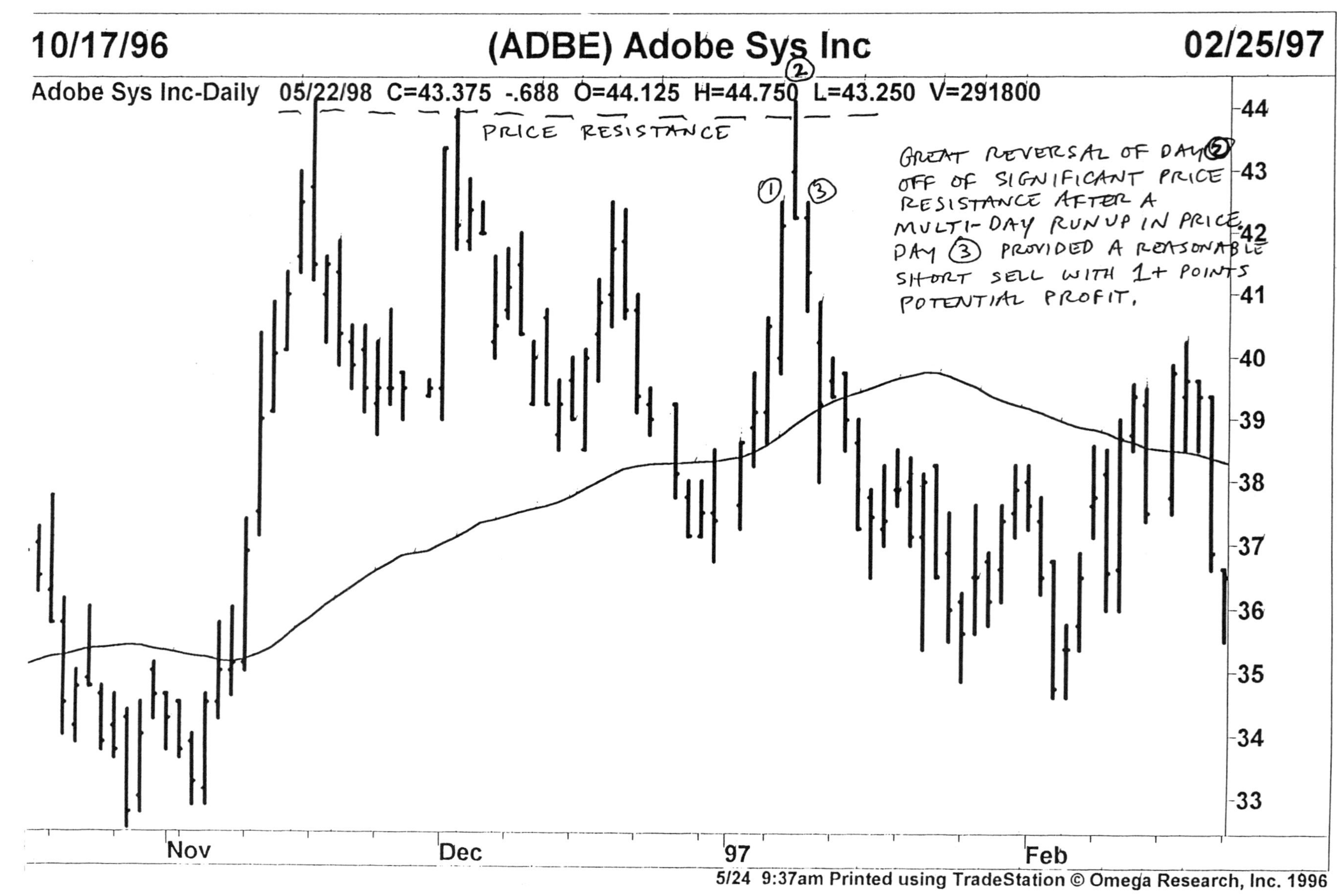
10/17/96
(ADBE) Adobe Sys Inc
02/25/97
Adobe Sys Inc-Daily 05/22/98 C=43.375 -.688 O=44.125 H=44.750 L=43.250 V=291800
PRICE RESISTANCE
1
2
3
GREAT REVERSAL OF DAY 2 OFF OF SIGNIFICANT PRICE RESISTANCE AFTER A MULTI-DAY RUNUP IN PRICE. DAY 3 PROVIDED A REASONABLE SHORT SELL WITH 1+ POINTS POTENTIAL PROFIT.
44
43
42
41
40
39
38
37
36
35
34
33
Nov
Dec
97
Feb
5/24 9:37am Printed using TradeStation © Omega Research, Inc. 1996

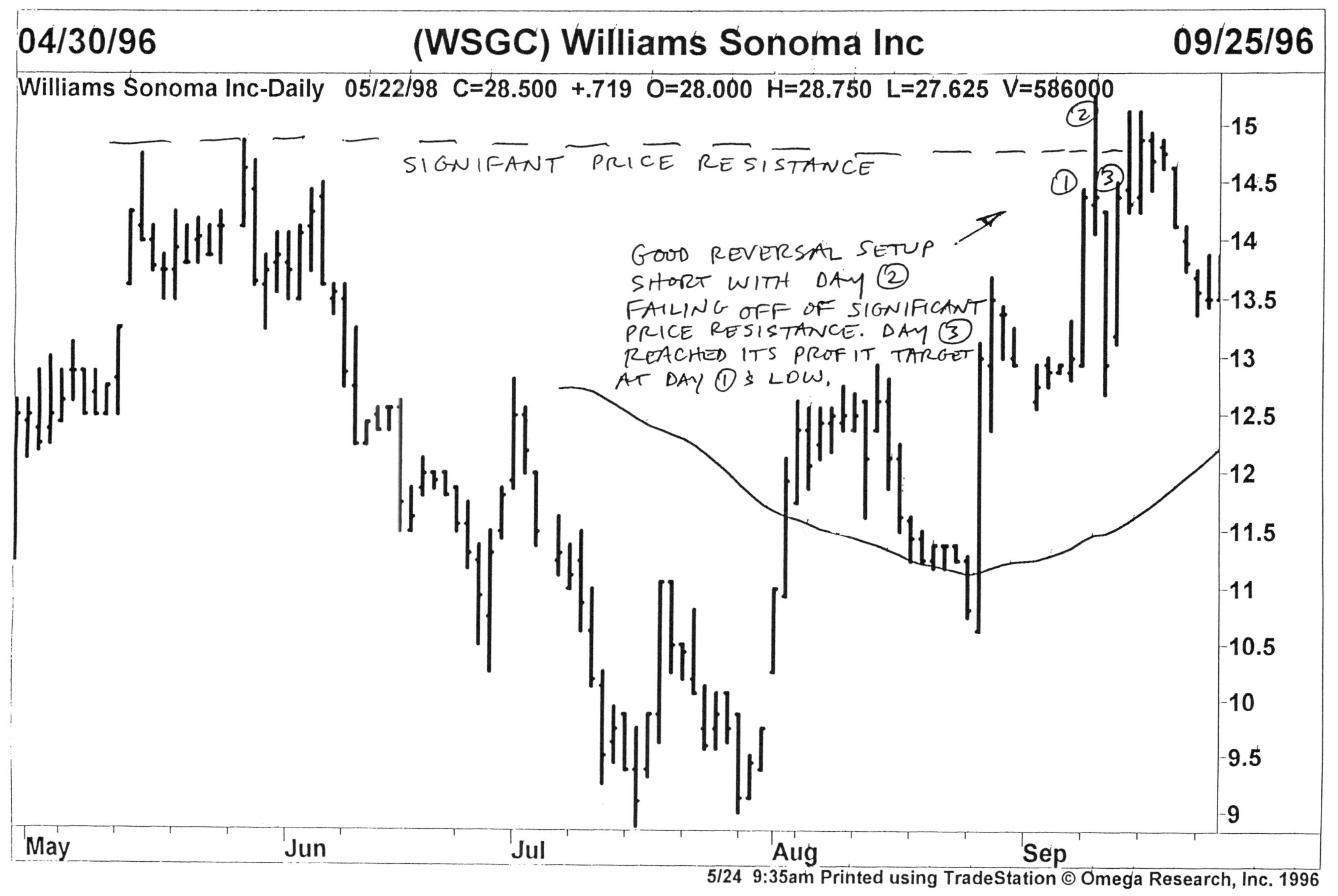
04/30/96
(WSGC) Williams Sonoma Inc
09/25/96
Williams Sonoma Inc-Daily 05/22/98 C=28.500 +.719 O=28.000 H=28.750 L=27.625 V=586000
SIGNIFANT PRICE RESISTANCE
GOOD REVERSAL SETUP
SHORT WITH DAY (2)
FAILING OFF OF SIGNIFICANT
PRICE RESISTANCE. DAY (3)
REACHED ITS PROFIT TARGET
AT DAY (1)'s LOW,
(1)
(2)
(3)
15
14.5
14
13.5
13
12.5
12
11.5
11
10.5
10
9.5
9
May
Jun
Jul
Aug
Sep
5/24 9:35am Printed using TradeStation © Omega Research, Inc. 1996

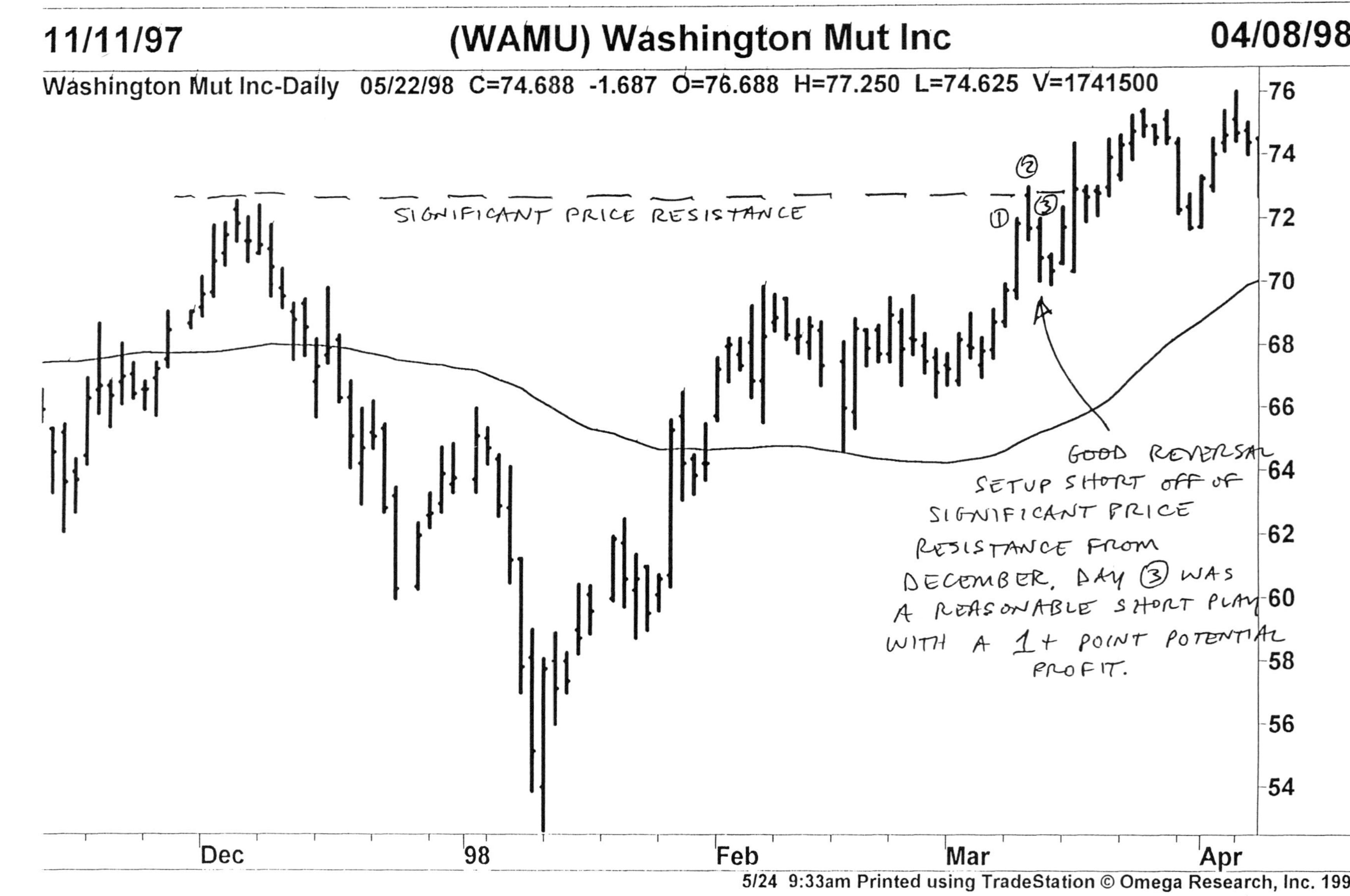
11/11/97
(WAMU) Washington Mut Inc
04/08/98
Washington Mut Inc-Daily 05/22/98 C=74.688 -1.687 O=76.688 H=77.250 L=74.625 V=1741500
SIGNIFICANT PRICE RESISTANCE
1
2
3
GOOD REVERSAL SETUP SHORT OFF OF SIGNIFICANT PRICE RESISTANCE FROM DECEMBER, DAY (3) WAS A REASONABLE SHORT PLAY WITH A 1+ POINT POTENTIAL PROFIT.
Dec
98
Feb
Mar
Apr
5/24 9:33am Printed using TradeStation © Omega Research, Inc. 1996

CONSOLIDATION

BREAKOUTS

CONSOLIDATION BREAKOUTS

"Consolidation breakouts on the 5 minute bar chart"

This price pattern setup is the one which is traded the most throughout the day as you type through your basket of stocks looking for the formation. Through my training of stock day traders, I have found that even someone with chart watching experience often has some initial difficulty recognizing a true setup. Although the setup seems relatively straightforward and simple, there are several specific criteria which it must meet to be a high probability pattern for trading.

Your ability to recognize and correctly enter this pattern is extremely important since it will comprise the majority of your trades. Therefore, I will reiterate the key components which must be met on the 5 minute bar chart so you can isolate only those consolidation breakout patterns that are to be traded. If any of these key components are missing then it is not a consolidation breakout pattern and should be passed up. Refer to the "Intraday Setups" section from the *"Stock Patterns"* book for the basic description and variations of this pattern.

CONSOLIDATION BREAKOUTS: KEY CRITERIA

1) First and foremost, the stock must currently be trading at its high or low of the day. This does not mean 1/8 below the high or 1/8 above the low. It means exactly what it says: at the high or low of the day. The way to ensure the stock is at its high is to look back to the left of the forming pattern and see if any 5 minute bar extends above the price where the stock is currently trading since the beginning of that day's trading session. If so, then you are not at the high of the day and should move on (the inverse is true for a pattern setting up at the current low of the day). If the pattern is forming exactly at a high set earlier in the trading session, this actually enhances the odds of success for a breakout trade once the pattern is formed. The same is true for a setup forming at the day's low.

2) The stock must be consolidating at its high or low of the day. Consolidation consists of at least four 5 minute bars that are trading up against the high or down against the low. Consolidation does not consist of just 1 or 2 bars! (3 bars are sometimes acceptable on rare occasions with the breakout occurring as the 4th bar is forming).

3) Hugging - The consolidation should tend to hug up against the high of the day or down against the low of the day. In effect, this reflects a build up of pressure against this price level in the direction of the breakout if it occurs. More initial follow-through in the price move can be expected.

4) A consolidation breakout setup at the high of the day can only be traded long. A consolidation breakout setup at the low of the day can only be traded short. No exceptions!

5) If you see a consolidation pattern that is tight and long and looks great, but is not at the current high or low of the day, do not trade it! Don't be too eager to jump on what may be a breakout of apparently great looking consolidation. If you fail to make sure that the consolidation is trading at the high or low of the day, then the odds of success fall dramatically. This is called trading "in the channel" and should be avoided.

These are 5 key criteria to be remembered and that must be met for a true consolidation breakout pattern. Resist the temptation to trade less than the best setups, apply all of the above analysis. Anything else is sloppy trading and translates into lost dollars.

Also, you will be frustrated with losing trades that did not satisfy the above criteria because you knew better than to take them. You want every edge in your favor, otherwise it's like throwing away money. Your focus should be to trade with quality. You should deem anything less as unacceptable to you as a professional day trader. Take pride in the craftsmanship of identifying and trading only the best setups.

CONSOLIDATION BREAKOUTS: ADDITIONAL NUANCES

- The tighter the consolidation is, the better the potential trade. This refers to the range from high to low for each 5 minute bar on your intraday chart. The smaller their range is as they consolidate against the day's current high or low, the better the odds of a strong breakout with follow-through.

- The longer the consolidation lasts, the greater the probability of success for the breakout trade. Four 5 minute bars should be a minimum, but if you have an hour or two of good consolidation then odds favor a stronger breakout trade.

- Trade these setups only in the direction of the intraday market indices. When the market is moving up on its 5 minute bar chart, look for stocks that are consolidating at their high. Look for stocks consolidating at their low when the market indices are moving down. Having the direction of the market in your favor enhances the odds of a successful consolidation breakout trade.

- If a stock has traded up to a certain price 1 or more times during the day (establishing a high for that session) and then trades back up to that same price and consolidates…it becomes a stronger trade.

These nuances simply increase the chances for a winning trade. Every odd that you can stack on your side adds to your overall success. I have diagrammed some examples of what consolidation both should and should not look like.

(perfect consolidation setups)

(occasionally acceptable consolidation setups)

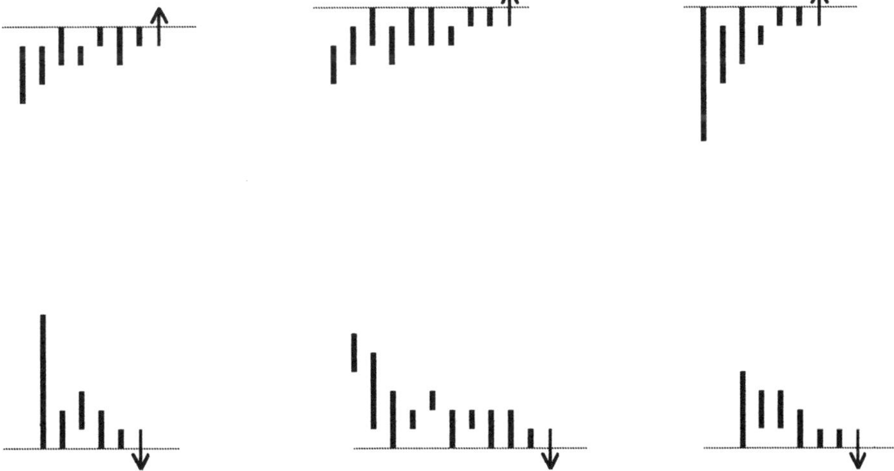

(consolidation setups - not)

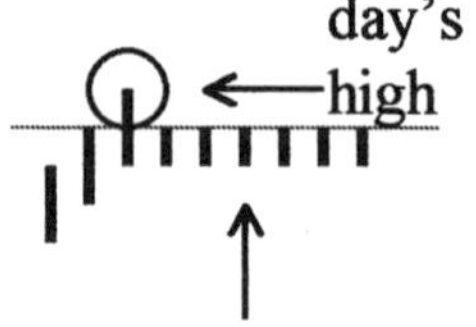

good consolidation but not at the high of the day

too much space here, needs to hug up against the day's high a bit better

decent consolidation hugging up against a price level but is not at the high of the day

Although the best setup has at least 4 bars of consolidation with every bar hugging against the high or low of the day prior to a breakout, sometimes a little leeway may be given. If a stock is very strong and has several bars consolidating at the high, one of the bars may not actually be touching the high. As long as all other factors point to a strong move (including the indices moving up decisively) then it may be considered.

Obviously the best "textbook-looking" setups provide the greatest odds of success. But in the real world of trading, they don't unfold this way all of the time. With experience in the market, some "acceptable" setups may be traded – especially with stocks where you have intimately familiarized yourself with their price-movement-personality by watching them trade day in and day out on the 5 minute bar chart.

Hopefully this will help you hone your ability to spot the real consolidation patterns and trade them as the stock breaks to a new high or low on the day. The next important ingredient is your entry point. Where do you enter the trade, and when is it too early or too late. This is best explained with a diagram showing a stock's level II market maker quote screen and comparing it to a diagram of the consolidation pattern.

MARKET MAKER SCREEN WITH 5 MINUTE CHART CONSOLIDATION

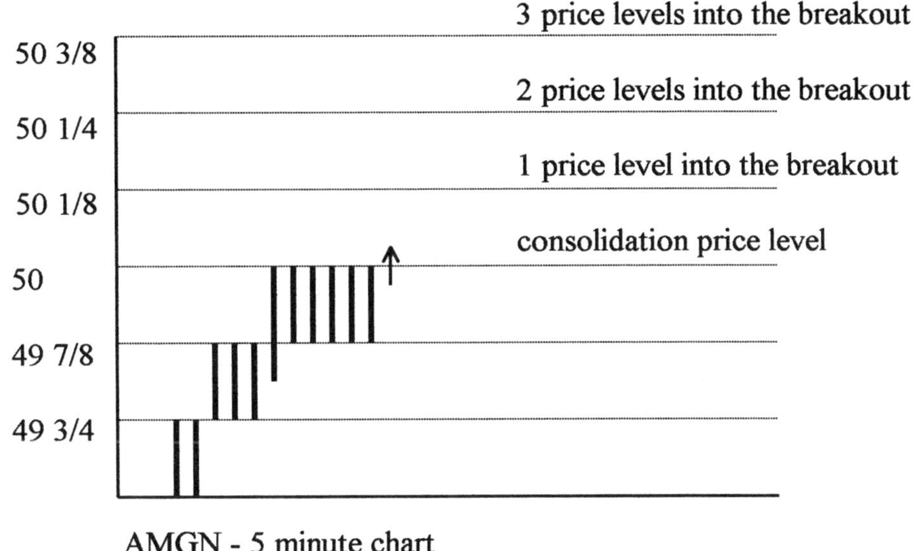

AMGN - 5 minute chart

Here is how the corresponding market maker screen would currently look for AMGN:

AMGN 50			
Bid		**Ask**	
GSCO	49 7/8	MLCO	50
INCA	49 7/8	SBSH	50
HRZG	49 7/8	MSCO	50
SHWD	49 3/4	NEED	50 1/8
TSCO	49 3/4	PWJC	50 1/8
WEED	49 3/4	NAWE	50 1/8
JEFF	49 3/4	HMQT	50 1/8
MONT	49 3/4	LEHM	50 1/4
FBCO	49 5/8	GSCO	50 1/4
PWJC	49 5/8	JEFF	50 1/4
		SHWD	50 3/8
		TSCO	50 3/8
		HRZG	50 3/8

AMGN has consolidated up against 50 and is a potential candidate for a breakout trade on the 5 minute bar chart. The market maker screen also reflects this with a bid price level of 49 7/8 and ask price level of 50 (the consolidation high of the day). Since you typically buy at the ask on these breakout trades, when and at what price do you enter your order to buy?

You would either buy at 50 or 50 1/8. The best price if the stock was about to move long would obviously be 50 in anticipation of the breakout. But you do not simply buy it and hope it breaks to the upside. Clues for timing your entry are given by the movement of market makers on the screen and prints of actual trades coming through on the time and sale screen (not shown). If the market makers begin to move up off of the inside ask of 50 as you also see time and sale prints of trades taking place at 50 then often the stock is about to penetrate through this price level as it begins its initial burst to the long side. If you observe this unfolding, many times you can try to execute a buy at the consolidation price of 50.

On the other hand, you may wish to wait for the bar chart and inside ask on the market maker screen to move to 50 1/8 to confirm the breakout. This is also an appropriate entry point. But if you cannot catch the stock by 50 1/8 before the market makers at this price level also move up off of the screen then pass up the trade. In other words you only want to enter a trade by buying or selling a stock either at the consolidation point or 1 price level into the breakout (50 1/8 in this case with AMGN).

Trading into a stock beyond 1 price level into the breakout is called "chasing" and will doom the trade to failure more often than not. Why? Because with this pattern you have not only isolated a good trade setup but also a low risk entry point where you can realistically risk no more than 1/4 of a loss if it goes against you. After the initial breakout where the stock may run up 1/4 to 1/2 point it usually stalls and has a pull back. If you entered at the correct price, you have a buffer of profit to easily ride through this initial "wiggle" without having it come back far enough against you to force you to exit with a 1/4 loss.

This is very important when intraday trend trading. If you enter the stock 2 price levels or more into the breakout, the initial pullback will often force you out of the trade for a loss as you then watch the stock resume its move in the direction of the breakout for what could have been a good profit. If you are scalping, your correct entry will allow you room to then offer the stock out 1/8 to 1/4 or more into the momentum of the initial price surge with a greater likelihood of getting filled for a quick profit before the stock stalls with its first pullback.

This is the strength of the 5 minute consolidation breakout setups for both intraday trend trading as well as scalping. Never chase a stock beyond 1 price level into the breakout. When scalping it is even better if you learn to anticipate the breakout successfully and can get filled at the actual consolidation level just prior to its penetration. This gives you an extra 1/8 profit if you are right and 1/8 less loss if you're wrong. Do the math. Over the course of days and weeks it adds up significantly as well as increases the percentage of successful trades. This has a very positive psychological impact that can further improve your trading.

CONSOLIDATION BREAKOUT – ALTERNATIVE ENTRY

If you missed the breakout entry on a stock there is an alternative way to enter. This approach should be used very sparingly and only on trades that have a high probability of successful follow-through. These confirming factors are based on a good pattern setup, "filtering" with the daily chart (covered in a later section), and making sure the indices are moving firmly in the direction of the trade. 90% of the time it is better to pass up the trade if you missed the initial breakout entry, but this is another tool in your arsenal.

Consider entering the trade once the initial pullback has stalled and it appears that the stock is about to continue its move in the direction of the breakout. As mentioned earlier, after the breakout surge in price, a pullback usually takes place. You do not want the breakout to have moved more than approximately 1/2 point beyond the consolidation price. When it then retraces some of this breakout move and begins to stall, consider bidding or offering into the direction of the breakout (depending upon whether it was a long or short move). Or you can simply buy the ask or sell at the bid to enter if the bid/ask spread is "tight" at that point.

Typically this pullback will retrace back near the breakout point. Once the trade is entered, do not risk more than 1/4 point as you do with any other trade. An example of a buy setup is diagrammed below. Again, this should not be utilized much at all in the normal course of trading.

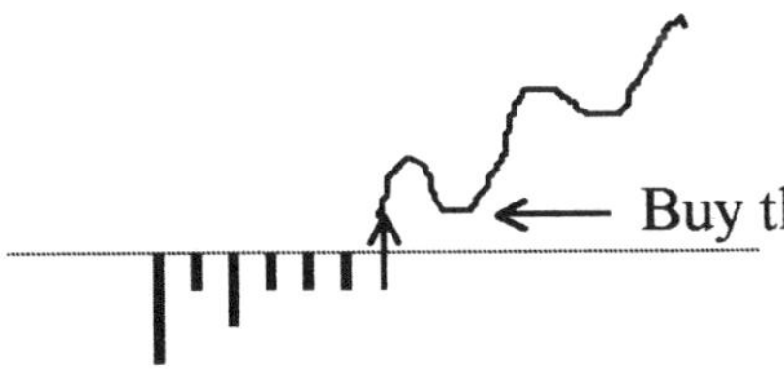

← Buy the dip of the initial breakout once it has stalled from its initial pullback...which <u>must be above the breakout price level</u>

The short scenario is the same, only inverted. After a breakout to the downside you would short the initial rally (pullback) once it has halted, assuming that the stock is about to resume its move down. <u>This entry is only for intraday trend trading, not scalping</u>!

VARIATION ON THE "INITIAL WIGGLE"

One approach to minimize the downside of your losing trades is to apply a variation on the first "wiggle" of a consolidation breakout trade on the 5 minute chart. This is best implemented if you are able to time your execution so that you enter the trade at the consolidation price as opposed to the actual breakout price. Time your order entry by the movement of the level II quote screen and "Time And Sale" prints as the stock begins initiating its breakout price surge.

If the stock moves up 3/8 beyond the consolidation entry point, then exit with a 1/8 loss (instead of the typical 1/4 point loss). Once the trade gives you a 1/2 profit, then exit at breakeven instead of the typical 1/8 loss if the stock pulls back to your entry point.

Once you have weathered this initial (first) "wiggle," then you'll probably want to let the standard wiggle guide the progression of the trade.

When intraday trend trading, this will usually still keep you in a good trade if you catch the consolidation price just prior to the breakout. Also, on a choppy non-trending day, you won't get hurt as bad when stocks do not follow through out of the breakout patterns.

This variation on the initial "wiggle" can be a powerful method for limiting losses on losing days while still generating big profits on trending days.

MORE 5 MINUTE BAR PATTERNS

5 MINUTE "L" PATTERN

Here is one of my favorite 5 minute setups for short plays that can unfold in the first one to two hours of trading as well as during the last hour of the session. I call it the "L" pattern. It is a variation on the typical consolidation breakout pattern seen on the 5 minute chart.

You want to see one (sometimes 2) 5 minute bar spiking down on a sharp quick selloff of 3/4 points or more, followed by 10 to 15 minutes without any significant price bounce. The stock should sit stagnant and show the semblance of 5 minute consolidation at the new, current low of the session, reflecting weakness. The next break in price should be to the downside.

As the pattern unfolds it should be accompanied by a downward move in the market indices. Attempt to short sell or short offer the stock, and risk no more than 1/4 point. You can see the reason I refer to this play as the "L" pattern below.

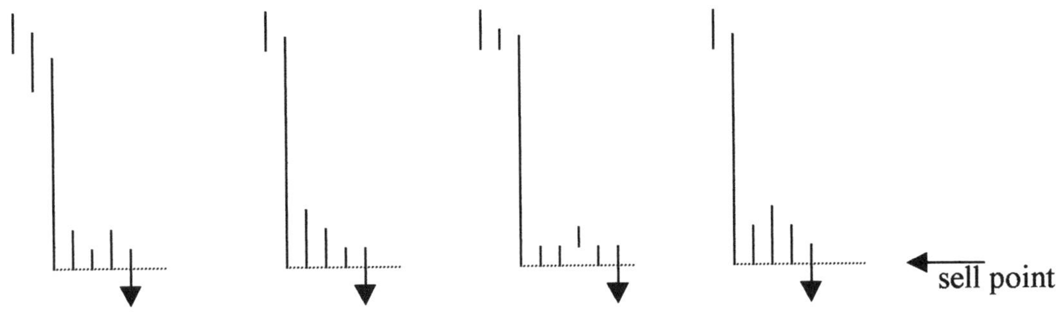

Since the next leg lower is often hard and fast, you may wish to "buy back in" to cover your trade after the next spike down. If the stock and overall market look weak, consider riding the trade for more profits by using the "wiggle."

The "L" pattern is only a short trade. Since the market and individual stocks sell off further and faster than they rally, a short trade like this one can offer the chance for larger quick profits.

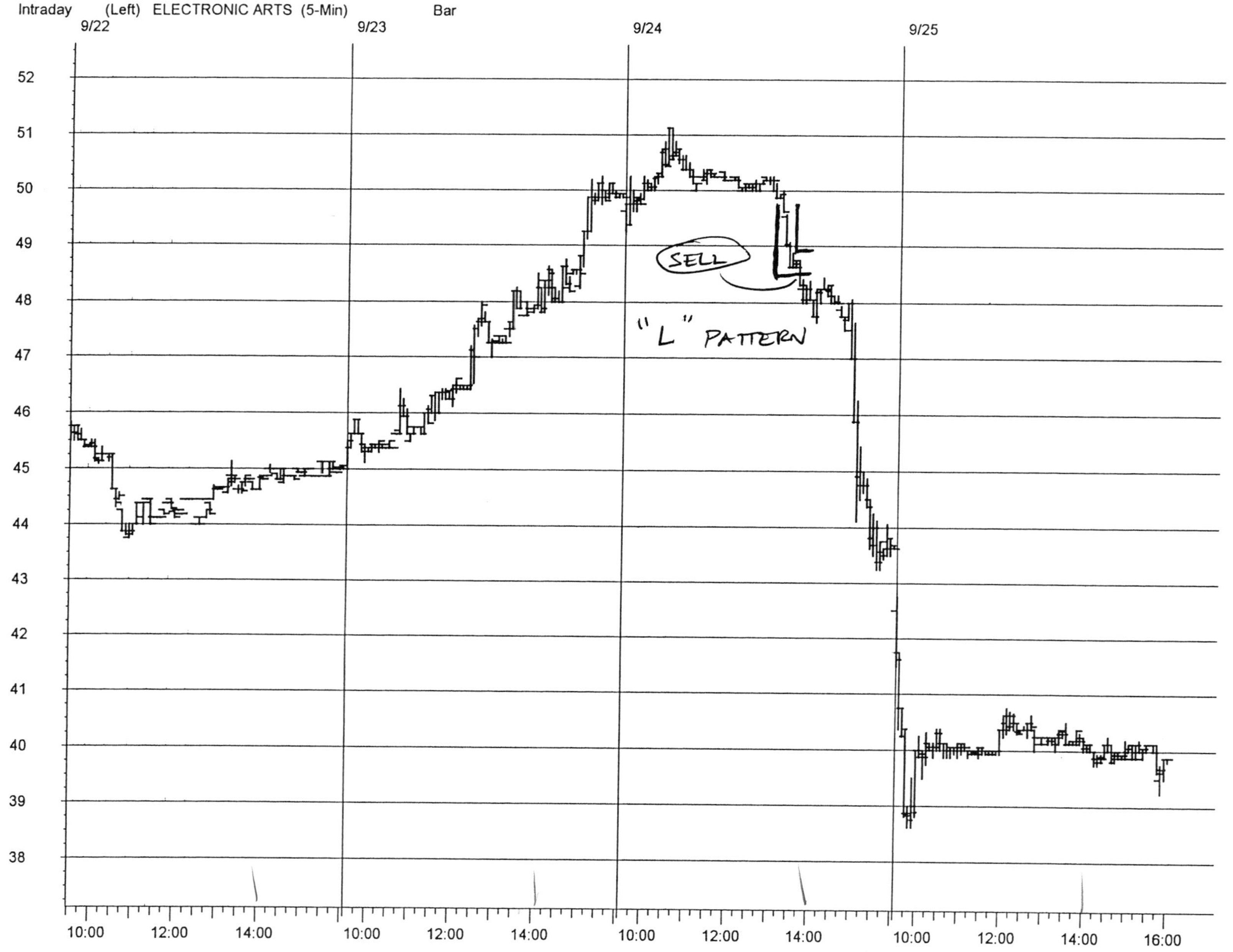

Intraday (Left) ELECTRONIC ARTS (5-Min) Bar
9/22
9/23
9/24
9/25
52
51
50
49
48
47
46
45
44
43
42
41
40
39
38
10:00
12:00
14:00
16:00
SELL
"L" PATTERN

Intraday (Left) JUST FOR FEET INC (5-Min)
Bar
8/05
8/06
8/07
8/09
"L" PATTERN
SELL
21 3/4
21 1/2
21 1/4
21
20 3/4
20 1/2
20 1/4
20
19 3/4
19 1/2
19 1/4
19
18 3/4
18 1/2
18 1/4
18
17 3/4
17 1/2
17 1/4
17
16 3/4
16 1/2
16 1/4
16
10:00 11:00 12:00 13:00 14:00 15:00
10:00 11:00 12:00 13:00 14:00 15:00
10:00 11:00 12:00 13:00 14:00 15:00 16:00

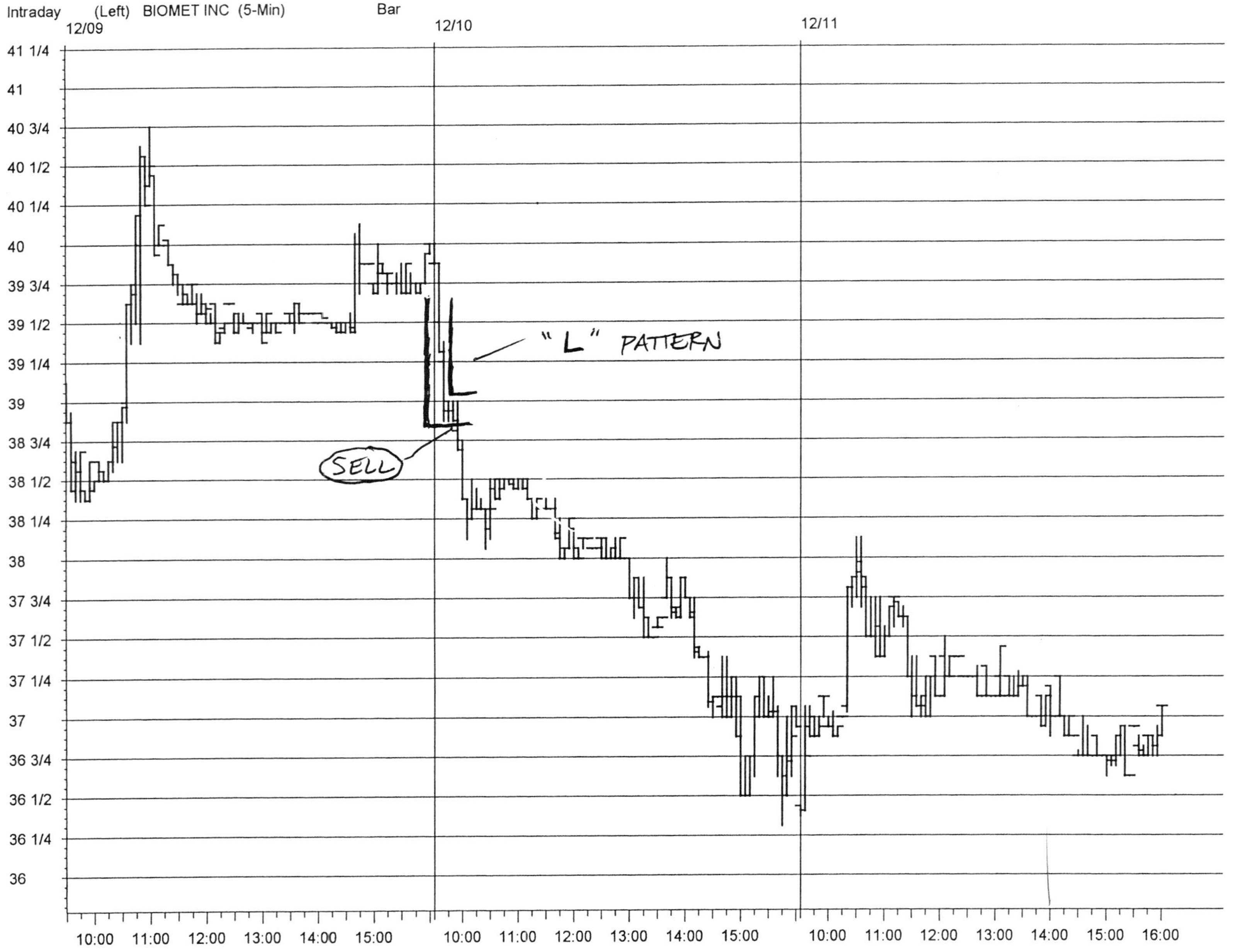
Intraday
(Left) BIOMET INC (5-Min)
Bar
12/09
12/10
12/11
41 1/4
41
40 3/4
40 1/2
40 1/4
40
39 3/4
39 1/2
39 1/4
39
38 3/4
38 1/2
38 1/4
38
37 3/4
37 1/2
37 1/4
37
36 3/4
36 1/2
36 1/4
36
"L" PATTERN
SELL
10:00 11:00 12:00 13:00 14:00 15:00 10:00 11:00 12:00 13:00 14:00 15:00 10:00 11:00 12:00 13:00 14:00 15:00 16:00

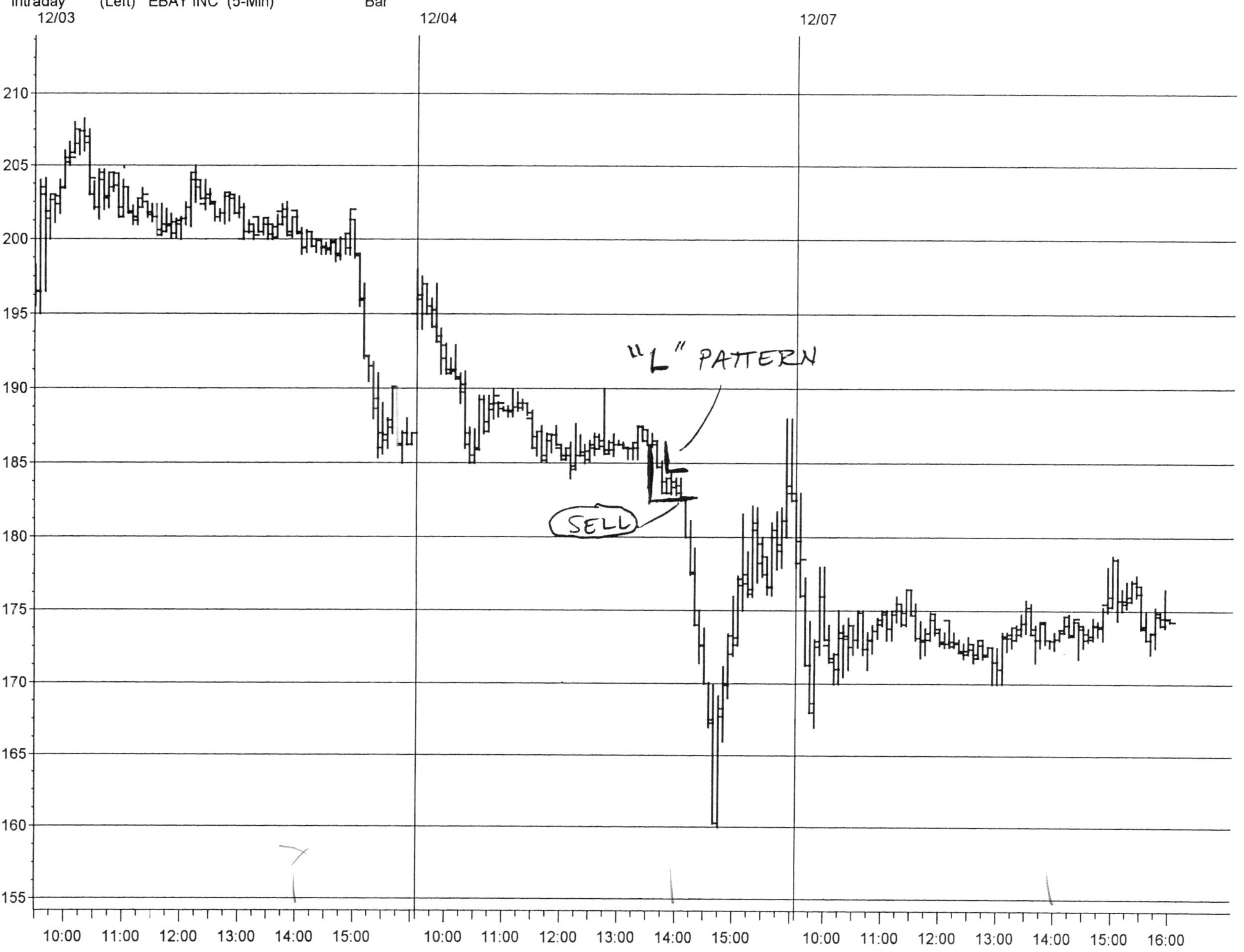
Intraday
12/03
(Left) EBAY INC (5-Min)
Bar
12/04
12/07
"L" PATTERN
SELL
210
205
200
195
190
185
180
175
170
165
160
155
10:00
11:00
12:00
13:00
14:00
15:00
16:00

THE FLASHBACK

The "flashback" pattern is a morning move off of the open. A stock can quickly fake one way, only to reverse back the other direction. The "headfake" pulls traders in and then forces them to cover as the stock heads in what is usually the true direction of the price move on the day. This setup should play itself out within the first 5 to 30 minutes of market activity for a stock. The quicker the reversal, the better the trade.

This pattern can be seen and used with the W/R day, extreme close as it bounces (reacts) off of a micro support or resistance level to follow through in the direction it bounced. But it will also unfold in many other situations and is a stand-alone pattern that can be traded early in the session.

For a buy setup the initial price moves down off of the open. The extent of the move may be anywhere from 1/8 to 1/2 (sometimes 5/8) point for stocks with a bid/ask spread of 1/4 or less. This initial down move should preferably occur during the first 5 to 10 minutes after the stock first begins trading.

The initial move should then halt and reverse direction relatively quickly (within 5 to 10 minutes). Next, the stock should quickly "flash back" through the high set in the first 5 minutes of trading, creating a long play.

The entry point is the current high that was set at the beginning of the session, or 1/8 point above it – no later. The trade is reinforced if the high on the first 5 minute bar was also the open of the day. The flashback short sell is the same as described above, only inverted.

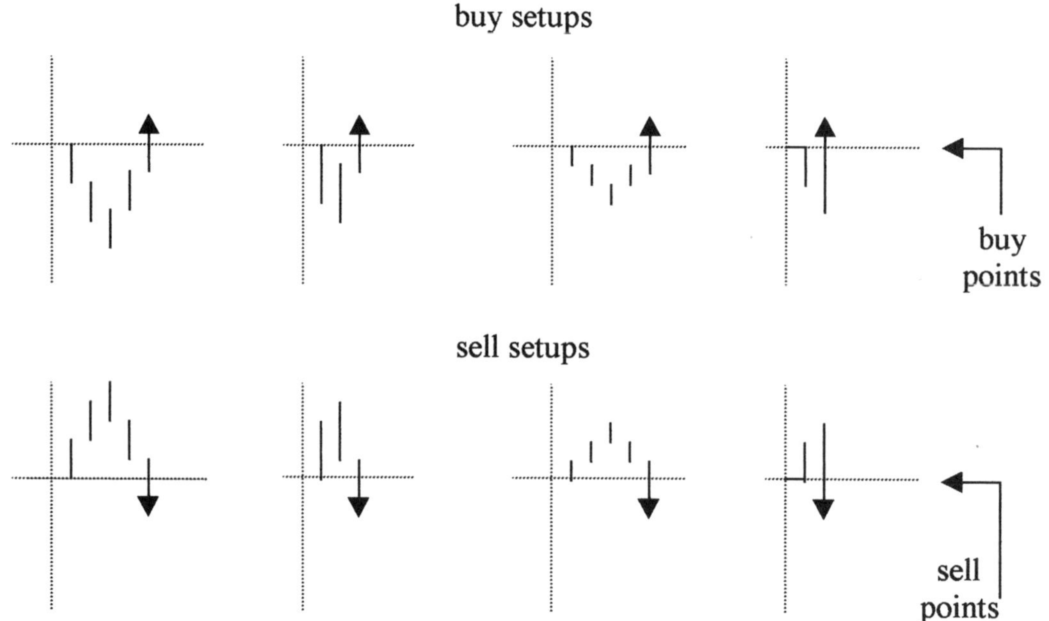

Make sure the trade is in the direction of the market indices.

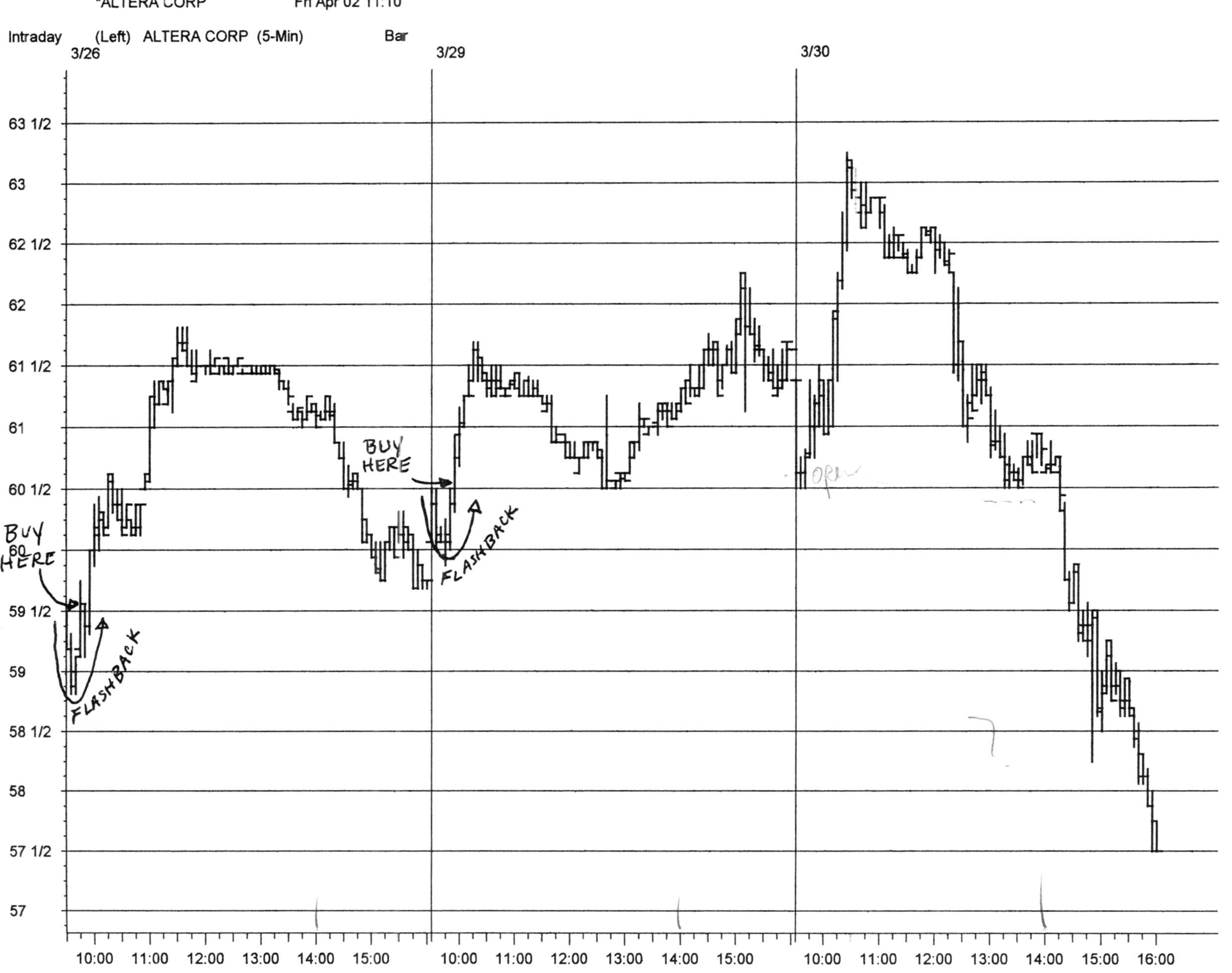
*ALTERA CORP
Fri Apr 02 11:10
Intraday
(Left) ALTERA CORP (5-Min)
Bar
3/26
3/29
3/30
63 1/2
63
62 1/2
62
61 1/2
61
60 1/2
60
59 1/2
59
58 1/2
58
57 1/2
57
10:00
11:00
12:00
13:00
14:00
15:00
10:00
11:00
12:00
13:00
14:00
15:00
10:00
11:00
12:00
13:00
14:00
15:00
16:00
BUY HERE
FLASHBACK
BUY HERE
FLASHBACK

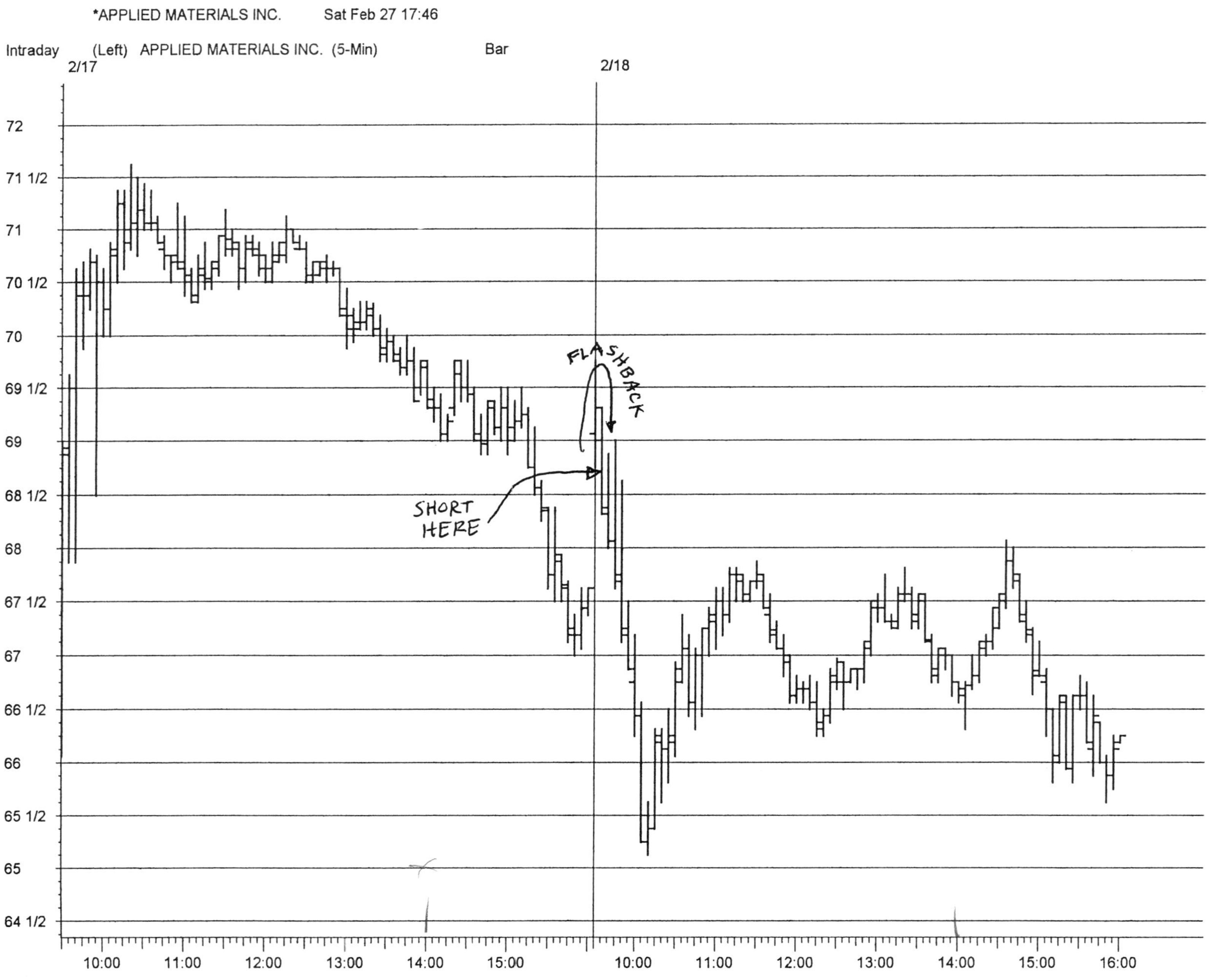
*APPLIED MATERIALS INC.
Sat Feb 27 17:46
Intraday
(Left) APPLIED MATERIALS INC. (5-Min)
Bar
2/17
2/18
72
71 1/2
71
70 1/2
70
69 1/2
69
68 1/2
68
67 1/2
67
66 1/2
66
65 1/2
65
64 1/2
10:00
11:00
12:00
13:00
14:00
15:00
10:00
11:00
12:00
13:00
14:00
15:00
16:00
FLASHBACK
SHORT HERE

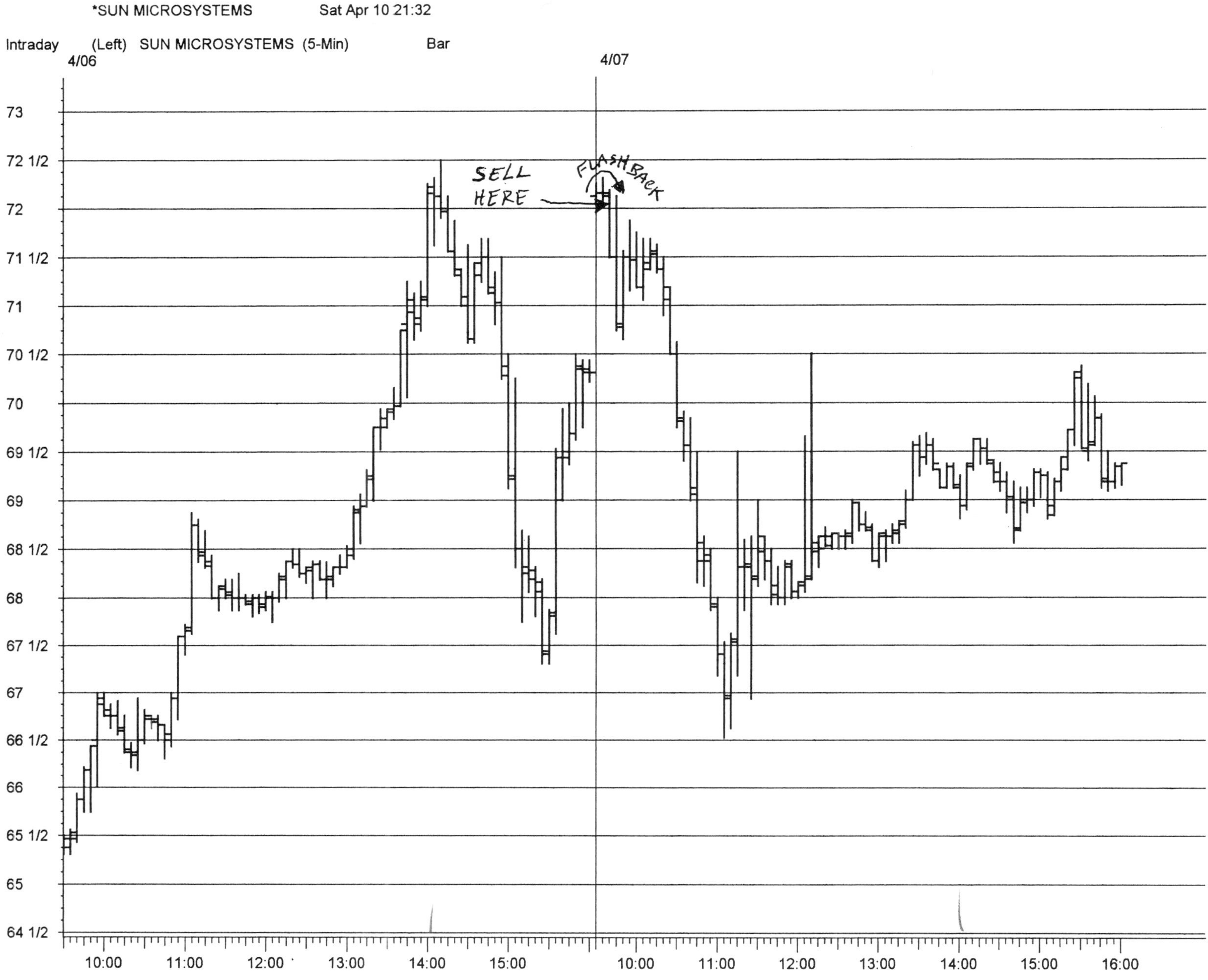
*SUN MICROSYSTEMS
Sat Apr 10 21:32
Intraday
(Left) SUN MICROSYSTEMS (5-Min)
Bar
4/06
4/07
SELL HERE
FLASHBACK
73
72 1/2
72
71 1/2
71
70 1/2
70
69 1/2
69
68 1/2
68
67 1/2
67
66 1/2
66
65 1/2
65
64 1/2
10:00
11:00
12:00
13:00
14:00
15:00
10:00
11:00
12:00
13:00
14:00
15:00
16:00

FAILED MORNING RALLY

A failed morning rally usually lasts from 30 minutes to 1 hour. A stock moves strongly up off of the open for a full point or more and begins to stall out. It then rolls over and almost as quickly, sells off back to or just below the low which was set at the open. This is different from the flashback in that the magnitude of the move is greater and takes longer to unfold.

By selling back down to its earlier low the stock is exhibiting weakness and portends a likely follow through further down out of this failed rally. Look for a 5 minute consolidation breakout pattern to form at the low, and consider shorting the stock when a break to the downside appears imminent.

As always, trade this short setup only if the indices are also moving down on the day. Here is how the pattern tends to look on the 5 minute bar chart.

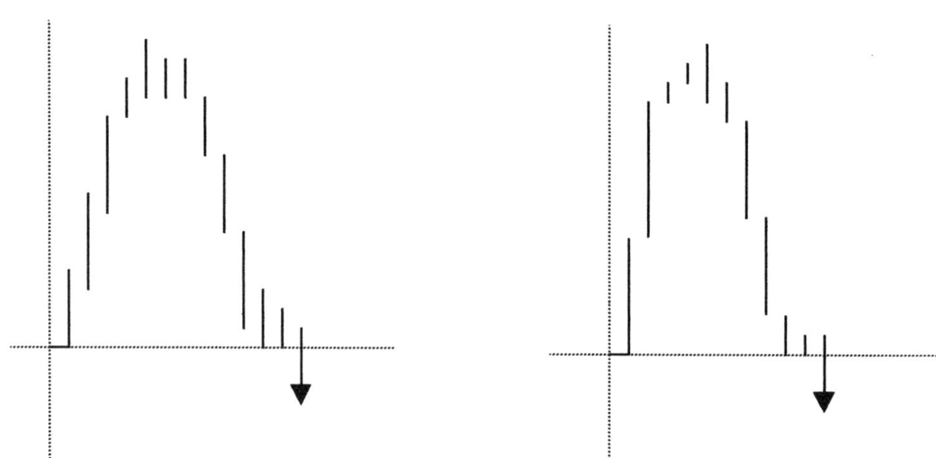

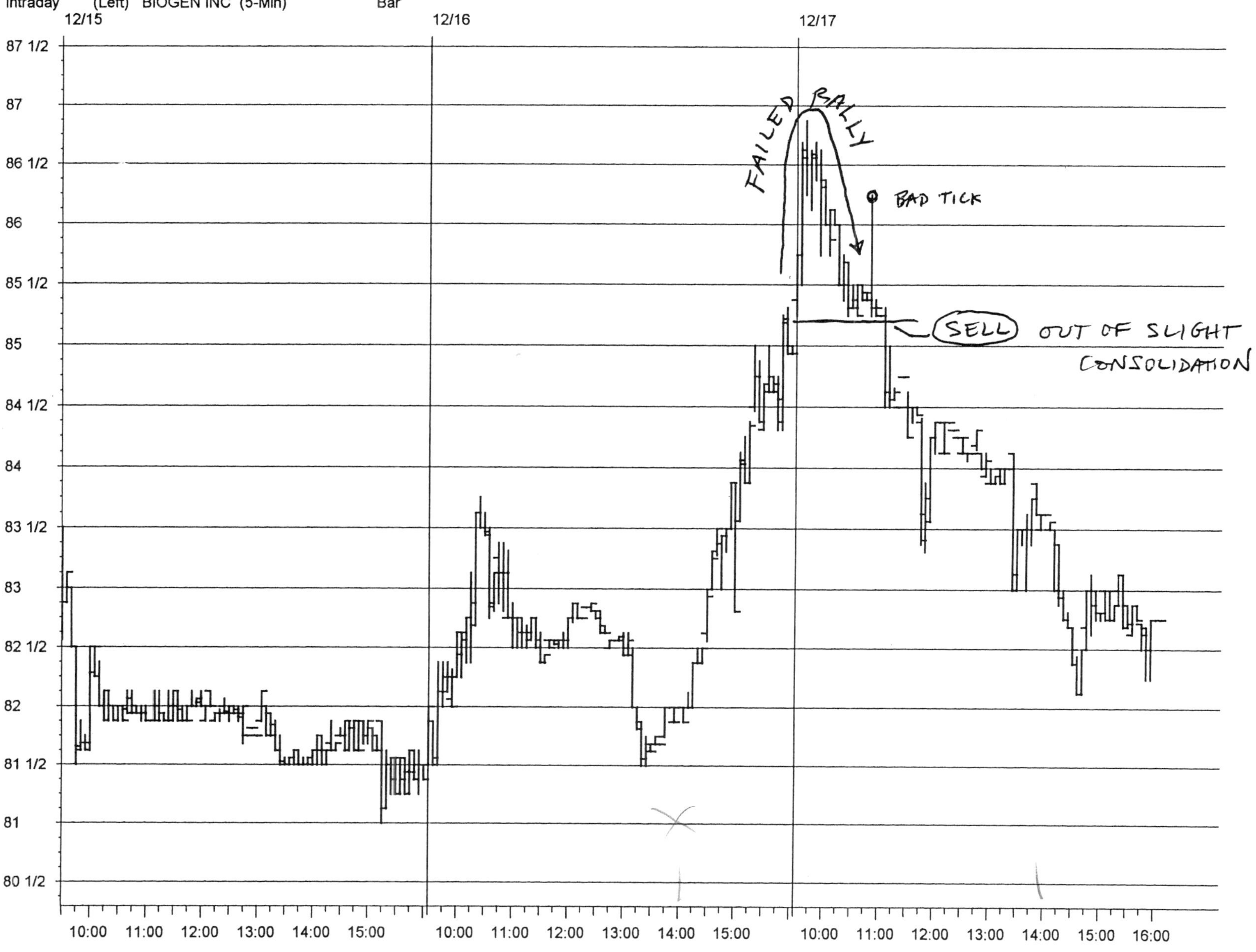

Intraday
(Left) BIOGEN INC (5-Min)
Bar
12/15
12/16
12/17
87 1/2
87
86 1/2
86
85 1/2
85
84 1/2
84
83 1/2
83
82 1/2
82
81 1/2
81
80 1/2
10:00
11:00
12:00
13:00
14:00
15:00
16:00
FAILED RALLY
BAD TICK
SELL
OUT OF SLIGHT CONSOLIDATION

SHOTGUN PATTERN – 5 MINUTE CHART

Many lower priced stocks in the 5 to 15 dollar range trade on low volume creating a sparse appearance on the 5 minute bar chart. It looks like a wall blasted by a sawed off shotgun (using birdshot). The daily range is often small (maybe 1/2 point from high to low) which doesn't offer enough intraday price movement to day trade.

On a semi-regular basis one of these issues will begin to reflect significant intraday volume coming into the stock. The 5 minute bar chart will start showing a more "fleshed out" appearance. Some significant event or news (perhaps unknown to the public) is usually responsible as the stock begins moving up in price. Often these stocks will then close at or near the day's high creating a wider range than is typical.

The next day tends to continue this activity presenting a reasonable day trading opportunity on a stock that has been "dead" for a number of weeks or months. Look to buy the stock the next day as long as it doesn't gap up significantly on the open.

Obviously, you can't monitor the massive number of stocks that are puttering around doing nothing as you wait for that one day when a "dead" stock comes alive. That would be a waste of your time and resources better spent on more active stocks and techniques that regularly present themselves.

But you will stumble across this phenomenon once in a while. Knowing what it looks like will keep you from just motoring past it and missing a low risk opportunity. These stocks will often have a two to three day run up in price, especially if they have put in an extended rounded bottom on the daily chart.

While this is primarily a buy setup, on occasion you'll see a similar phenomenon for a sell off as a short trade. Although much less common, make sure that the stock isn't too low in price. You want room for the stock to move down enough intraday to justify a day trade with reasonable profit potential.

This trade setup works best for buys to the long side. The most effective way to communicate how they appear is with the following actual chart examples showing several days of 5 minute bar chart activity.

Intraday (Left) ECI TELECOM LTD., ORD (5-Min) Bar
12/15
12/16
12/17
12/18
38 3/4
38 1/2
38 1/4
38
37 3/4
37 1/2
37 1/4
37
36 3/4
36 1/2
36 1/4
36
35 3/4
35 1/2
35 1/4
35
34 3/4
34 1/2
34 1/4
10:00
12:00
14:00
16:00
★ NOTICE THE INCREASED VOLUME TODAY SHOWN BY MORE SOLID 5-MINUTE BARS
WEAKNESS
SELL
ON BREAKOUT OF CONSOLIDATION
"SCATTER SHOT" APPEARANCE OF LOW VOLUME

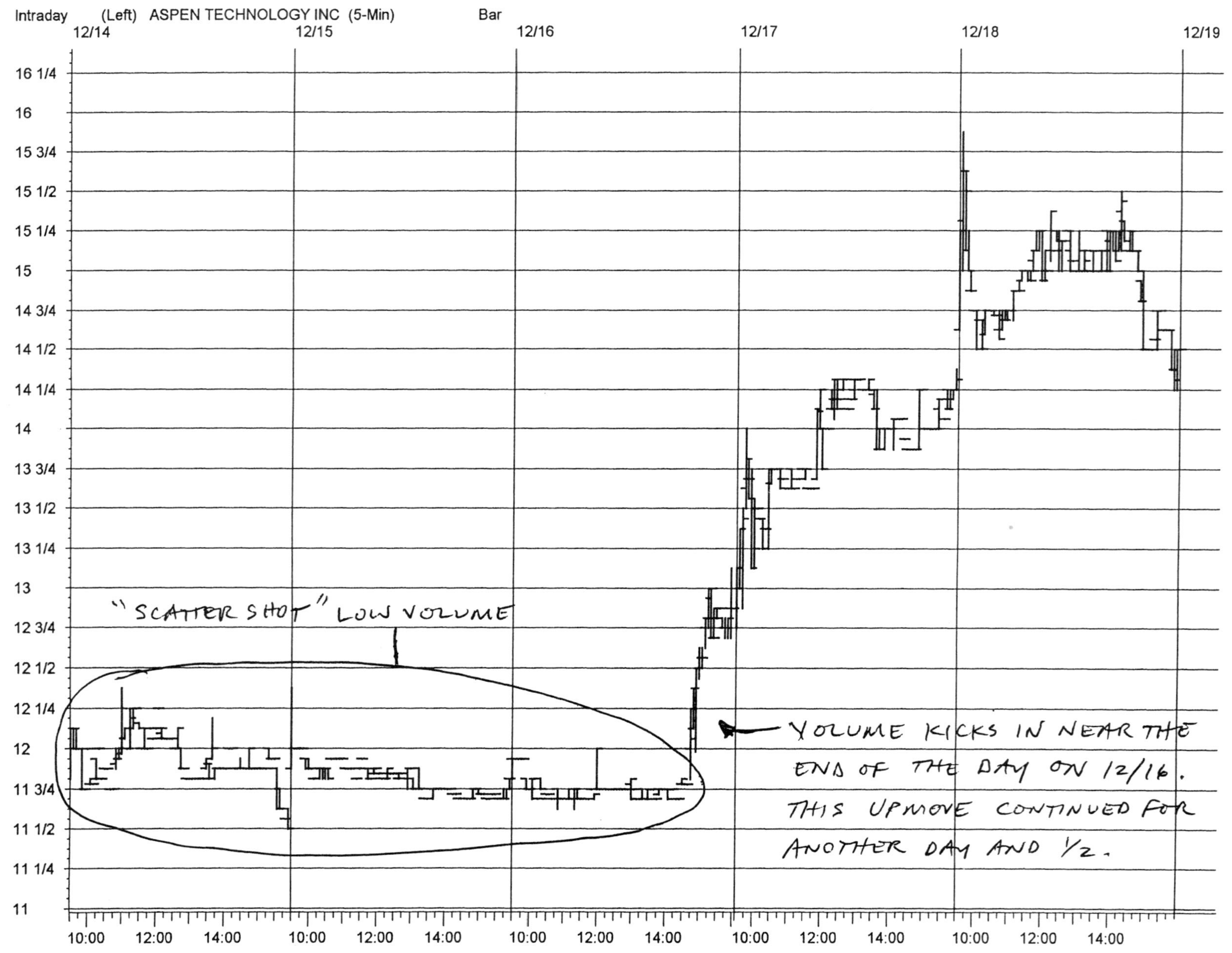

Intraday
(Left) ASPEN TECHNOLOGY INC (5-Min)
Bar
12/14
12/15
12/16
12/17
12/18
12/19
16 1/4
16
15 3/4
15 1/2
15 1/4
15
14 3/4
14 1/2
14 1/4
14
13 3/4
13 1/2
13 1/4
13
12 3/4
12 1/2
12 1/4
12
11 3/4
11 1/2
11 1/4
11
10:00
12:00
14:00
"SCATTER SHOT" LOW VOLUME
VOLUME KICKS IN NEAR THE END OF THE DAY ON 12/16.
THIS UPMOVE CONTINUED FOR ANOTHER DAY AND 1/2.

MICRO SUPPORT/RESISTANCE IN STOCKS

While you can see support and resistance on the daily bar chart of stocks and indices, the intraday price activity of both also reacts off of "micro" support and resistance. These micro support and resistance price levels can be observed on the 5 minute bar chart of a stock. Having several days of 5 minute bar chart displayed will help you see a price where a stock tends to halt its move.

Micro support/resistance levels are prices that tend to halt a stock's move intraday. Therefore, if you find a trade setup that is too near one of these halting points, then the stock has a lower likelihood of following through decisively.

When micro support is broken to the downside, that price will often function as micro resistance if the stock rallies back up. Conversely, when micro resistance is penetrated as the stock moves up through it, the same price level serves as micro support.

A stock's micro support and resistance price levels are another tool to help guide your trading decisions. If a daily or 5 minute trade setup is forming right up against a micro support or resistance level, then the trade usually holds greater potential of follow through.

Micro support and resistance levels can unfold during one trading session or may also be seen for several days back. This is one reason why I watch a four day chart of 5 minute bars. It's easier to see the price levels that are impacting a stock if you have a multiple day "picture" of the stock's intraday price activity.

This concept is best shown with actual examples, but the diagram below will give you an idea of what to look for.

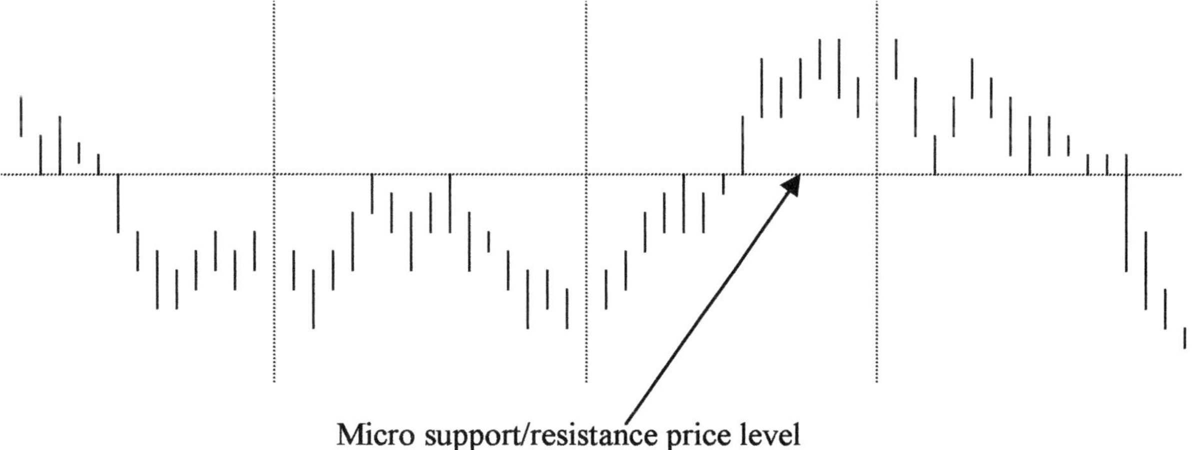

Notice how the above price level tended to halt the stock's price move. It is best used with 5 minute consolidation breakout trades that are also hugging up or down against this same price. When the breakout happens, it often has good strength and follow through.

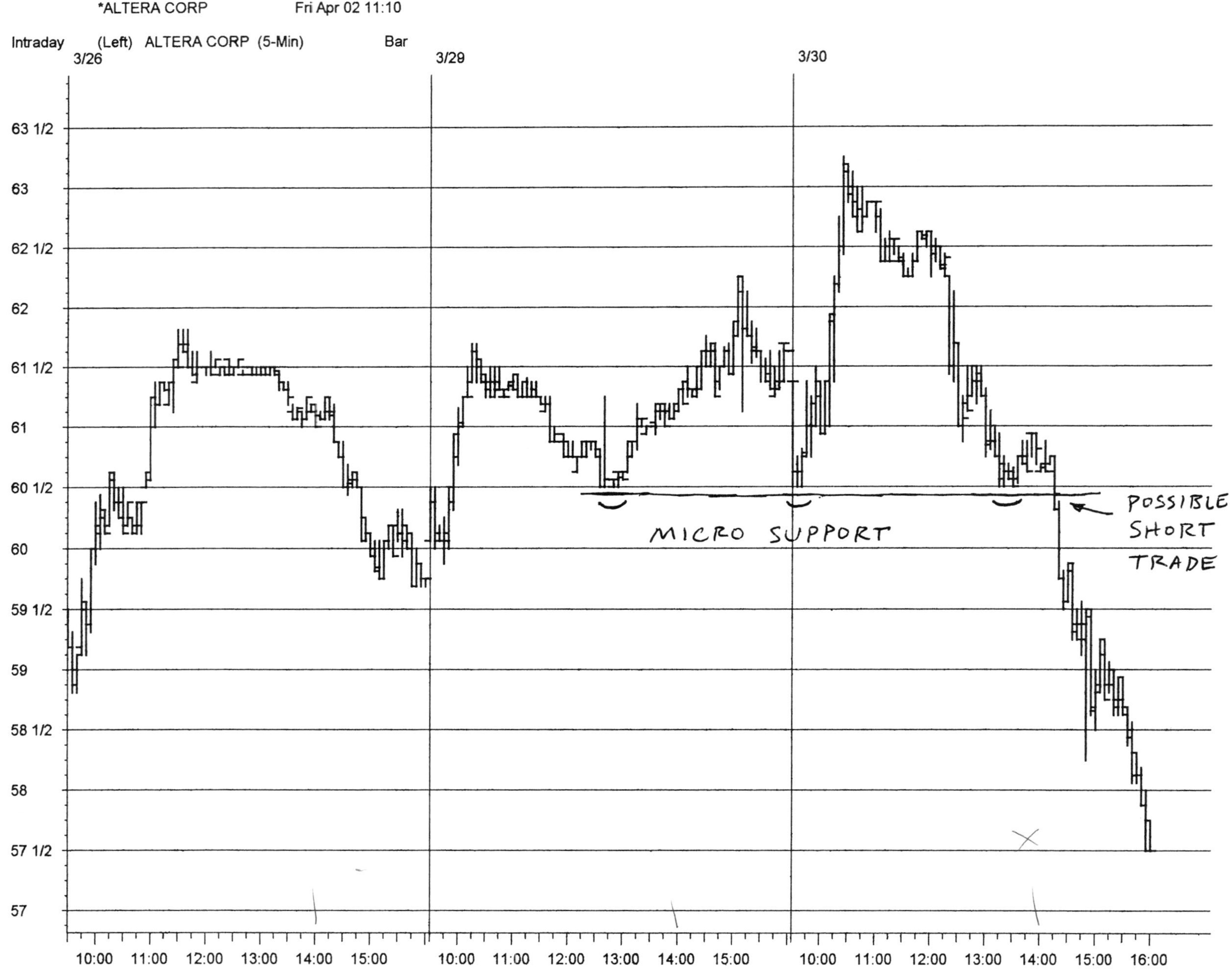
*ALTERA CORP
Fri Apr 02 11:10
Intraday
(Left) ALTERA CORP (5-Min)
Bar
3/26
3/29
3/30
63 1/2
63
62 1/2
62
61 1/2
61
60 1/2
60
59 1/2
59
58 1/2
58
57 1/2
57
10:00
11:00
12:00
13:00
14:00
15:00
16:00
MICRO SUPPORT
POSSIBLE SHORT TRADE

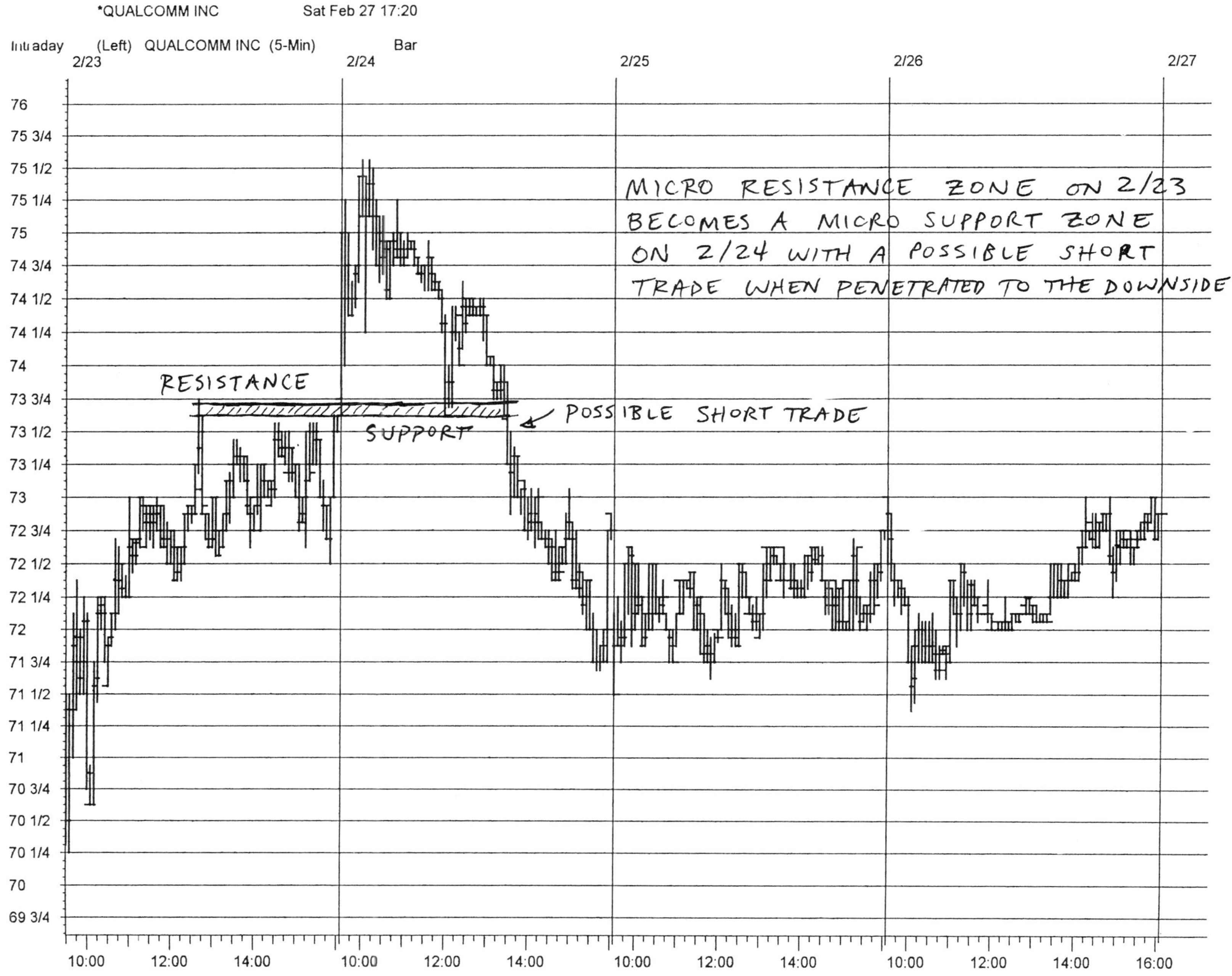

*QUALCOMM INC
Sat Feb 27 17:20
Intraday (Left) QUALCOMM INC (5-Min)
Bar
2/23
2/24
2/25
2/26
2/27
76
75 3/4
75 1/2
75 1/4
75
74 3/4
74 1/2
74 1/4
74
73 3/4
73 1/2
73 1/4
73
72 3/4
72 1/2
72 1/4
72
71 3/4
71 1/2
71 1/4
71
70 3/4
70 1/2
70 1/4
70
69 3/4
10:00
12:00
14:00
16:00
MICRO RESISTANCE ZONE ON 2/23
BECOMES A MICRO SUPPORT ZONE
ON 2/24 WITH A POSSIBLE SHORT
TRADE WHEN PENETRATED TO THE DOWNSIDE
RESISTANCE
SUPPORT
POSSIBLE SHORT TRADE

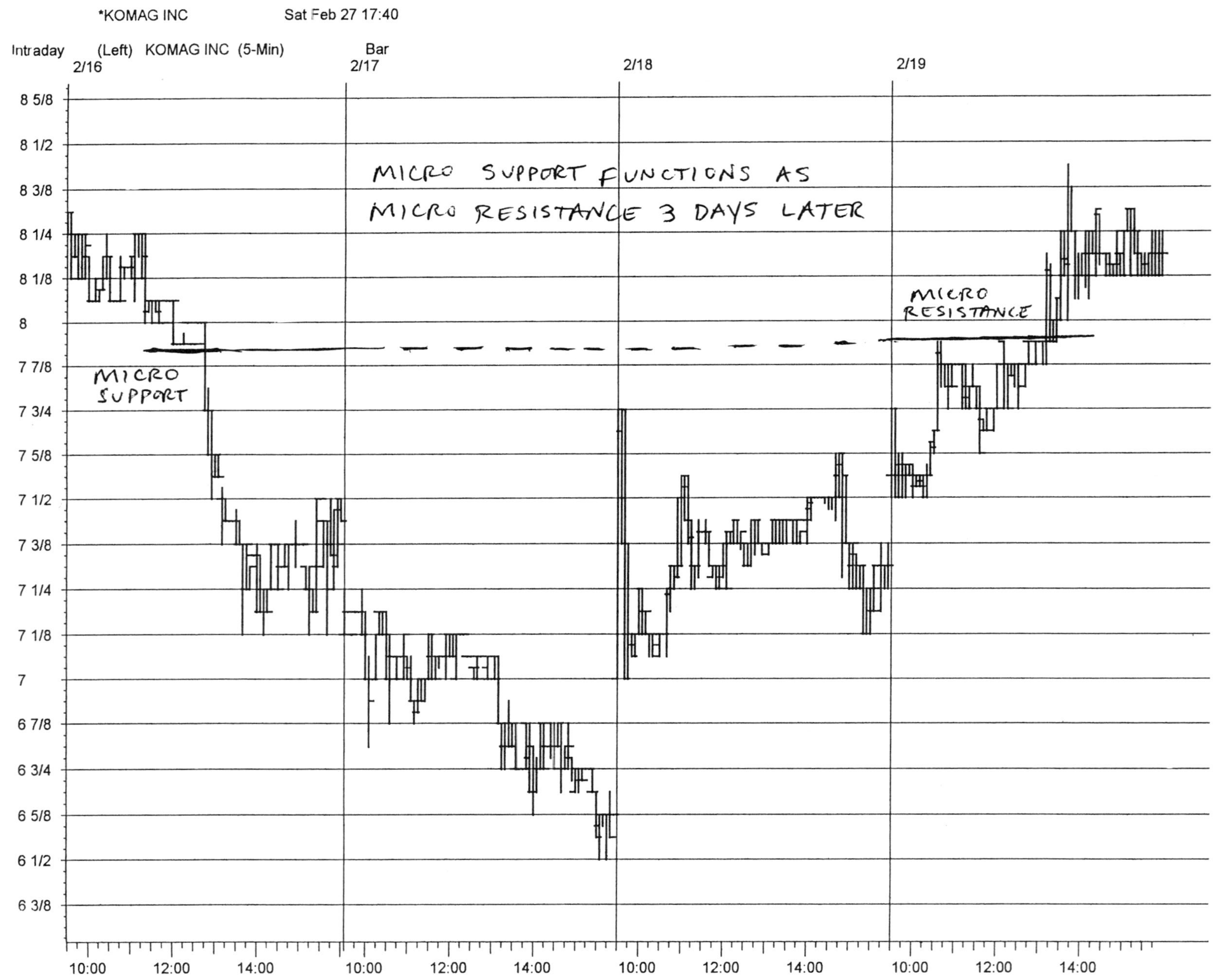
*KOMAG INC
Sat Feb 27 17:40
Intraday
(Left) KOMAG INC (5-Min)
Bar
2/16
2/17
2/18
2/19
MICRO SUPPORT FUNCTIONS AS
MICRO RESISTANCE 3 DAYS LATER
MICRO SUPPORT
MICRO RESISTANCE
8 5/8
8 1/2
8 3/8
8 1/4
8 1/8
8
7 7/8
7 3/4
7 5/8
7 1/2
7 3/8
7 1/4
7 1/8
7
6 7/8
6 3/4
6 5/8
6 1/2
6 3/8
10:00
12:00
14:00

PROFIT TARGETS

PROFIT TARGETS

Whether you are intraday trend trading (giving a stock the "wiggle") or scalping, it is important to know where likely price areas are that will often halt a stock's move. These are referred to as potential profit targets. There are 7 primary profit targets when trading both the daily setup patterns as well as 5 minute bar chart setups. These profit targets impact your trading decisions in 4 ways:

1) They can serve as exit points from a current trade where you would no longer use the wiggle.

2) They help you screen out seemingly good price pattern setups (as a ***filter***). If a stock is forming a setup pattern and a profit target is just beyond the entry point for the trade, then there is no room for the stock to run. You don't want a profit target just above the price where you are buying a stock. This is because it significantly reduces the odds of follow-through. Therefore, you would pass up the trade since you are looking to "cherry pick" only the best ones. This means you want trades with 1+ point potential moves when intraday trend trading. At times less is okay when scalping.

3) They can also be used to enhance the odds of success if your trade setup is at or just beyond these specific areas that tend to halt price moves. This assumes you are entering a trade in the direction that is breaking through an area that usually serves as a profit target. How can a profit target be an entry? Doesn't the term "target" imply an exit point? Yes, but often these targets serve as support or resistance areas. If they are penetrated then the stock has room to move. If you have a buy setup forming on the chart which hugs up against a profit target, then if the stock breaks long it tends to follow through. You will understand better when you view the following diagrams.

4) They can be used as trade entry points in a second way. Once price has been halted by the profit target, a stock can react off of this area in a rebound effect for a trade in the opposite direction. In other words, when price has moved to one of these points and halts and begins to reverse direction, there are occasional opportunities for "fades."

The 7 profit targets are listed below.

1. Support or resistance on the daily bar chart
2. Retracement of a Wide Range Day, Extreme Close
3. The 50 day or 200 day simple moving averages
4. The closing of a price gap
5. Reversal setup profit target
6. A price spike
7. A ***significant*** reversal in market index direction against the direction of your trade

We'll look at diagrams of the 7 primary profit targets and further illustrate how some can be used as both a potential exit point or entry point. The examples represent daily bar charts with any *squiggly* line representing the intraday move of the stock for a day trade.

THE 7 PRIMARY PROFIT TARGETS

1) Support or resistance on the daily bar chart

(exit point)

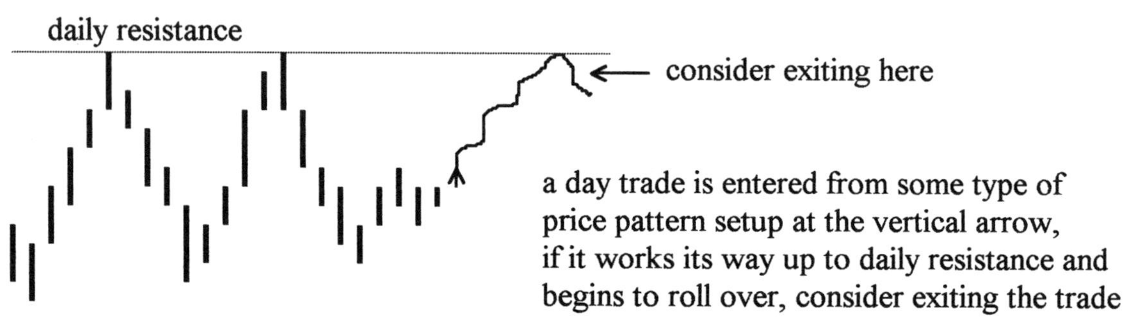

(filter)

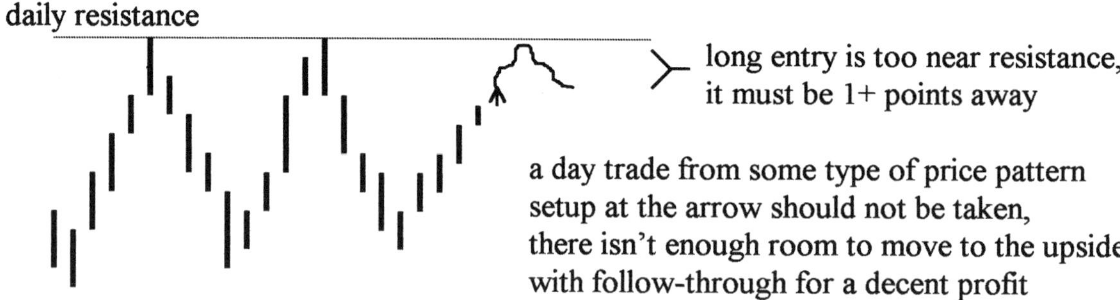

(a trade entry point if penetrated)

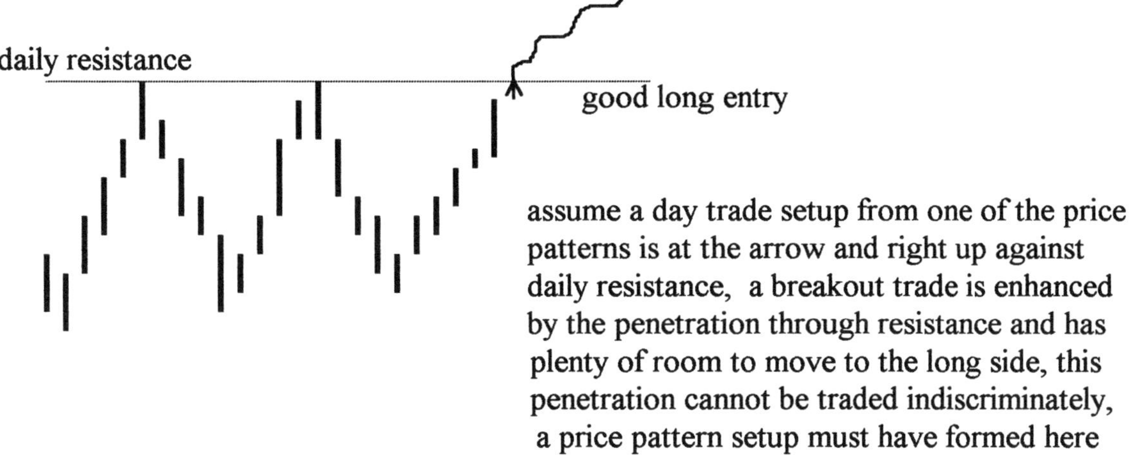

assume a day trade setup from one of the price patterns is at the arrow and right up against daily resistance, a breakout trade is enhanced by the penetration through resistance and has plenty of room to move to the long side, this penetration cannot be traded indiscriminately, a price pattern setup must have formed here

(a trade entry point in the reverse direction)

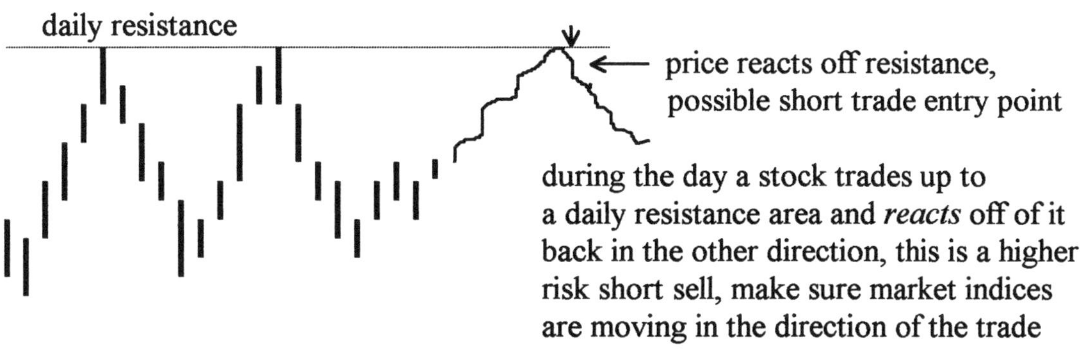

during the day a stock trades up to a daily resistance area and *reacts* off of it back in the other direction, this is a higher risk short sell, make sure market indices are moving in the direction of the trade

Each of the above scenarios shows how to play off of daily resistance. Daily support functions in the same way if you simply invert the 4 diagrammed examples.

2) Retracement of a Wide Range Day, Extreme Close

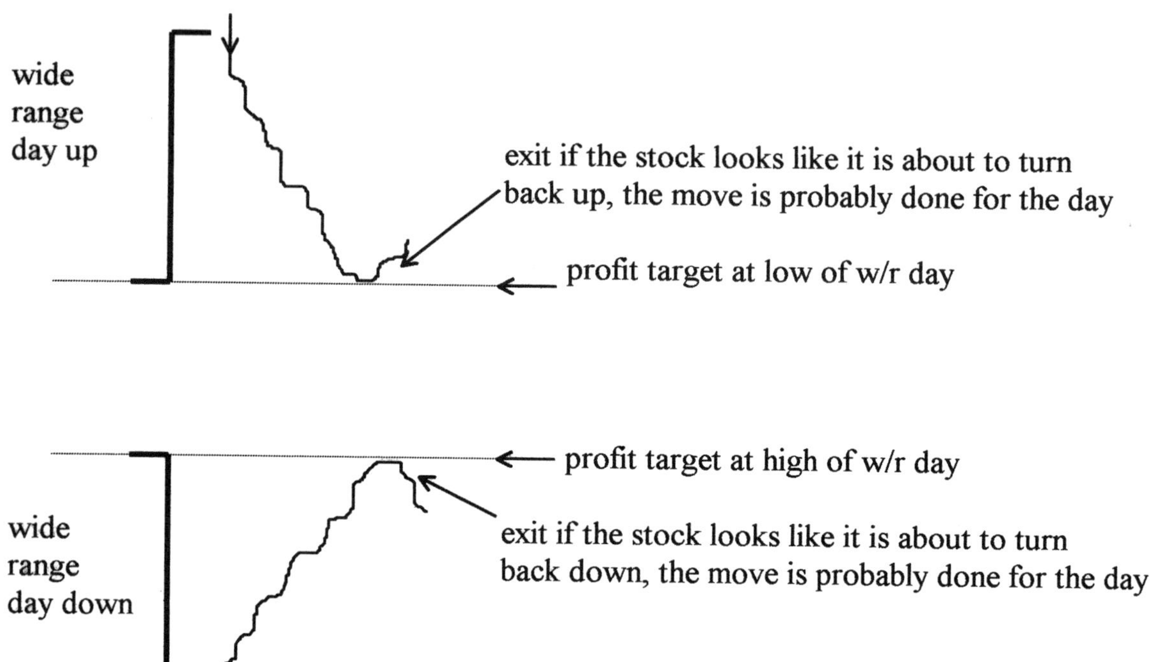

The w/r day retracement should only be used as an exit from a current trade.

3) The 50 day or 200 day simple moving averages

(exit point)

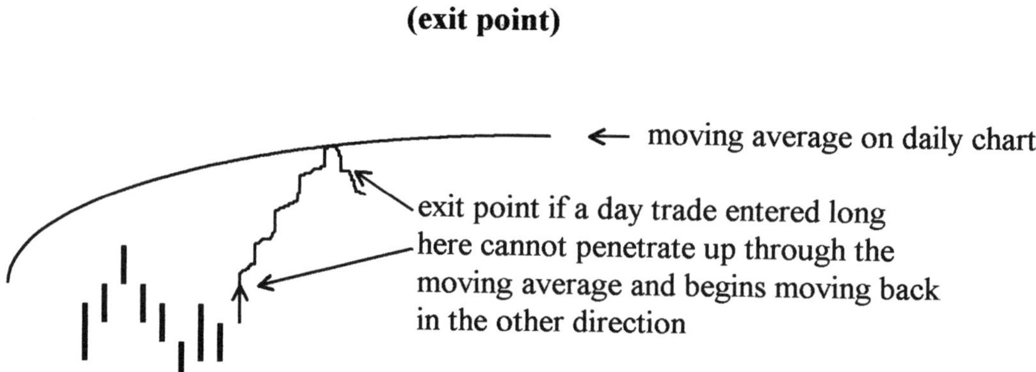

(filter)

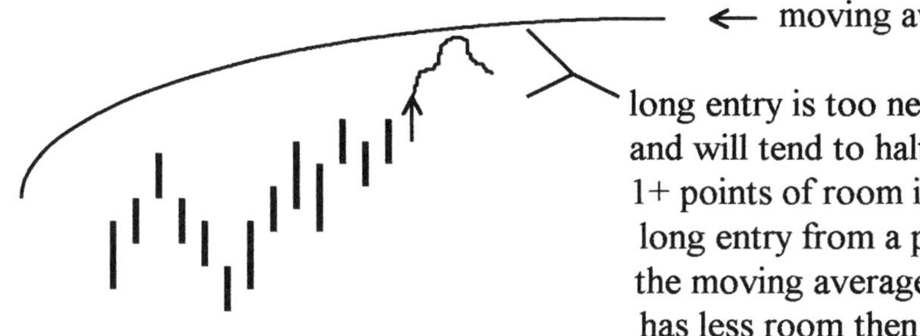

long entry is too near the moving average and will tend to halt the up move, 1+ points of room is needed between the long entry from a price pattern setup and the moving average for a day trade, if it has less room then pass up the trade

(a trade entry point if penetrated)

← moving average on daily chart

assume a day trade setup from one of the price patterns is at the arrow and right up against the moving average, a breakout trade is enhanced by the penetration through the moving average with room to run to the long side, this penetration must coincide with one of the price pattern setups

(a trade entry point in the reverse direction)

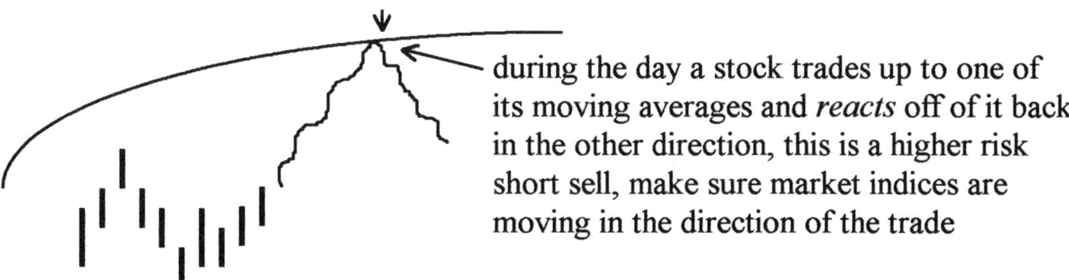

during the day a stock trades up to one of its moving averages and *reacts* off of it back in the other direction, this is a higher risk short sell, make sure market indices are moving in the direction of the trade

Each of the above scenarios shows how to play off of the 50 or 200 day moving averages when the stock is below the moving average line on the daily chart. These moving average lines function in the same way when a stock has been trading above them. Simply invert the 4 diagrammed examples. These averages often act as support or resistance.

4) The closing of a price gap

This is usually associated with the wide range day, extreme close setup where the next day gaps open significantly outside of the w/r day's close. But it may also be applied to any significant gap up or down in a stock as these are often great day trades. Below are some examples.

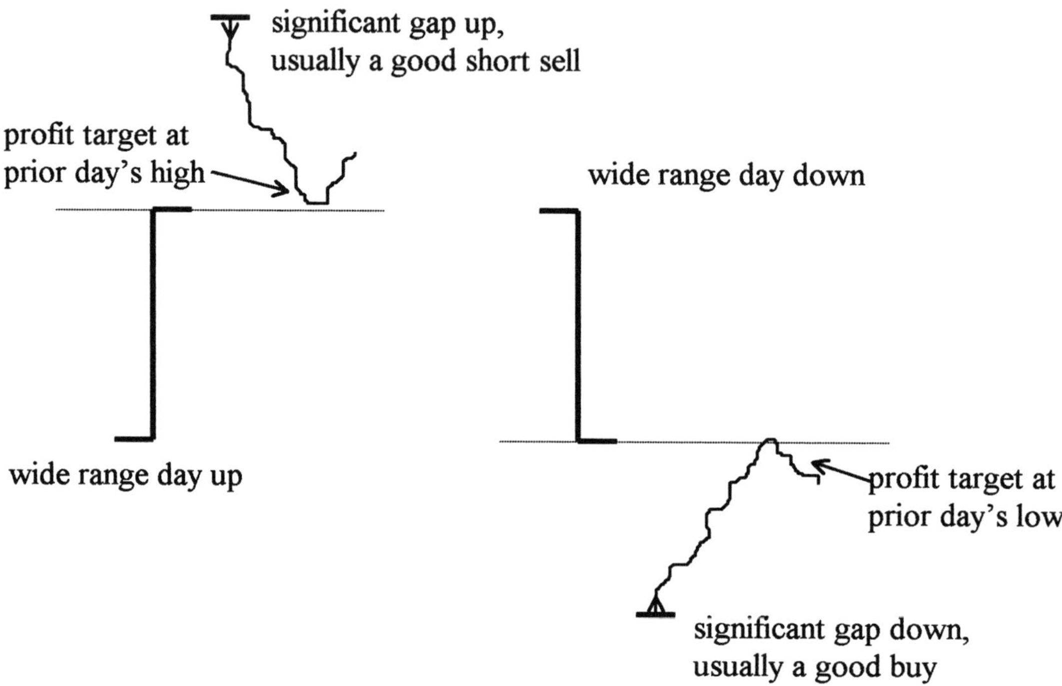

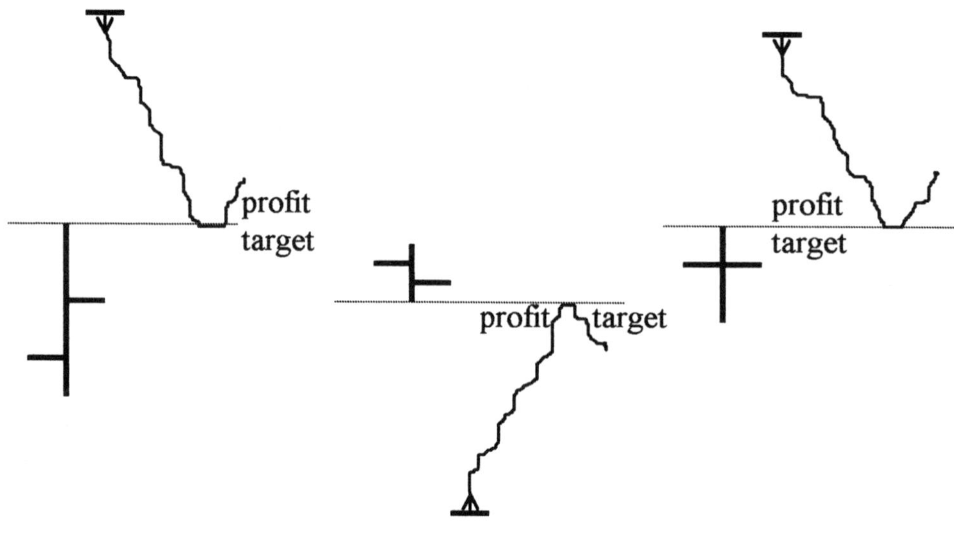

The gap should be at least over 1 point, the larger the gap the better the trade potential...usually 3% to 5% of the stock's price. Look for an attempt to close the gap back to the prior day. This is the point where price will often halt and sometimes reverse. This profit target should only be used as an exit from a current trade.

Also, don't be too quick to exit if it appears that price is continuing to move in the direction of your trade. Only exit if the stock begins to react off of this target back in the other direction.

5) Reversal setup profit target

profit target at high of day prior to reversal bar

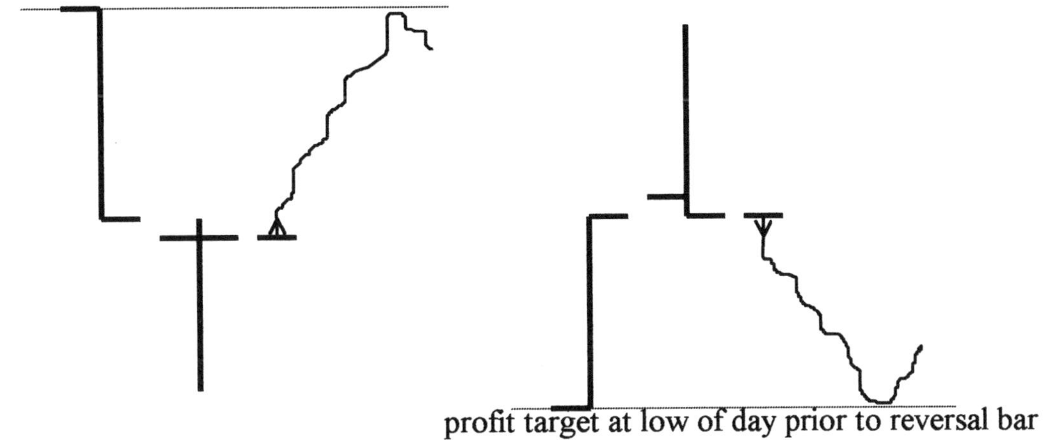

This profit target is also used only as an exit point for a current trade.

6) A price spike up or down of 3/4 point or more within 5 minutes.
   (this applies to stocks that typically have bid/ask spreads of 1/8 to 1/4)

This usually ends up displaying a "rubber band" effect. Price has moved too far too quickly and often whips right back in the opposite direction beyond what you would give for a "wiggle." Therefore, from a probability perspective, it is better to take this profit if you're in the trade than to hand money back to the market.

You will find this occurring with the 5 minute consolidation breakouts more often than strong stock moves in the first 15 minutes of trading. This is due to the large volume hitting the market in the early morning. These morning spikes often continue in the same direction of the initial move and typically do not have a rubber band effect. Focus on price spikes out of the consolidation breakouts on the 5 minute bar chart after the first hour or so of trading.

This profit target not only serves as an exit if you took a consolidation breakout trade, it also may serve as an entry point in the opposite direction once the price move has stalled and begins to reverse.

(exit point)

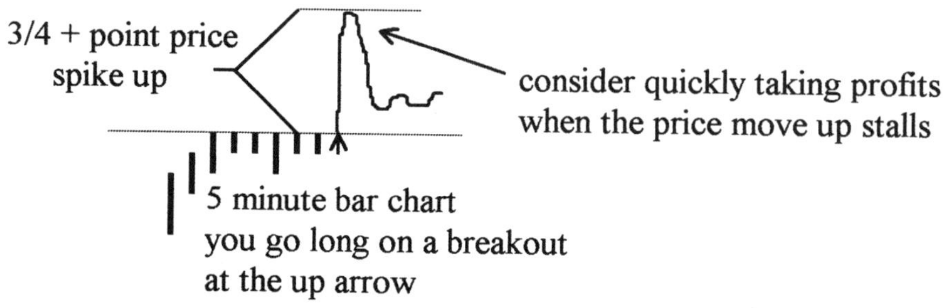

(a trade entry point in the reverse direction)

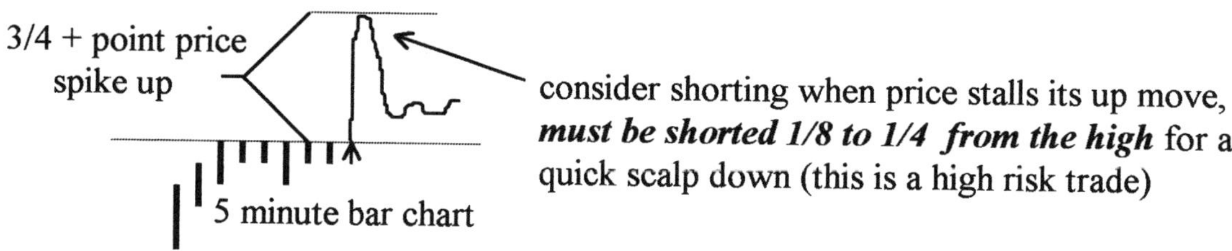

Both of the above scenarios are breakouts to the upside. The breakouts to the downside are the same, just inverted. Be careful with the "fade trade" where you enter in the opposite direction of the breakout after a price spike. Be quick to exit if you are wrong. Also, make sure that when you enter, the bid/ask spread is narrow and the level II quote screen looks favorable.

7) A ***significant*** reversal in the market indices against the direction of a current open trade

This is not your typical "wiggle." It means that you may be long and the market indices have been moving up supporting your position as you trade in the direction of the intraday market trend. If the 5 minute bar chart of the indices all of a sudden begin a sharp, strong move in the opposite direction of your trade, and the trade also seems to be reversing direction, seriously consider exiting and booking profits. Although this sounds like a general guideline, you will see it happen with experience and recognize it early. Obviously this provides only an exit criterion…no entries.

FADING

FADING

"Counter trend trading techniques"

Fading refers to a trade in the opposite direction of a stock's current intraday price move. In essence you are attempting to pick the top or bottom of a price swing. It may be an area on the intraday or daily chart which halts a price move (such as a profit target) with the expectation of a rebound in the opposite direction. It is very difficult to actually pick tops and bottoms. Therefore, you should only play these setups after you've developed experience in day trading and also come to know the "price personality" of a basket of stocks that you follow and regularly trade.

THESE ARE HIGHER RISK TRADES! They should comprise no more than 5 - 10% of your trades if any. There is plenty of opportunity and money in the market without even trading these fade setups, so don't feel that these techniques even need to be incorporated into your arsenal. I know this is like saying "don't pull the trigger on this gun, but here's how you do it." Just be careful! These trades are presented here only because at times they do offer reasonable day trading opportunities when conditions are right. They are usually scalping type trades requiring quick entry and quick exit with low tolerance of a move against you.

Your intention should not be to pick the high or low to the tick. You will be reacting to the market and the specific criteria for each setup. Again, these trades mandate a quick exit if it appears that you are wrong.

Here is a listing of the 6 fade techniques that we'll cover in detail:

1) Price spike
2) 2 waves up (or down)
3) Tagging
4) Big stack and a rainbow
5) Profit target reaction
6) Double roll-overs & double turn-ups

None of the six setups should be traded in the first 45 minutes to 1 hour of trading. Morning volume can put you in front of a freight train if you are wrong, leading to a greater loss than should be allowed for a fade trade. Also, the entries of these trades should be keyed off of the 5 minute bar chart although the overall trade evaluation often includes the daily bar chart. Most of these trades are designed for stocks that typically have a 1/8 to 1/4 bid/ask spread to minimize the risk if you are wrong.

1) PRICE SPIKE

The price spike is based on the "rubber band" effect for when a stock moves too far, too fast. It often snaps back in the opposite direction to retrace some of the price move. This can sometimes happen on a consolidation breakout of the high or low of the day. Here are the criteria:

- The price must have spiked up or down <u>at least</u> 3/4 of a point within 5 minutes (this assumes a stock that typically has a narrow bid/ask spread)

- The price move must have halted

- The side of the level II quote screen where you would exit if you are wrong must offer the opportunity to cover with a 1/8 loss with a reasonable number of market makers at that price level (if shorting a price spike up it would be the ask side and vice versa for fading a price spike down)

- On a short trade of a price spike up, either offer 1/16 or 1/8 inside of the current ask or simply sell the inside bid if the bid/ask spread is no more that 1/8

- Look for a 1/4 profit or more as prices whip back in the other direction, exiting quickly when the move seems to be coming to a halt

- Be ready to take only a 1/8 profit or a flat (break even trade) if the stock only retraces slightly and halts

- If you are wrong, attempt to bid or offer at break even...if you are not filled and the stock begins to surge against you, exit the trade for the 1/16 or 1/8 loss

As you can tell, timing is of the essence and these are trades that you definitely do not want to chase...otherwise they'll give you just enough rope to hang yourself. Also, the market indices must not be screaming in the direction of the price spike, the stock will not typically retrace and can rip against you costing you more than a small loss. Here is an example of both a price spike up and price spike down on a 5 minute bar chart. The squiggly line represents the price spike and subsequent retracement. Remember, the price spike should take no more than 5 minutes before it halts and should be 3/4 point or more.

(price spike up)

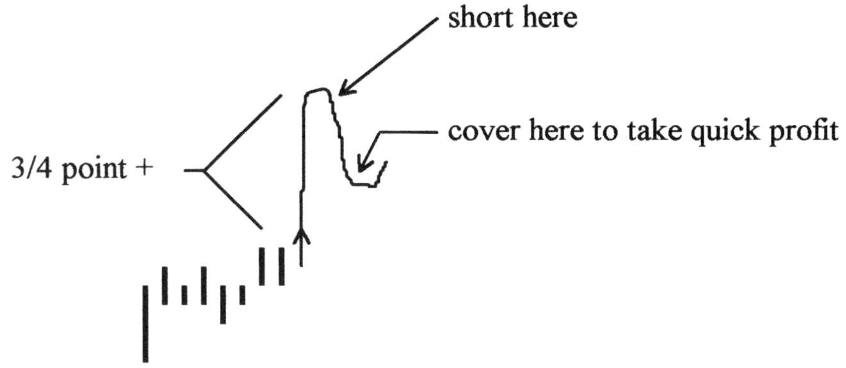

short here

cover here to take quick profit

3/4 point +

(price spike down)

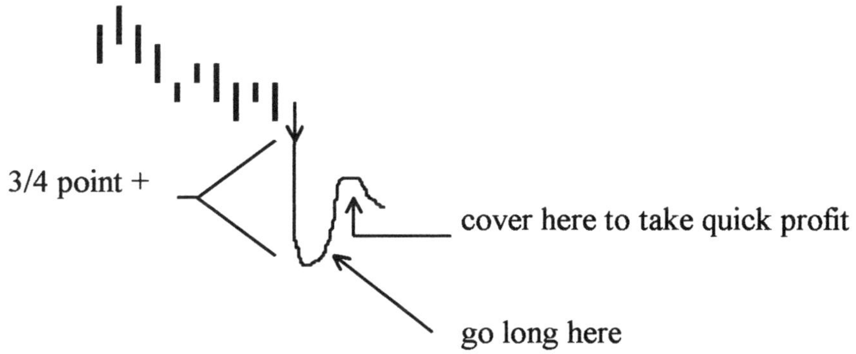

3/4 point +

cover here to take quick profit

go long here

2) TWO WAVES UP (OR DOWN)

Two waves refers to 2 price surges in the same direction that take place within 5 - 10 minutes and is very similar to the price spike. Looking back on a 5 minute bar chart you will not be able to see each wave (price surge) up or down. Instead, it is seen as it unfolds in real time by watching the level II market maker screen on a stock that spikes up or down with 2 distinct momentum surges creating a quick 3/4 or more move.

The first wave may push the stock's price 3/8 to 5/8. Then the move halts and may retrace, but no more than 1/8 (or 1/4 if it ran 5/8 or more) before it quickly surges back in the direction of the initial move taking it anywhere from 3/4 to over 1 point from where the first price wave began. When price stalls at the end of the 2nd wave, the rubber band effect is usually about to take place. Refer to the entry and exit criteria from the prior price spike fade trade to trade this setup as it is very similar. Here is how it might look for both a 2 wave up and a 2 wave down for a day trade:

(2 waves up)

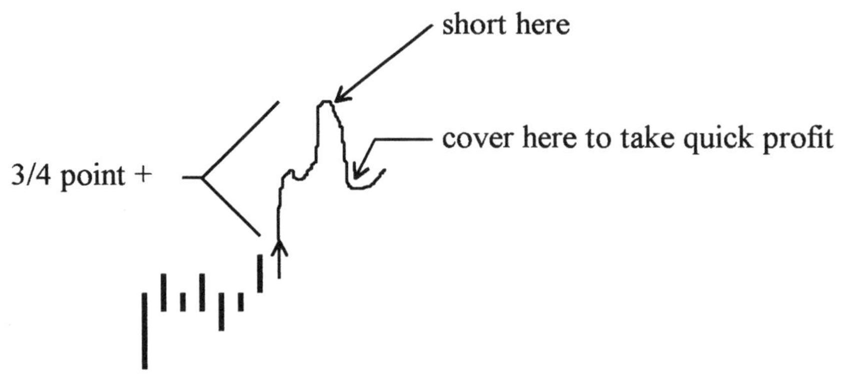

(2 waves down)

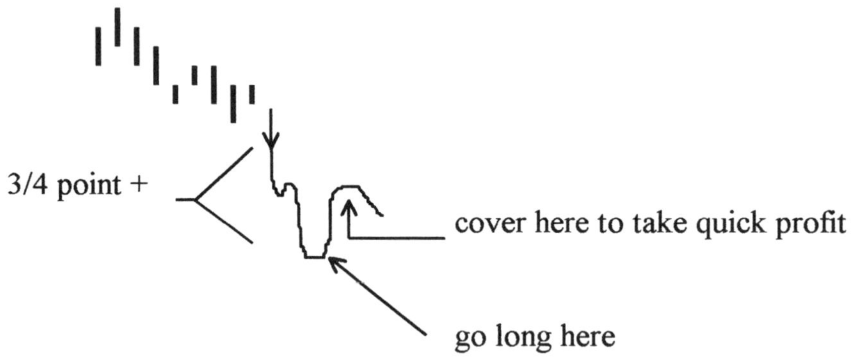

Although it is very similar to the price spike, the 2 waves can take a few minutes longer and usually help to more strongly confirm that a rubber band retracement is about to unfold. With both the price spike setup and 2 waves variation, make sure the stock is not reacting to a news announcement and that the market indices are not ripping strongly against the direction in which you are about to fade the stock.

3) TAGGING

Tagging is a setup that involves what a market maker occasionally will do on the level II market maker screen after a stock has made a directional move by either selling off or running up from several minutes to an hour or two. This pattern typically works best during a sell-off once price has stalled and offers a buying opportunity for a fade long. With this in mind, the example simply depicts the before and after appearance of the market maker screen for tagging a buy. This technique is intended for stocks that typically have a 1/8 to 1/4 bid/ask spread that has widened.

(before)

AMGN 50			
Bid		Ask	
GSCO	50	MLCO	50 1/2
INCA	50	SBSH	50 1/2
HRZG	50	MSCO	50 1/2
SHWD	50	NEED	50 1/2
TSCO	50	PWJC	50 5/8
WEED	49 7/8	NAWE	50 5/8
JEFF	49 7/8	HMQT	50 5/8
MONT	49 7/8	LEHM	50 3/4
FBCO	49 3/4	GSCO	50 3/4
PWJC	49 3/4	JEFF	50 7/8

(after)

"TAG" PWJC…buy @ 50 1/8

AMGN 50			
Bid		Ask	
GSCO	50	PWJC	**50 1/8**
INCA	50	MLCO	50 1/2
HRZG	50	SBSH	50 1/2
SHWD	50	MSCO	50 1/2
TSCO	50	NEED	50 5/8
WEED	49 7/8	NAWE	50 5/8
JEFF	49 7/8	HMQT	50 5/8
MONT	49 7/8	LEHM	50 3/4
FBCO	49 3/4	GSCO	50 3/4
PWJC	49 3/4	JEFF	50 7/8

When a stock that typically has a 1/8 to 1/4 bid/ask spread which widens to 3/8 or 1/2, a market maker occasionally pops in that you can then "Tag" or buy and risk only 1/8 loss. The important factor here is that PWJC came in on the offer at 50 1/8 and there is a big stack of 50's on the bid side to get out if you are wrong for a 1/8 loss. More importantly, PWJC is only one market maker at 50 1/8 with the next price level behind him at 50 1/2.

If price has stalled and you can enter a limit order to buy at 50 1/8 from PWJC, then with any price bounce, this market maker will move out of the way and you can offer out your shares below 50 1/2 and become the inside ask price. In addition, the bid will often fill in with 50 1/8, then 50 1/4, giving you the chance for a quick 1/8 profit by simply selling on the bid. If you are wrong about the trade, it still will often give you the chance to get out flat at break even. In any case, you are risking no more than 1/8.

If the stock does bounce strongly, then you may end up with a windfall profit of 3/8 or more. Although these setups on the market maker screen do not come along very often, when they do, tagging that 1 market maker can offer a good trade with a reasonable risk reward ratio.

Tagging setups often occur at round numbers which tend to halt price movement. Examples of round numbers are 33, 47, 50, etc. as opposed to fractional prices such as 33 5/8 and 27 7/8.

The above example shows a tag setup for a buy once a stock has made a move down. The mirror image is true for a tag setup for a short once a stock has made a move up. As always, make sure the market indices are not moving strongly against the direction of this fade trade.

4) BIG STACK AND A RAINBOW

This is a descriptive name for how a level II market maker screen occasionally looks after an intraday move up or down. It is similar to tagging except that your focus is on how big the stack of market makers is on the bid side when considering a long position, or ask side when considering a short position. The other side of the market maker screen should have only 1 or 2 market makers at each price level for several levels. With a color coded market maker screen, a different color for each price level creates the appearance of a rainbow look. Thus the name big stack and a rainbow.

You would also like to see the market indices turning back in the direction of the trade you are about to attempt. Here is how this setup looks after a price move down. As with tagging, this trade also tends to unfold at round numbers.

(big stack and a rainbow - buy)

AMGN 50			
Bid		Ask	
GSCO	50	PWJC	50 1/8
INCA	50	MLCO	50 1/4
HRZG	50	SBSH	50 3/8
SHWD	50	MSCO	50 1/2
TSCO	50	NEED	50 5/8
WEED	50	NAWE	50 3/4
JEFF	50	HMQT	50 3/4
MONT	50	LEHM	50 7/8
FBCO	50	GSCO	50 7/8
PWJC	50	JEFF	50 7/8

big stack (Bid side) — rainbow (Ask side)

After a sell off, price has stalled at 50 and the stock appears due for a bounce. You could either attempt to bid in at 50 1/16 or just buy at 50 1/8 with a limit order to PWJC on the ask. If the stock bounces, it will be easier for price to go up quickly with only 1 or 2 market makers on the ask moving away as they sell their shares. Once the bounce begins to stall, you can offer out as the current inside ask or simply sell your shares on the bid.

You are only risking 1/16 to 1/8 for a potential gain of anywhere from 1/8 to 1/2 or more depending on how brisk the bounce is and how quickly the market makers move up off of the ask and subsequently fill in on the bid. If you are wrong about the trade and the stock begins trading down through the 50's on the bid side, quickly cover your trade.

The mirror image of this example is the setup for a short trade. The big stack would be on the ask and the rainbow would be on the bid. This represents another fade trade with a reasonable risk to reward ratio which sometimes offers windfall profits if the stock bounces strongly in the direction of your trade providing good follow-through.

5) PROFIT TARGET REACTION

Two of the exit points from the earlier "profit targets" section can also serve as trade entry points for fade trades. These targets often halt price intraday, signaling the end of the move and often indicating a rebound in the opposite direction. These fade trade candidates are designed to get you in at a low risk entry point once it is apparent that the profit target is reversing the stock's direction.

The profit target reaction setups are listed below:

1. Support or resistance on the daily bar chart
2. The 50 or 200 day simple moving averages
3. ("price spikes" have already been covered earlier in this section)

Refer back to the "profit targets" section to review how these targets tend to function to halt a stock's price move. If a stock has had a reasonable price move during the day that takes it up to or down to one of these areas which then halt the move, be ready for a reaction back in the opposite direction. These fades can be scalps but may also be intraday trend traded, especially if the market is moving strongly in the direction of your entry.

I have diagrammed both examples for a profit target reaction, fading short an up move that has met resistance on the daily chart as well as at one of the moving averages. These examples were listed under the "profit targets" section but are incorporated here since they are specifically fade trades.

(a fade entry point off daily resistance)

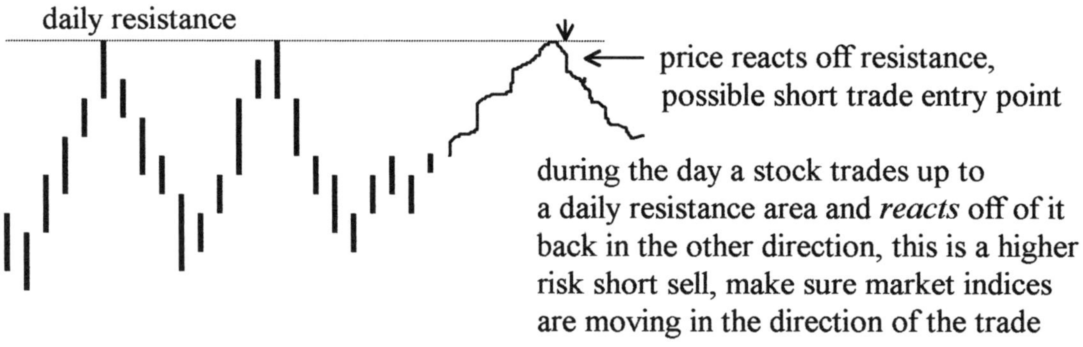

(a fade entry point off either the 50 or 200 day m.a.)

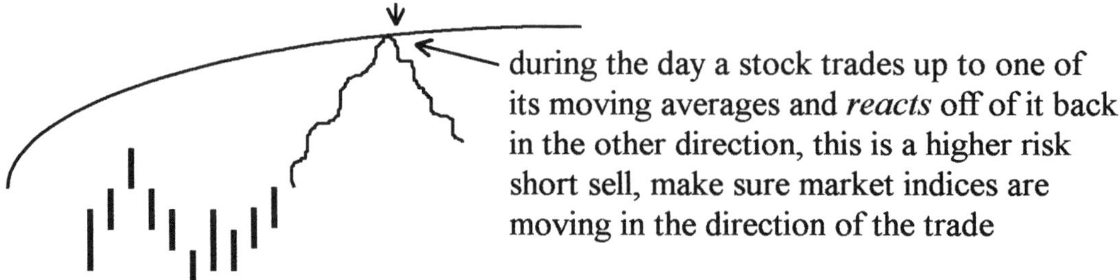

In both of the above examples you want to enter within 1/8 to 1/4 from the reversal point at resistance when shorting the stock. The buy setups are the same as the above diagrams, simply inverted.

Your initial focus should be to ascertain that the stock has actually been halted and appears about to reverse. Look to the market indices, they must be moving in the direction of the trade you are about to enter for the best odds of success. Finally, you are isolating a low risk entry point by looking at your risk on the market maker screen. You should risk no more than 1/8 or occasionally 1/4 and be quick to exit if you are wrong.

This trade may either be scalped, or on many occasions, it will follow through and retrace much of its earlier move on the day, offering more significant profit.

6) DOUBLE ROLL-OVERS & DOUBLE TURN-UPS

Roll-overs are short trades and turn-ups are long trades that are fades. They typically have the lowest success rate of any of the other fade trades. So why am I including them? Because with experience, you come to know how certain stocks react after they have had a reasonable move up or down intraday. All of a sudden the market indices begin a strong move in the opposite direction. Some of these stocks have the nifty little habit of following the indices as they roll-over from their high in an ensuing sell off, or turn-up on an ensuing rally...often with good follow-through for a decent profit.

Both setups are distinctly designed to be played based on a strong move in the market indices to create an acceptable risk to reward ratio. These often play out in the afternoon as the market reverses direction in the last hour or two of trading. Roll-overs and turn-ups work best with the more liquid stocks. Here are the diagrams using a 5 minute chart.

(double roll-over)

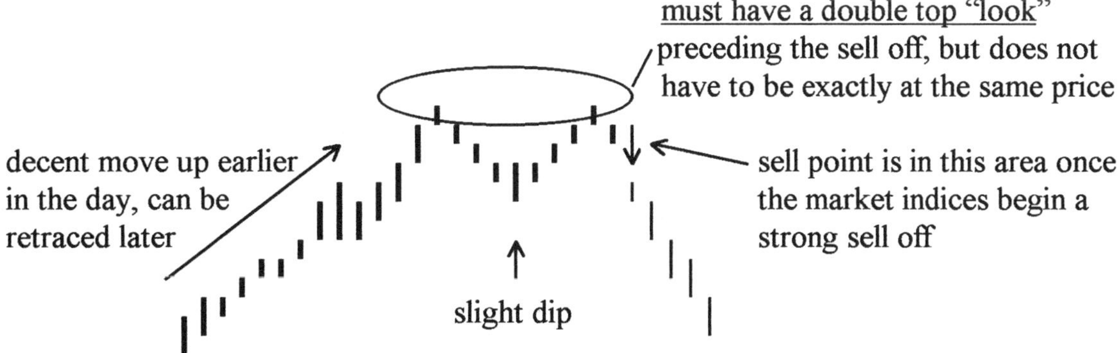

The stock had a relatively smooth and reasonable move up during the day. It rolled over once without moving back down much, then rallied back near or slightly beyond the prior high creating a double top look. The market indices (not shown) begin to sell off strongly. As the stock rolls over the 2nd time, quickly enter short and risk no more than 1/8 (or occasionally 3/16 to 1/4) and ride the stock down as it will often attempt to retrace a good portion of the day's earlier up move.

Take profit when the market indices stall their move down and the stock begins to bounce. If you are wrong about the trade, quickly exit with a flat if possible or no more than a 1/8 loss.

One important feature of the roll-over fade is the double top appearance. This enhances the trade by reflecting a price area during the day which is tending to serve as micro resistance. It reinforces the short trade once the 2nd roll-over begins.

Sometimes these trades will retrace all of the day's rally and give you over a point profit. Since this is a higher risk trade, be ready to take profits or exit if you are wrong. The next diagram is of a turn-up which is exactly the same as a roll-over, only inverted.

(double turn-up)

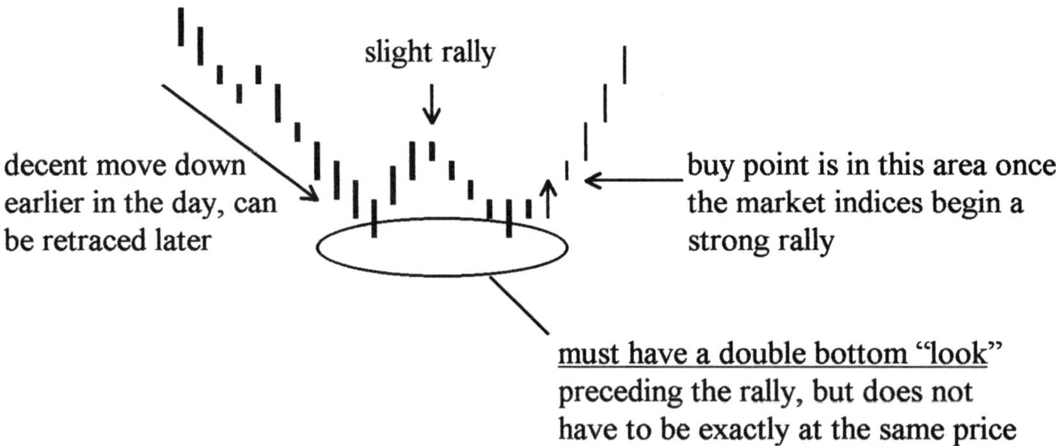

Well, there you have it, the 6 fade trading techniques. In conclusion, trading these techniques can bring your trading career to a swift conclusion unless you strictly adhere to all of the rules and nuances laid out for each fade setup. Also, as mentioned earlier, these should comprise no more than 5 - 10% of your trades at most. But once you watch these unfold over time, you will be able to incorporate them into your own trading and bring additional profits to your bottom line.

FILTERING

FILTERING

"Filtering out only the best trade setups"

I believe that the best way to day trade is to find a good price pattern setup and then look for a reason not to take the trade…to rule it out. If after looking (filtering), the setup is still staring you in the face, then it almost has to be traded. It's a way to force you to "cherry pick" only the best trades with the highest potential for success.

This section covers the filtering process. None of the price pattern setups should ever be traded in a vacuum simply because they look like a great setup. You have to further evaluate other factors that can either support or negate the potential trade. If you fail to do this and not consider the overall big picture for each individual trading candidate, then you will never excel or grow as a trader!

Therefore, read and digest the content from this section while in your mind you actively think about how you will incorporate all of the bits of information into the different trade setups in this manual. Start assimilating each component and continually exercise your mind to evaluate all of the puzzle pieces that allow you to uncover only the best trades.

We are in effect putting a puzzle together. We take each piece and attempt to thoroughly understand it and how it is applied. Then at a certain point we start linking the pieces together one by one until we comprehend how they all relate to each other in the decision making process.

With practice this process can be done with speed to quickly evaluate a potential trade and act on it decisively or know immediately to pass it up. Our goal is to complete the puzzle and see the big picture as we day trade.

Carry this theme with you throughout the manual, and continually review earlier portions. Start assimilating all of the ideas and methods that began with the *"Stock Patterns"* book. Continue to actively assimilate the progression of ideas through this manual on enhanced and advanced techniques.

As you read through the description of each filtering factor, you will often be referred to other sections in this manual and in the *"Stock Patterns"* book where diagrams and descriptions have already been covered in detail.

Now, on to filtering…

You will typically spend your time scanning through your basket of stocks during the trading session looking for a price pattern setup. This refers to the daily bar setups that typically play out early in the morning as well as to the 5 minute bar chart patterns that unfold throughout the rest of the trading day.

When you find a pattern that has formed, you must filter the trade by evaluating supporting and negating factors that will affect the potential trade. These factors are broken down into these two categories in this section: *supporting and negating*. Negating factors will be covered first followed by supporting factors. They will both be summarized at the end as a quick reference and to help tie it all together.

NEGATING FACTORS

1) TOO NEAR A PROFIT TARGET

If a potential profit target lies just beyond the direction of a trade setup then it may halt the stock's move. If you are intraday trend trading, you must have room for at least a 1+ point move. A profit target cannot be within this distance without decreasing the odds of your trade following through in the intended direction.

This is one of the most important negating factors. It doesn't matter how good the trade setup looks, it is better to move on to greener pastures. If you are scalping you do not want a profit target any nearer than 1/2 point away.

Review the profit target section to visualize what you will be looking for when evaluating if there is enough room for the stock to move. The profit targets which function as filters are listed below.

1. Support or resistance on the daily bar chart
2. Retracement of a Wide Range Day, Extreme Close
3. The 50 day or 200 day simple moving averages
4. The closing of a price gap

2) INTRADAY TREND OF INDICES NOT IN DIRECTION OF INTENDED TRADE

This is straightforward. Keep an eye on a 5 minute bar chart of the indices to know if you are trading in the direction of the trend, whether long or short. Trading against the direction of the overall market is like swimming upstream. The stock will not follow through nearly as well. Focus on trades that are in synch with the market. If you are trading a NASDAQ stock, follow the NASDAQ Composite or 100. If you are trading a NYSE issue, follow the NYSE Composite and DOW. In both cases, it is also preferable that the S&P 500 futures contract is also trading in the same direction.

3) CONGESTION ON THE DAILY BAR CHART

Look at the daily bar chart for the stock. If it is in a sideways, choppy trading range then you probably won't see much directional follow-through, even with a good setup. Do not trade a stock that is in congestion on the daily chart. There are plenty of other opportunities out there. Eventually that stock will break out of the daily congestion area and phase into several days to several weeks of price swings. You will see it plainly on the daily chart. This is when a stock becomes tradable again with more predictability of follow-through from the setups. Every stock cycles in and out of this "trader friendly" mode on the daily chart.

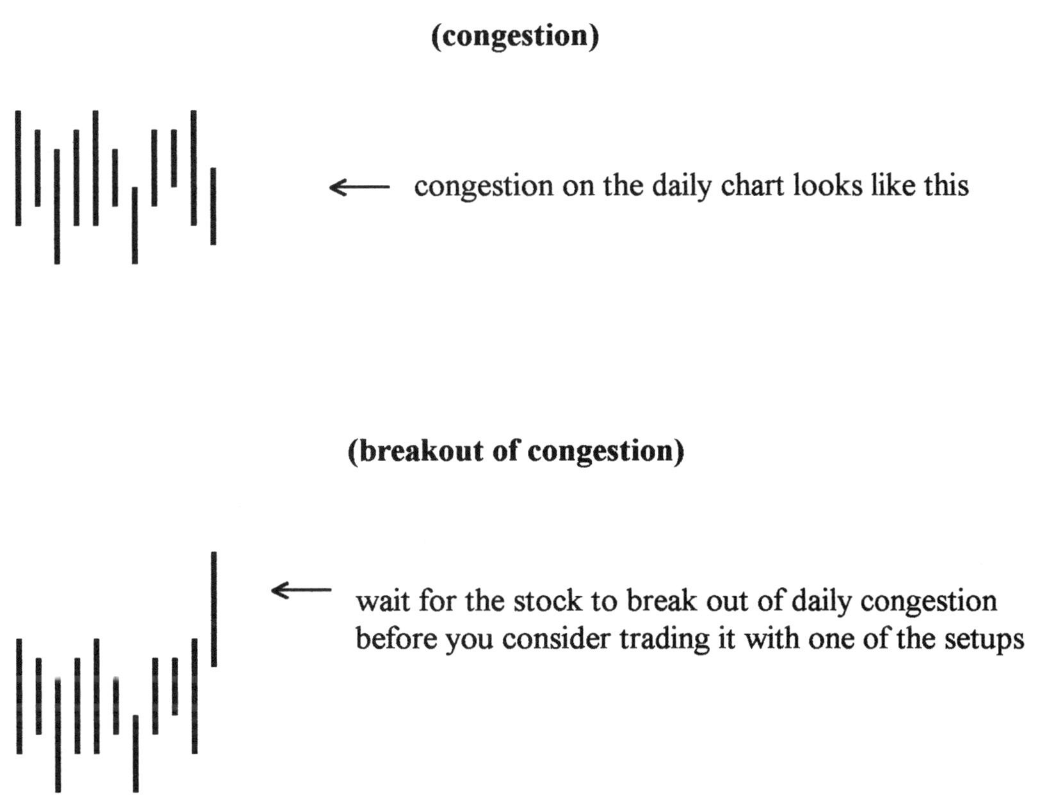

4) THE PRICE LEGEND ON THE DAILY BAR CHART

Occasionally you will see what looks like a great setup with plenty of profit potential that actually doesn't move much at all. Look at the price legend on the side of the daily chart and make sure that the average daily range for that stock (from high to low) isn't just 1/2 point. This can be deceptive with many charting software packages expanding a chart to fit the screen. A stock with an average daily range of over 2 points may appear the same as one with an average daily range of only 1/2 point. It is hard to squeeze a 1+ point profit or even a good scalp trade out of a stock that doesn't move much. *Be aware of the price legend.*

5) RELATIVE STRENGTH

Relative strength can work for or against you. This refers to how strong or weak a stock is relative to the index. If the index is moving down and a stock holds firm or even moves up, then once the index reverses direction, the stock will usually follow through long more strongly than others. Therefore you would not want to short this stock in this case. If the market is moving up and a stock is not following suit, then if the market reverses direction, the stock would be one of the first stocks to sell off. You would not want to buy this stock even if it had a good price pattern setup to the long side. Make sure you are aware of how the stock reacts to market movement up or down during the day to gauge its relative strength or weakness. It will keep you out of trades that will not go anywhere. **Relative strength is extremely important to monitor by observing the 5 minute bar chart of the stock and how it moves with the index during the day.**

6) NEARBY HIGH OR LOW OF THE PRIOR DAY OR TWO

These often serve as micro support or resistance points that may halt a stock's move. If you have a buy setup which is 3/8 away from the prior day's high and the high of 2 days back is also near the prior day's high then think twice before taking the trade. It may stall out at these highs as they serve as a micro resistance area. Also, since you have 2 prior days with the same high, look to see if you are in congestion on the daily chart.

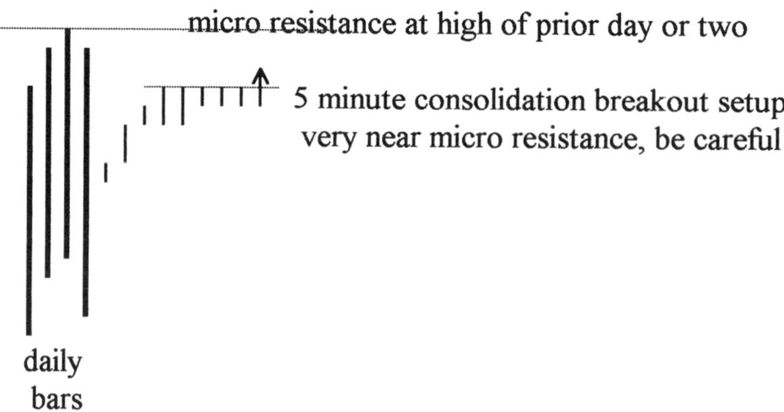

SUPPORTING FACTORS

1) DAILY BAR OR 5 MINUTE SETUPS AT 50 OR 200 DAY MOVING AVERAGE

When you have a price pattern setup long and it is also hugging up against one of these moving averages, the break to the upside is enhanced and will have even better follow-through. The inverse is true for a sell setup that is hugging down against one of the moving averages. Since these averages can serve as support or resistance, a penetration usually signals a significant move in price which is a great day trade opportunity.

2) DAILY OR 5 MINUTE SETUP AT DAILY SUPPORT OR RESISTANCE LEVEL

This is similar to the support and/or resistance provided by the moving averages. If you have a good setup long that is also hugging up against resistance on the daily chart (either nearby or longer term) then a break to the upside offers more potential follow-through with room for the stock to run. The inverse is the case with a sell setup hugging down against price support on the daily chart. Be cognizant of where recent and long term support and resistance areas are on the daily chart. They can help you map your way to greater profits.

3) SERIES OF DAYS WITH THE SAME HIGHS OR LOWS

If you have a cluster of 2 or more daily highs at or very near the same price, a trade setup that is hugging up against them will tend to break out more strongly. The same is true for a series of same daily lows with a sell setup hugging down against the same price.

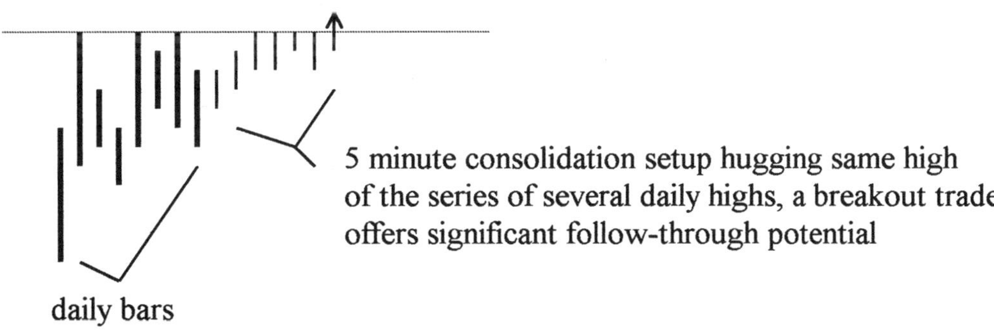

4) SWINGING ACTION ON THE DAILY CHART

This is the opposite of congestion. When a stock is moving around on the daily chart in a swinging fashion with wider range daily bars, it is usually in a more tradable mode. These are the times when a good setup will also provide good follow-through as the stock is in a "trader friendly" mode. Take advantage of it while it is offering higher odds of successful trades and greater profit swings.

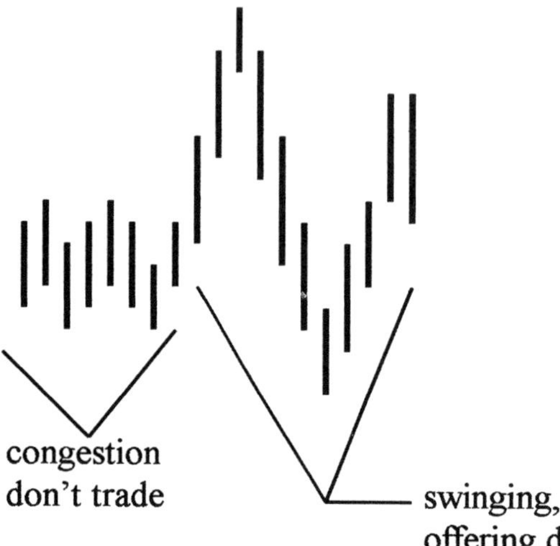

5) RELATIVE STRENGTH (revisited)

Relative strength can be an incredibly helpful tool for uncovering setups with more explosive potential. If the market is selling off and a stock is holding its own or moving up slightly, when the market reverses direction, this stock will usually be one of the first ones to break long and tend to move further. The same dynamics unfold when the market is rallying and a stock sits stagnant or sells off slightly. When the market reverses short, this stock has greater potential of a good short trade than most others. Keep an eye out for how stocks are reacting to the market direction during the day. Relative strength will clue you into some great trades. But remember, you still must have a price pattern setup to enter that stock. Relative strength serves as an enhancement as a supporting factor. The following example diagrams relative strength.

(relative strength)

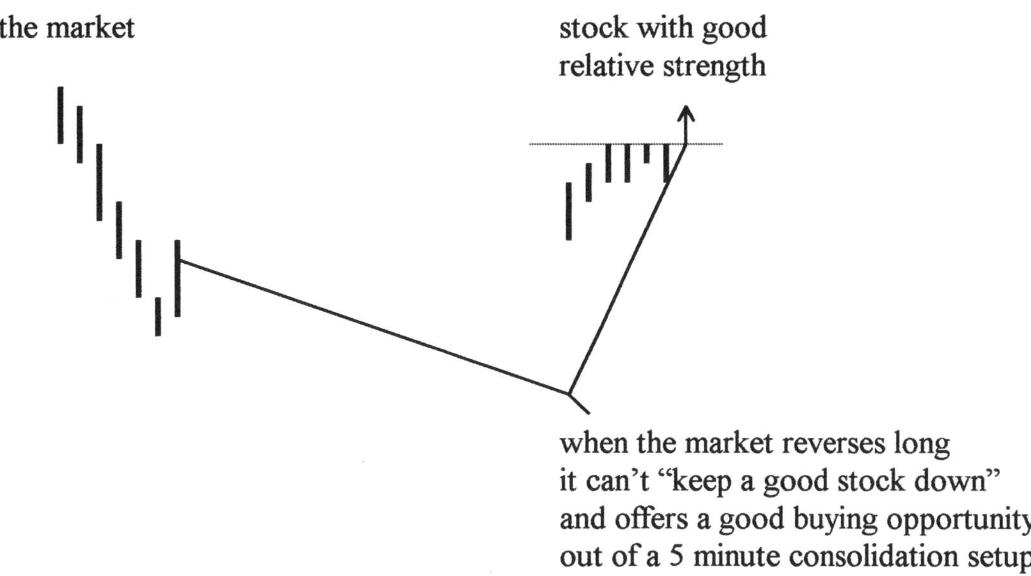

This completes the filtering section. As mentioned earlier, review the profit targets section that details some of the more important points on a chart where you can more easily rule out a trade or confirm it. You can see how important the role of the daily bar chart and intraday market index direction are when evaluating a trade setup. You want as many odds in your favor as possible when taking a trade. This is the "cherry picking" process.

As a quick reference and to help you integrate filtering into your decisions, a summary of this section is provided below.

NEGATING FACTORS	SUPPORTING FACTORS
1. Too near a profit target	1. Daily bar or setup or 5 minute setup is right up against the 50 or 200 day m.a.
2. Intraday trend of indices not in direction of intended trade	2. Daily or 5 minute setup is hugging up or down against daily chart support or resistance level
3. Congestion on the daily bar chart	3. Series of days with the same hi's or lo's
4. The price legend on the daily chart shows avg. daily range not enough	4. Swinging price action on the daily chart
5. Relative strength not in your favor	5. Relative strength in your favor
6. Nearby high or low of prior day or two is just beyond the direction of a potential trade entry point	

This summarizes the supporting and negating factors of the filtering process when evaluating a good trade setup using the daily and 5 minute bar charts. The final filter is the level II quote screen appearance. You must assess the level II quote screen to determine what your risk is. Ask yourself: "If I am wrong about this trade and it goes against me, where will I likely get filled if I have to immediately exit the position?" This is covered in more detail with market maker screen examples and commentary in the *"Stock Patterns"* book beginning on page 99.

It does not matter how good the price pattern setup is or how good the trade still looks on the charts after the mental filtering. If the market maker screen presents too much risk for that particular trade, then do not take it. This is the final step in the filtering process, and one that will cost you dearly if you do not pay it very close attention for each day trade candidate.

CONGESTION

2/30/97
(ORCL) Oracle Corp
07/22/98
'acle Corp-Daily 07/22/98 C=25.938 -1.812 O=27.000 H=27.063 L=25.625 V=8883200
32
30
28
26
24
22
20
18
98
Feb
Mar
Apr
May
Jun
Jul
DON'T TRADE A STOCK WHEN IT IS IN A CONGESTION AREA OF SIDEWAYS, CHOPPY PRICE ACTION. THERE IS LESS LIKLIHOOD FOR TRADES TO OFFER DECENT DIRECTIONAL FOLLOW-THROUGH FOR PROFIT
7/25 6:16pm Printed using TradeStation © Omega Research, Inc. 1996

CONGESTION

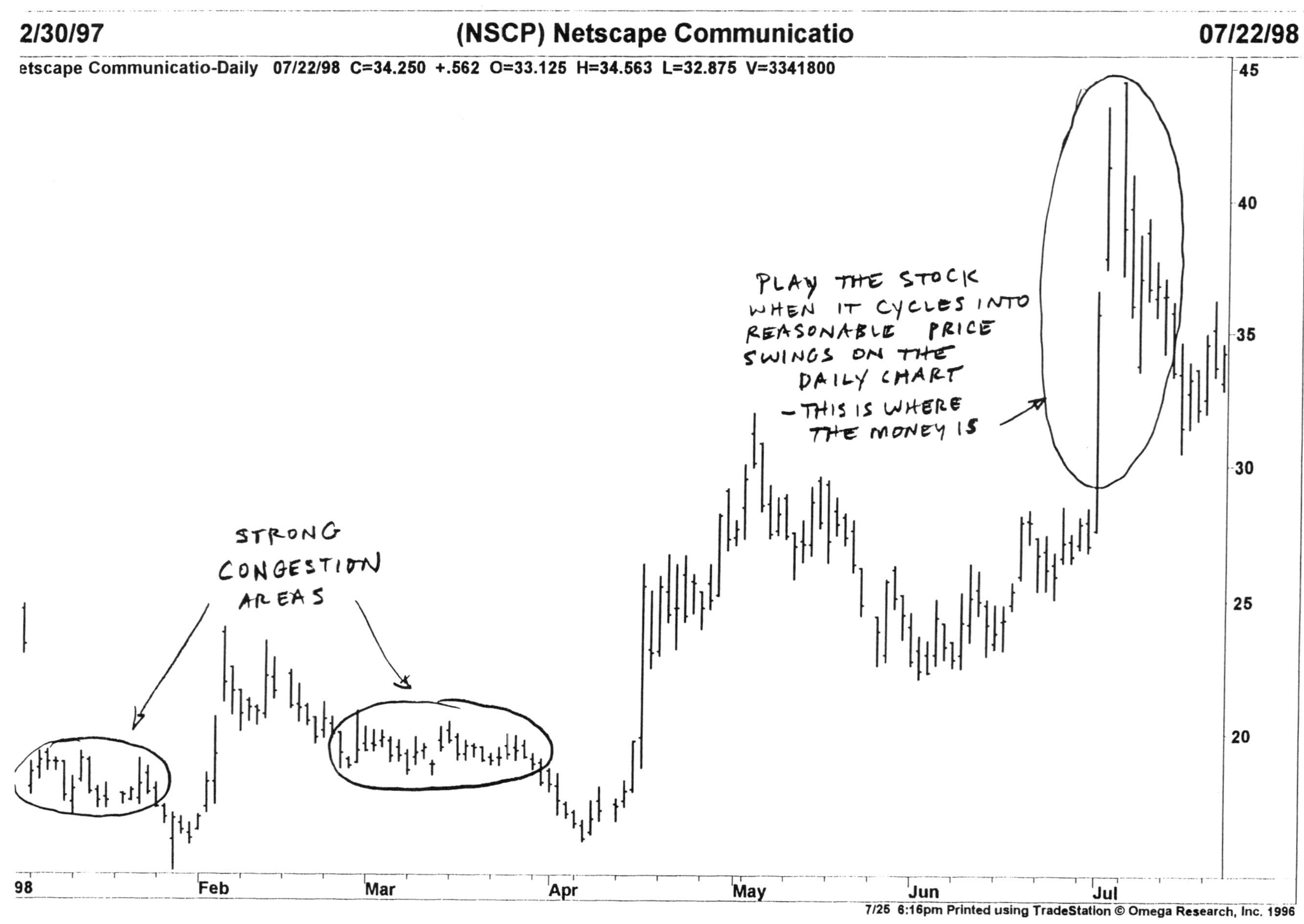

2/30/97
(NSCP) Netscape Communicatio
07/22/98
etscape Communicatio-Daily 07/22/98 C=34.250 +.562 O=33.125 H=34.563 L=32.875 V=3341800
45
40
35
30
25
20
98
Feb
Mar
Apr
May
Jun
Jul
7/25 6:16pm Printed using TradeStation © Omega Research, Inc. 1996
STRONG CONGESTION AREAS
PLAY THE STOCK WHEN IT CYCLES INTO REASONABLE PRICE SWINGS ON THE DAILY CHART
- THIS IS WHERE THE MONEY IS

CONGESTION

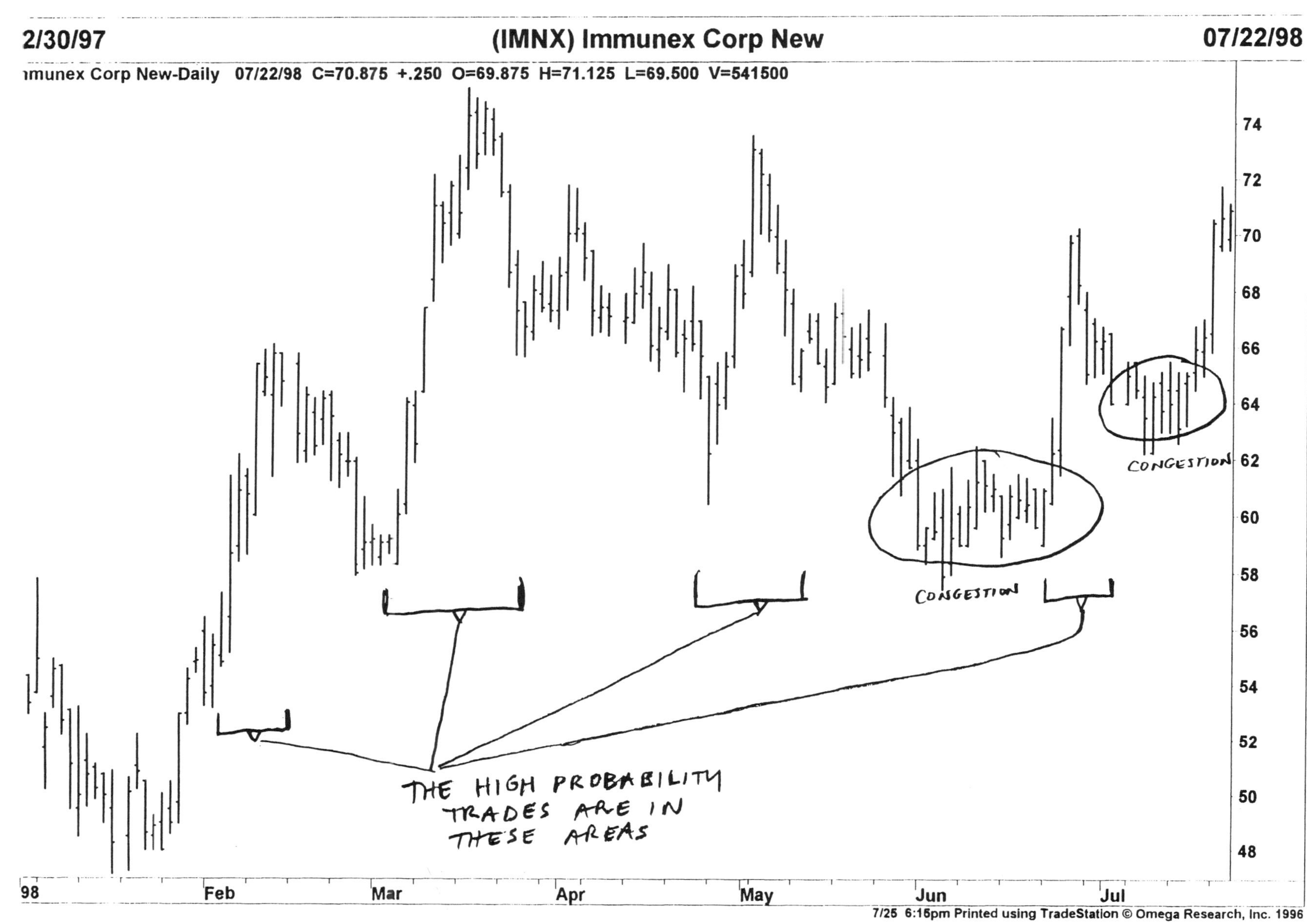
2/30/97
(IMNX) Immunex Corp New
07/22/98
ımunex Corp New-Daily 07/22/98 C=70.875 +.250 O=69.875 H=71.125 L=69.500 V=541500
74
72
70
68
66
64
62
60
58
56
54
52
50
48
98
Feb
Mar
Apr
May
Jun
Jul
CONGESTION
CONGESTION
THE HIGH PROBABILITY TRADES ARE IN THESE AREAS
7/25 6:15pm Printed using TradeStation © Omega Research, Inc. 1996

CONGESTION

2/30/97 (CIEN) CIEN 07/22/98

IEN-Daily 07/22/98 C=88.313 +.375 O=87.250 H=88.500 L=85.375 V=2504200

90
85
80
75
70
65
60
55
50
45
40

98 Feb Mar Apr May Jun Jul

GOOD MOVEMENT ON THE DAILY CHART ALERTS YOU TO TRADE PRICE PATTERN SETUPS WITH HIGHER ODDS OF SUCCESS

CONGESTION

CONGESTION

CONGESTION

7/25 6:15pm Printed using TradeStation © Omega Research, Inc. 1996

CONGESTION

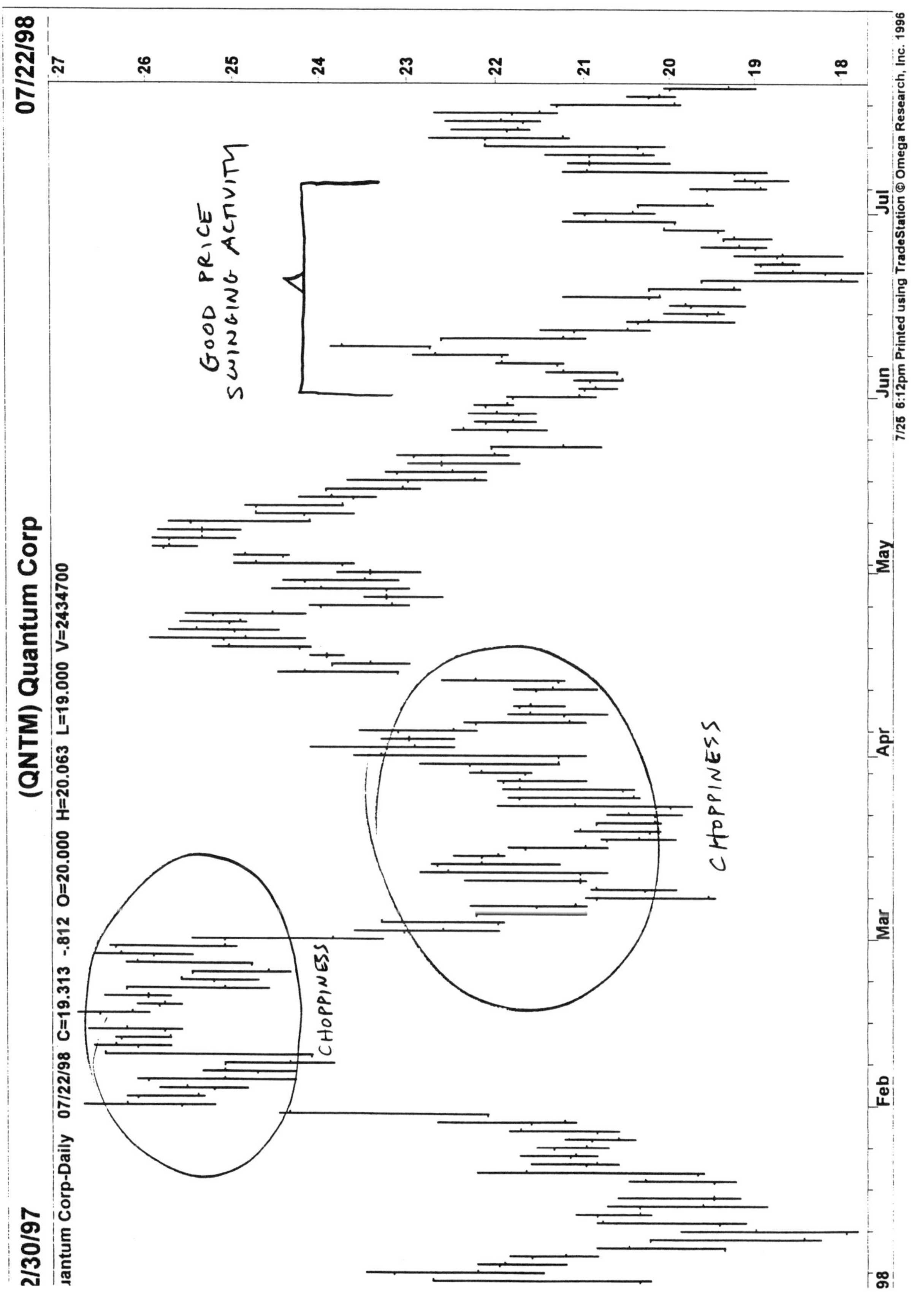

2/30/97 (QNTM) Quantum Corp 07/22/98

ıantum Corp-Daily 07/22/98 C=19.313 -.812 O=20.000 H=20.063 L=19.000 V=2434700

27
26
25
24
23
22
21
20
19
18

98 Feb Mar Apr May Jun Jul

CHOPPINESS

CHOPPINESS

GOOD PRICE SWINGING ACTIVITY

7/25 6:12pm Printed using TradeStation © Omega Research, Inc. 1996

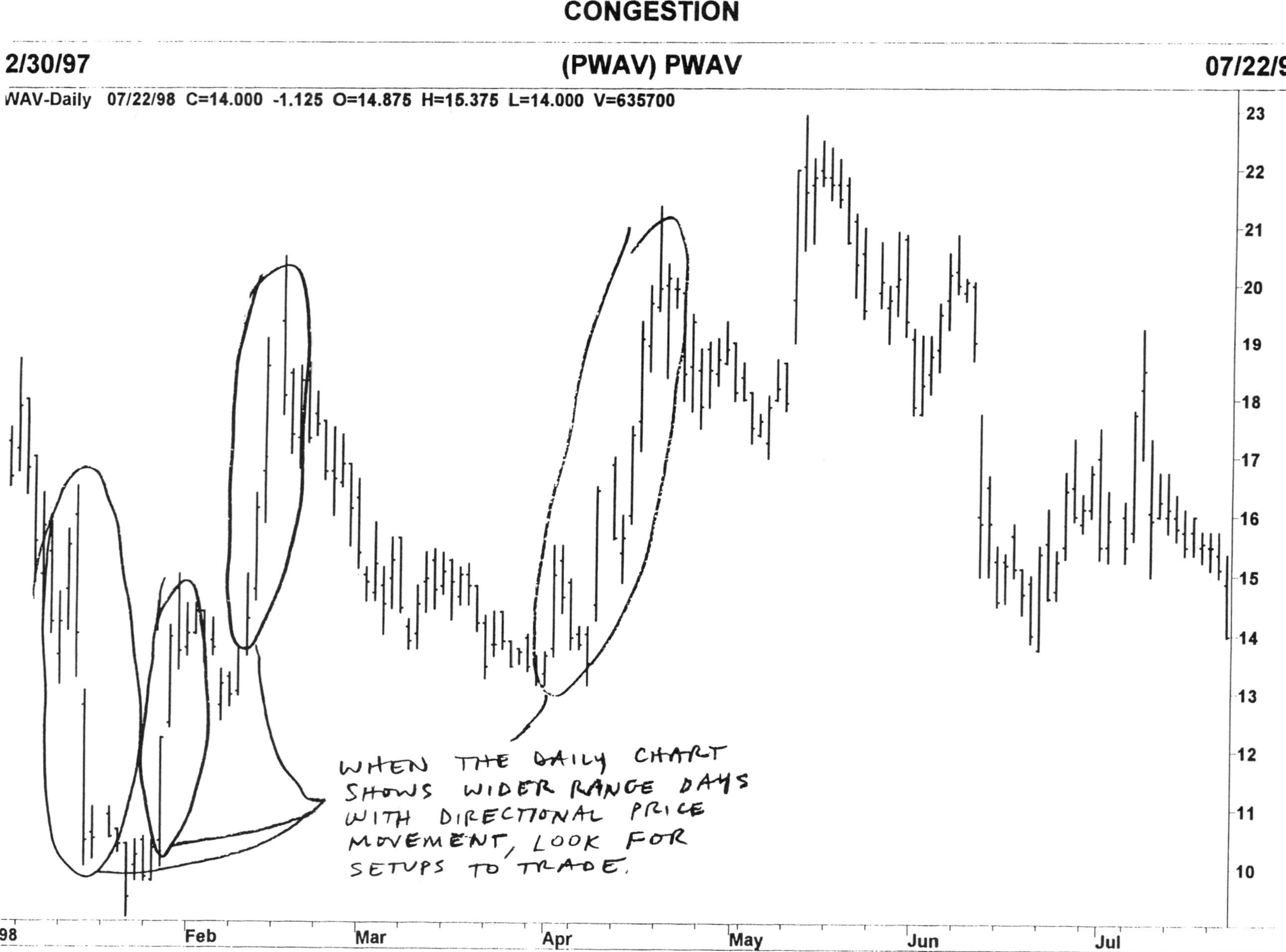
CONGESTION
2/30/97
(PWAV) PWAV
07/22/98
WAV-Daily 07/22/98 C=14.000 -1.125 O=14.875 H=15.375 L=14.000 V=635700
23
22
21
20
19
18
17
16
15
14
13
12
11
10
98
Feb
Mar
Apr
May
Jun
Jul
WHEN THE DAILY CHART SHOWS WIDER RANGE DAYS WITH DIRECTIONAL PRICE MOVEMENT, LOOK FOR SETUPS TO TRADE.
7/25 6:10pm Printed using TradeStation © Omega Research, Inc. 1996

TRADABLE DAILY CONGESTION

As a day trader it is usually best to avoid trading a stock that is in congestion on the daily chart. There is less directional follow-through up or down in price moves – even out of good price pattern setups. But I've noticed one particular phenomenon that unfolds occasionally in some stocks where they can be traded in daily congestion.

Sometimes a stock will have several successive days where each day retraces the prior day's move. One day will open near the low and trade up during the session to close near its high. The next day will open near that prior day's high and trade back down to close at or near its low, retracing the move from the day before. The following days will tend to retrace each prior day's move. It looks something like this:

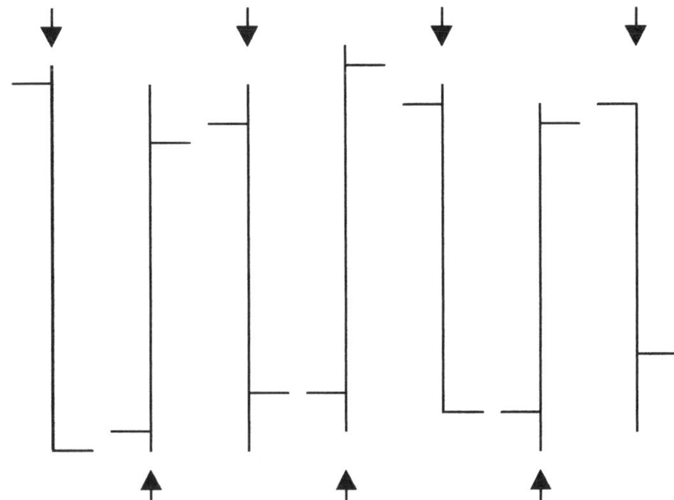

The daily range from high to low for these bars should be 1 ½ points or more to generate reasonable day trade potential. Often you can utilize the wide range day, extreme close trading strategies to enter and trade these stocks during this unique type of congestion. *Refer to the stock's 5 minute chart to make sure the intraday price activity bears out the retracement of each prior day without too much whipsawing action.*

This type of congestion and trading opportunity doesn't come along very often. But when it does, recognize it and capitalize on these high probability day trade plays. You can see this phenomenon recur in the same stock again and again on the daily chart as it traded into these congestion phases during the past year or two.

Don't force this pattern. It needs to be obvious to your eye when reviewing the charts. Once you know how it looks though, you can pick them out quickly and be prepared to trade them. Enter these trades early in the market session to capture the majority of the move.

Use the "wiggle" once you are in the trade. When the stock has retraced the majority of the prior day's move, you may want to exit the position since it has neared a probable halting point at the profit target of the high or low of the previous day.

Daily (Left) QUALCOMM INC Bar MA (P=50)
1997
66
64
62
60
58
56
54
52
50
48
46
44
42
40
27 29 31F 5 7 11 13 18 20 24 26 28M 5 7 11 13 17 19 21 25 27 A 3 7 9 11 15 17 21 24 28 30M 5 7 9 13 15 19 21 23 28 30J 4
CONGESTION
WHERE EACH DAY TENDS
TO RETRACE THE PRIOR
DAY'S MOVE

Daily
1997
(Left) LAM RESEARCH CORP
Bar MA (P=50)
POTENTIALLY
TRADABLE
CONGESTION

Daily
(Left) ELECTRONIC ARTS
1997
Bar MA (P=53)
POTENTIALLY TRADABLE
CONGESTION
38
37
36
35
34
33
32
31
30
29
28
27
26
25
24
23
22
21
20
19
18
27 A 3 7 9 11 15 17 21 24 28 30M 5 7 9 13 15 19 21 23 28 30J 4 6 10 12 16 18 20 24 26 30J 3 8 10 14 16 18 22 24 28 30 A 5

CLOSE AT HIGH OR LOW OF DAILY CONGESTION

As a stock cycles through "price swinging" activity and congestion on the daily chart, be on the lookout. When a stock is in a congestion period, watch for a day that closes at or near its high that is also at or very near the upper side of the daily congestion area. Conversely, don't miss a stock that has closed at or near its low of the day that is also at or very near the lower side of the daily congestion area.

The breakout move out of daily congestion, or "resting" period for a stock, is often preceded by a daily bar as described above. The next trading session often provides a strong move out of the consolidation area for a great day trade opportunity.

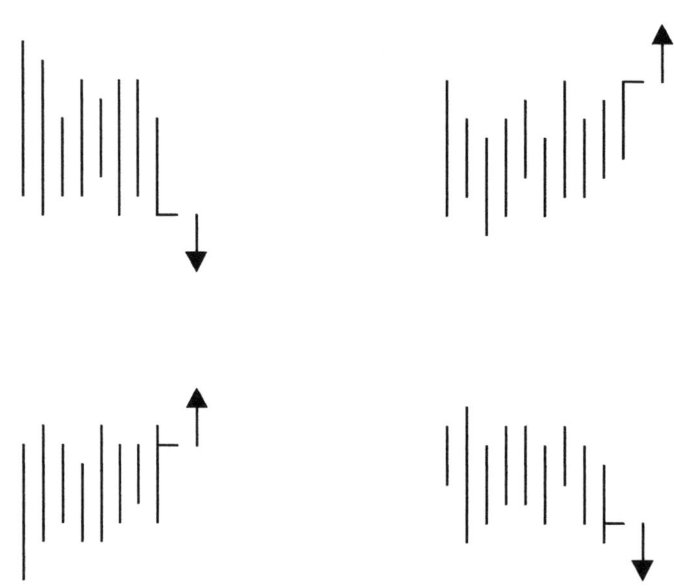

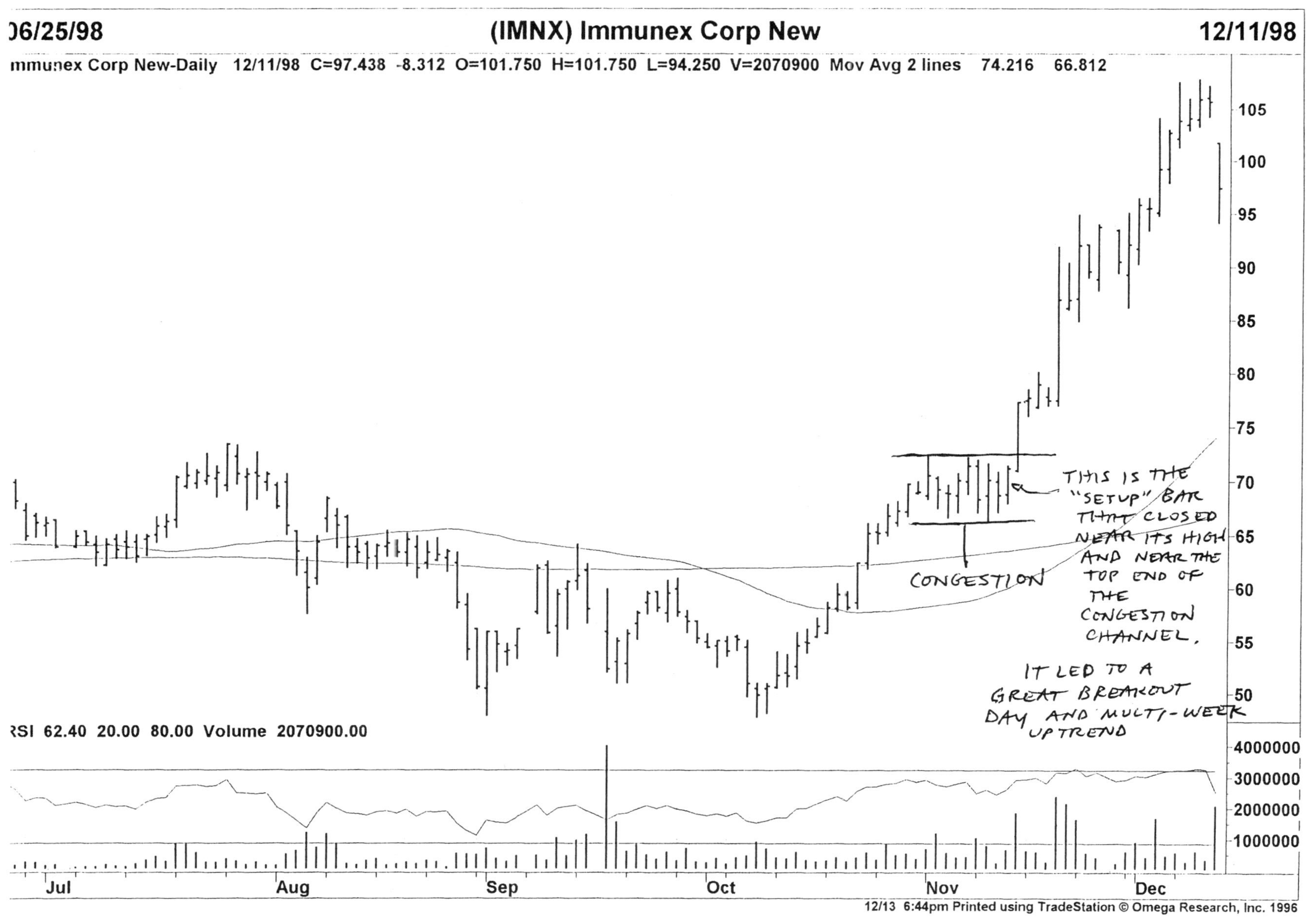
06/25/98
(IMNX) Immunex Corp New
12/11/98
mmunex Corp New-Daily 12/11/98 C=97.438 -8.312 O=101.750 H=101.750 L=94.250 V=2070900 Mov Avg 2 lines 74.216 66.812
105
100
95
90
85
80
75
70
65
60
55
50
THIS IS THE "SETUP" BAR THAT CLOSED NEAR ITS HIGH AND NEAR THE TOP END OF THE CONGESTION CHANNEL.
CONGESTION
IT LED TO A GREAT BREAKOUT DAY AND MULTI-WEEK UPTREND
RSI 62.40 20.00 80.00 Volume 2070900.00
4000000
3000000
2000000
1000000
Jul
Aug
Sep
Oct
Nov
Dec
12/13 6:44pm Printed using TradeStation © Omega Research, Inc. 1996

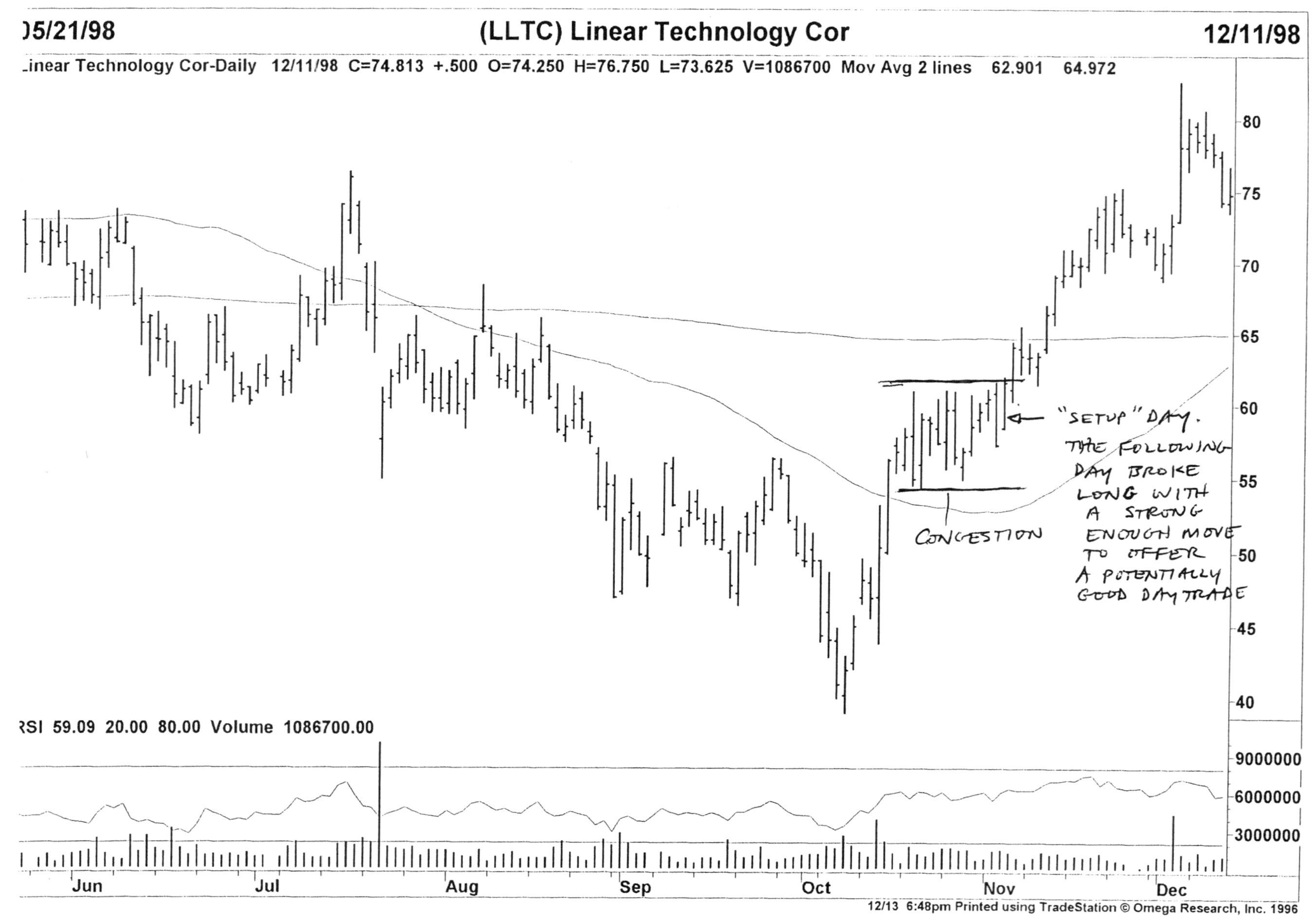

5/21/98
(LLTC) Linear Technology Cor
12/11/98
Linear Technology Cor-Daily 12/11/98 C=74.813 +.500 O=74.250 H=76.750 L=73.625 V=1086700 Mov Avg 2 lines 62.901 64.972
80
75
70
65
60
55
50
45
40
"SETUP" DAY.
THE FOLLOWING DAY BROKE LONG WITH A STRONG ENOUGH MOVE TO OFFER A POTENTIALLY GOOD DAY TRADE
CONGESTION
RSI 59.09 20.00 80.00 Volume 1086700.00
9000000
6000000
3000000
Jun
Jul
Aug
Sep
Oct
Nov
Dec
12/13 6:48pm Printed using TradeStation © Omega Research, Inc. 1996

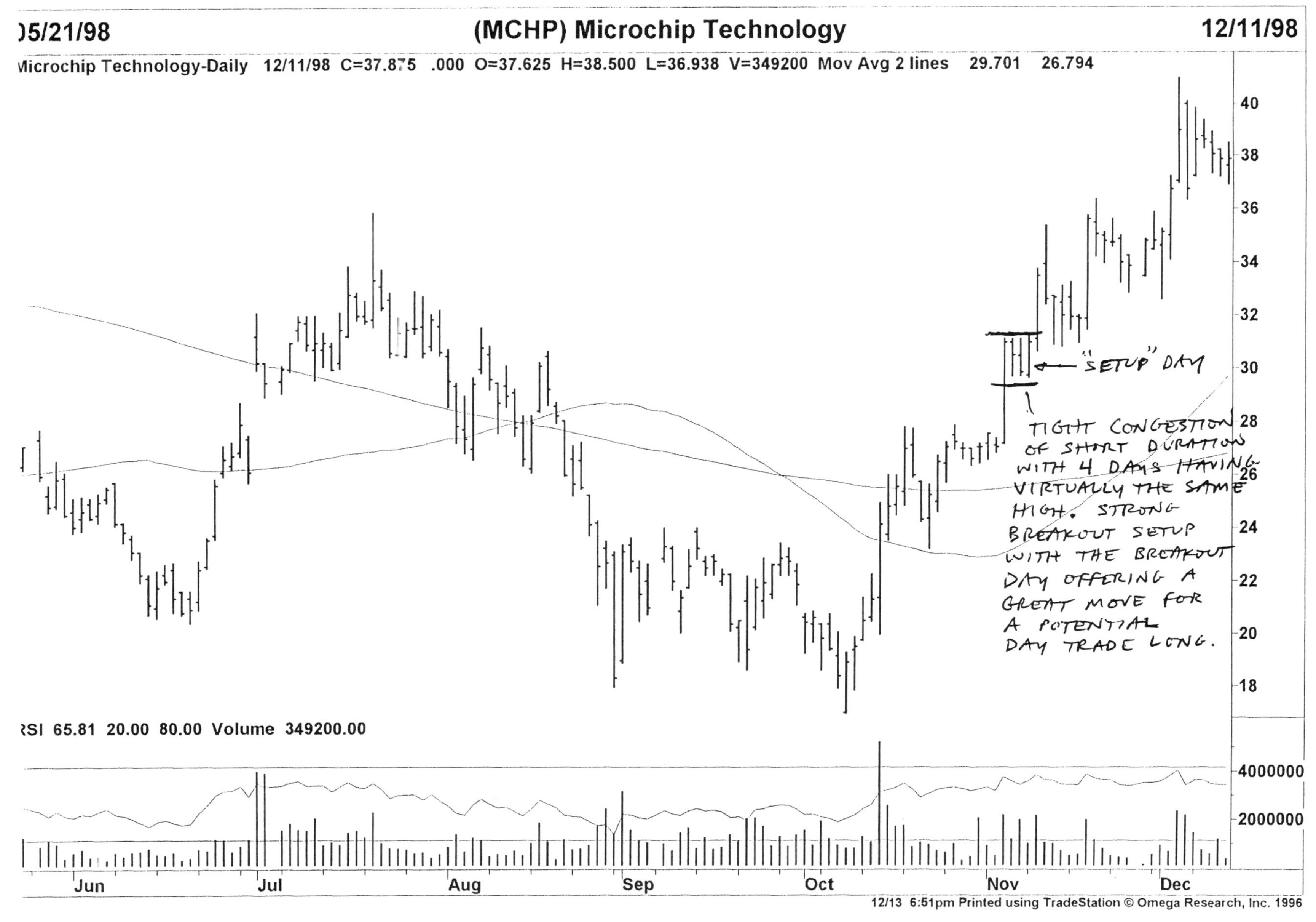

)5/21/98
(MCHP) Microchip Technology
12/11/98
Aicrochip Technology-Daily 12/11/98 C=37.875 .000 O=37.625 H=38.500 L=36.938 V=349200 Mov Avg 2 lines 29.701 26.794
40
38
36
34
32
30
28
26
24
22
20
18
"SETUP" DAY
TIGHT CONGESTION OF SHORT DURATION WITH 4 DAYS HAVING VIRTUALLY THE SAME HIGH. STRONG BREAKOUT SETUP WITH THE BREAKOUT DAY OFFERING A GREAT MOVE FOR A POTENTIAL DAY TRADE LONG.
RSI 65.81 20.00 80.00 Volume 349200.00
4000000
2000000
Jun
Jul
Aug
Sep
Oct
Nov
Dec
12/13 6:51pm Printed using TradeStation © Omega Research, Inc. 1996

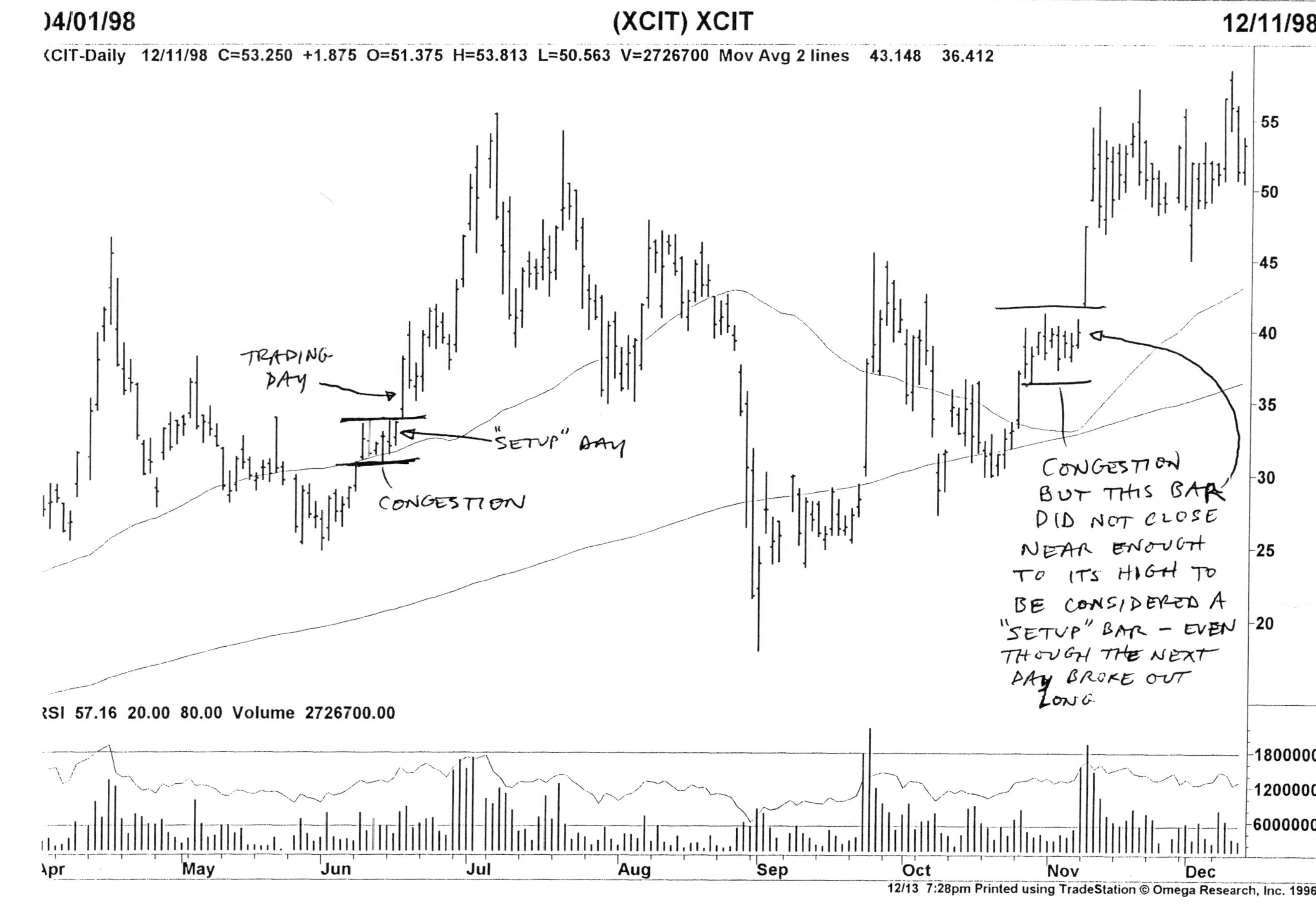
)4/01/98
(XCIT) XCIT
12/11/98
(CIT-Daily 12/11/98 C=53.250 +1.875 O=51.375 H=53.813 L=50.563 V=2726700 Mov Avg 2 lines 43.148 36.412
55
50
45
40
35
30
25
20
TRADING DAY
"SETUP" DAY
CONGESTION
CONGESTION BUT THIS BAR DID NOT CLOSE NEAR ENOUGH TO ITS HIGH TO BE CONSIDERED A "SETUP" BAR – EVEN THOUGH THE NEXT DAY BROKE OUT LONG
RSI 57.16 20.00 80.00 Volume 2726700.00
1800000
1200000
6000000
Apr
May
Jun
Jul
Aug
Sep
Oct
Nov
Dec
12/13 7:28pm Printed using TradeStation © Omega Research, Inc. 1996

DAILY BARS OF INDECISION

DAILY BARS OF INDECISION

"Beware the significance of the close"

When day trading, the prior day's close poses significance as to how the stock will tend to move the next day. One of the prime indicators of a choppy day or a day lacking direction with follow-through is provided by the nature of the prior day's close. If the stock closed near the middle of the range from its high and low of the day, then the market is reflecting indecision for that stock. This indecision will usually carry on into the following day…so beware of the close.

Often, it is best to steer clear of trading these stocks even if they have a good intraday setup on the 5 minute bar chart. Directional follow-through is not very likely, and you want to stack all of the odds in your favor for a good day trade. To avoid getting caught in these lower probability trades, evaluate the following diagrams to better understand how these days of indecision tend to look.

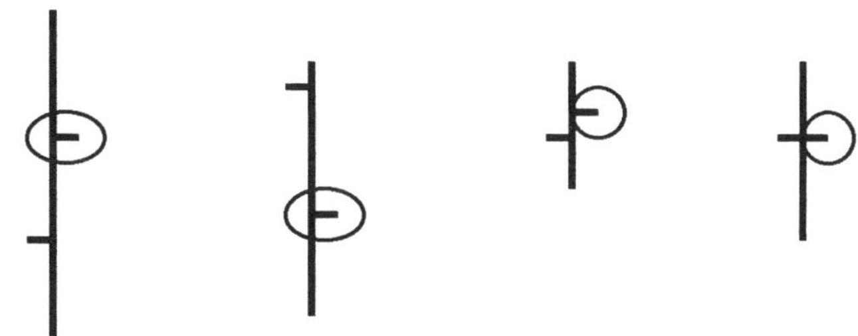

The underlying principle for indecision lies in how the stock closes near the middle of the range of the day. If a stock closes in the area shown below, then be more cautious with any day trade setup.

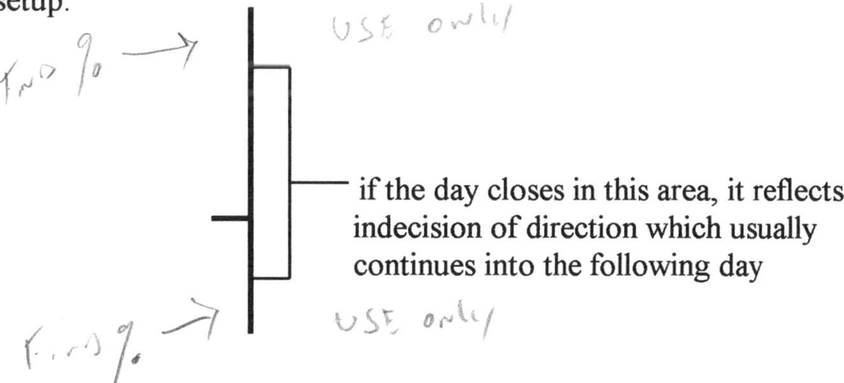

Some trades have enough compelling factors (covered in this manual) to consider worthwhile, even with this type of prior day. But, unless you have a significant reason for a trade following this type of prior day, then consider passing it up. Remember, we want to "cherry pick" only the best ones.

II

SUPPORTING TOOLS AND TACTICS

MARKET INDEX BEHAVIOR

MARKET INDEX BEHAVIOR

"Typical scenarios for overall market movement"

You always want the market indices moving in the direction of any trade setup that you are wanting to enter. Trading in the direction of the market only enhances the chances for a successful day trade. If you trade against the market's direction, you are not "cherry picking" your trades.

The best way to follow the market is with a 5 minute intraday bar chart. This would include the NASDAQ Composite and/or NASDAQ-100 when trading a NASDAQ stock, the NYSE Composite and Dow Jones Industrial Average when trading a New York issue. Having these charts displayed along with a chart of the S&P-500 futures contract provides a backdrop of market activity and direction.

By setting the charts to show 2 to 3 days worth of data, you can easily recognize intraday support and resistance areas (often at the high or low of a prior session), trending and non-trending days. Simple trendlines and trend channels can also be drawn on the chart with most software packages. This is all of the information you need as a reference point about the current character of the market while you look for good trade setups. At a glance, the indices serve as guideposts indicating whether to look for long or short trades and whether it's a good or not-so-good, choppy market.

Market indices regularly display several typical patterns of behavior. Knowing how these scenarios usually play out will provide you an advantage. And since the market direction is such an important component of successful trading, these scenarios will give you an edge, or bias, for whether you should be looking for longs or shorts. It also will help you gauge when to enter trades and when to stand aside.

Much of the focus will be on how the market opens in relation to the prior day's close followed by how it moves within the first hour of trading. The typical market index behavior scenarios set the stage for what is likely to be the direction of follow-through for the market.

Typical market index behavior categorizes your expectations into three different areas:

1) Big gap opening
2) Slight gap opening
3) An open even with or very near the prior day's close

Although you will be using bar charts, the diagrams are drawn with a line for simplicity.

BIG GAP OPENING

(big gap up, sell-off)

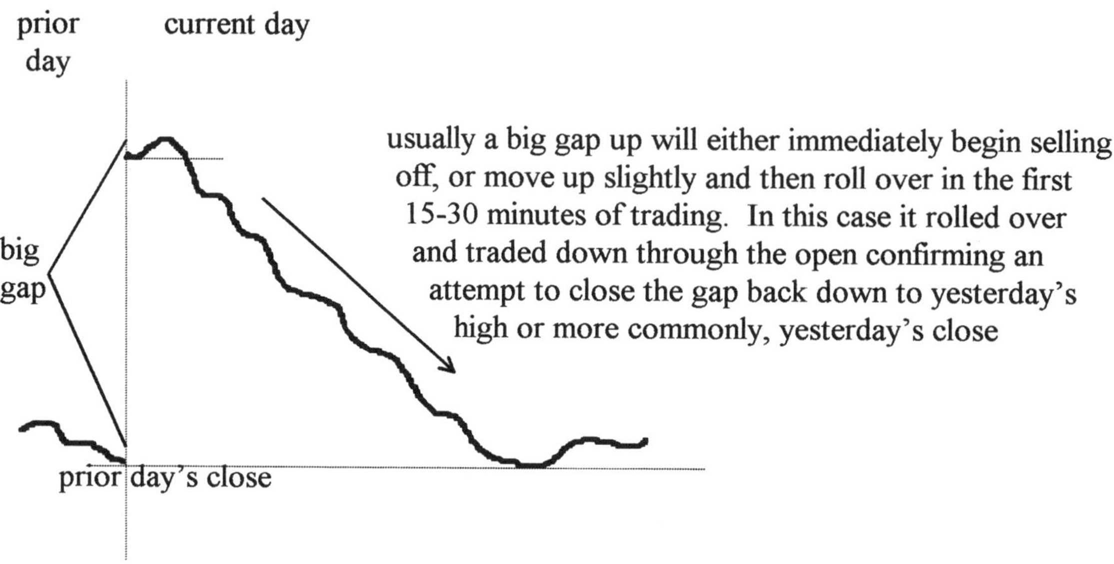

<u>This is the most frequent pattern for how a big gap plays out</u>.

On a big gap up, don't rush into any long trades. Wait for the market to roll over and begin selling off. Scout out some good potential short trades, and when the market gives way, consider trading them short.

This is where relative strength can play a significant role. With such a substantial gap up, a number of stocks have also gapped up from their prior day's close. If you find some stocks that did not gap up, but instead opened near or slightly below the prior day's close, then they have weak relative strength. These are often good short candidates out of a price pattern setup to the down side.

Also, any stock that gaps up *significantly* with the market may encounter a sell-off in conjunction with the market sell-off. It may offer a strong move down as the stock attempts to close the gap back to its prior day's high.

A big gap down plays out the same way except it is the inverse of the diagram and explanation above. A big gap down usually provides good buying opportunities.

The next scenario of the big gap up happens much less frequently. It is diagrammed and explained next.

(big gap up, rallies long)

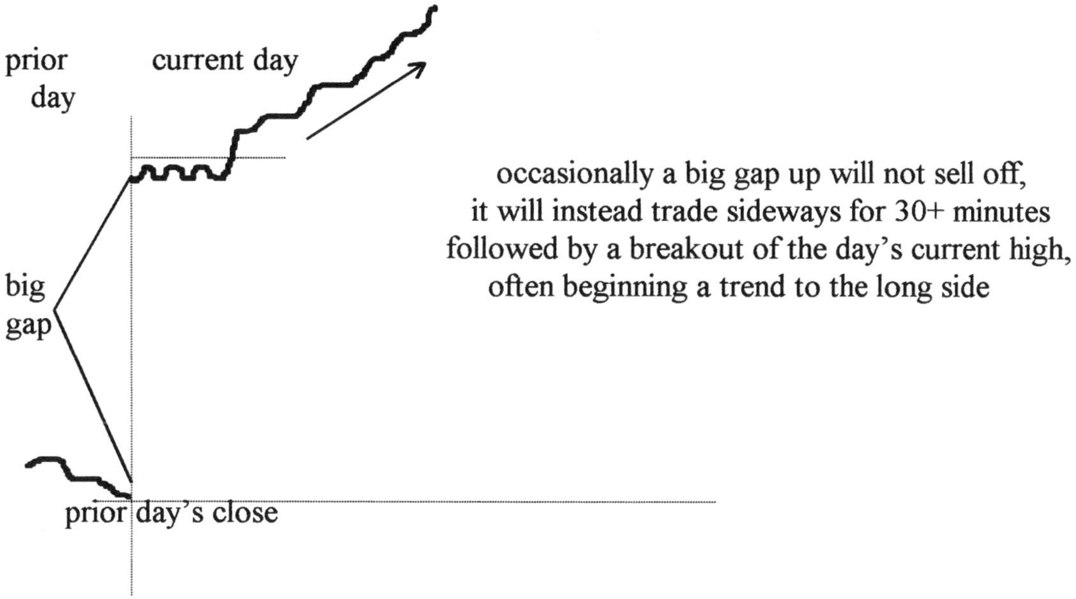

This scenario does not unfold very often. The first sign is that it does not sell off. It continues to hold the gap as it trades sideways in a tight range. If this lasts over 30 minutes and the index breaks out to a new high on the day, it will usually trend that direction for a while. This is when you should be looking for good long setups in individual stocks.

Simply invert the diagram to understand how a big gap down would look. It would hold the gap, trading sideways and finally break down through the day's current low for some good short trading potential.

Let's summarize the big gap opening. The bias is usually for a big gap to close. This way you can better anticipate and trade in the direction the market is most likely taking. It will also keep you from getting in on the wrong side by trading too soon when you see a big gap. Your entries should also be better since you have an expectation that the market is going to close the gap and are prepared by having certain stocks already picked out to trade. If the gap holds and then breaks the other direction you will see it unfolding before the "break." In either case you will know how to react to the market and find the best stocks to trade and get the best entry price.

SLIGHT GAP OPENING

(slight gap up, rebound long)

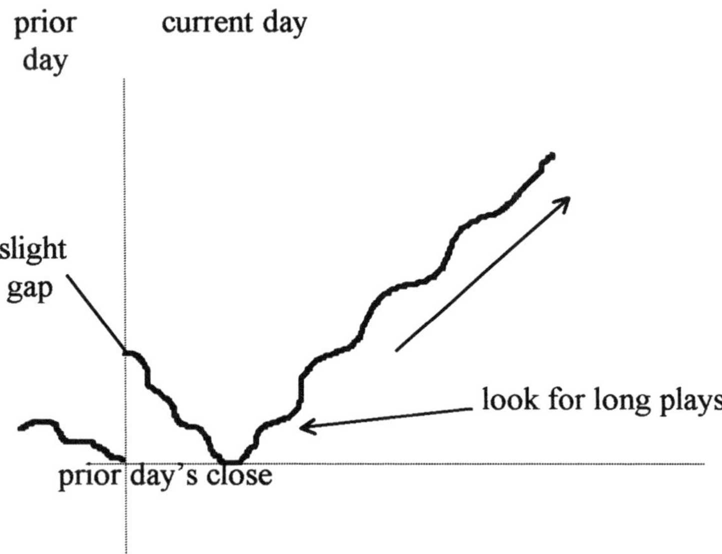

<u>This is the most common scenario for a slight gap up</u>.

If the market has a slight gap up, the expectation is for it to close the gap quickly by selling off to the prior day's close, where it should find support, and *rebound relatively quickly* back to the long side. Usually this offers an intraday trend up during the morning and sometimes for the whole day. Look for stocks with good setups long and consider entering them on the reaction bounce off of the prior day's close of the index.

Invert this example in your mind to see how the slight gap down would look. The index should trade back up to the prior day's close (resistance) and rebound back to the downside for some potentially good short trades.

The slight gap opening will occasionally close the gap and *not rebound*. Instead, it may trade sideways for 20+ minutes against the prior day's close and then decisively penetrate through it. This break can initiate a trend in the direction of the penetration with decent follow-through.

Here is how it should look for a slight gap up that breaks down.

(slight gap up, break down)

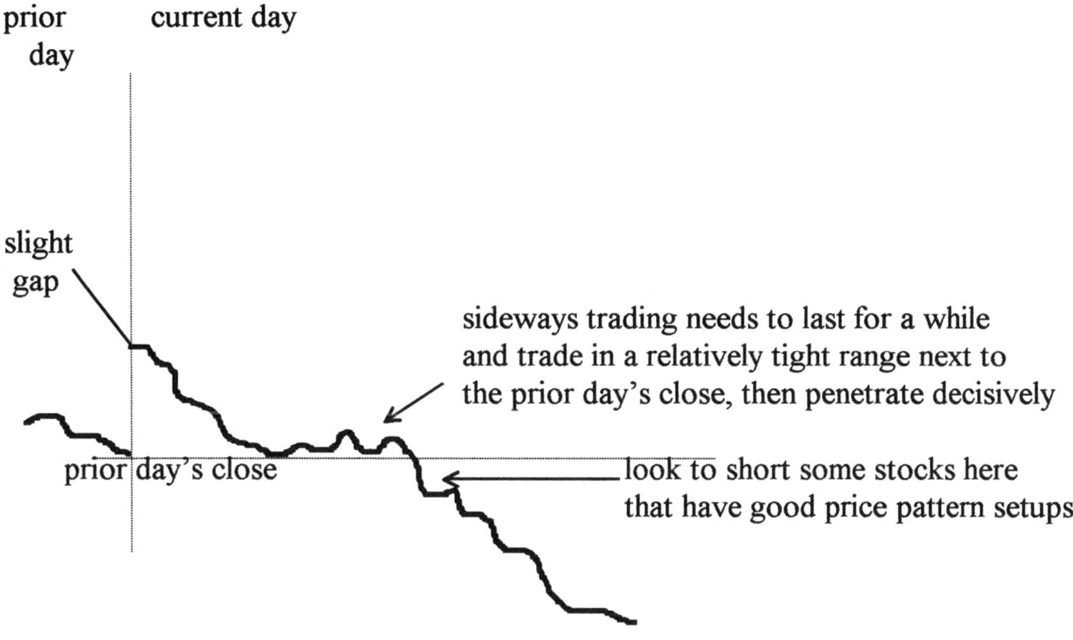

If the index does not trade in a tight range near the prior day's close then the odds of a successful follow-through of a break to the downside diminish considerably. In this case it may be just a choppy market to be traded only lightly.

OPEN NEAR PRIOR DAY'S CLOSE

Many good intraday trending days begin with an open very near the prior day's close. On the other hand many choppy, trendless days also begin this way. So how do you tell the difference? You can't right away. If the market opens and trades sideways in a *tight* range for 20+ minutes and then breaks firmly through the current high or low, then odds favor a trend in that direction for at least part of the morning.

If the index instead trades up slightly and rolls over, then down slightly and turns back up, beware. This portends a choppy market until the current intraday high or low is decisively penetrated.

Here is how a trending market might unfold.

(opening near prior day's close, trending)

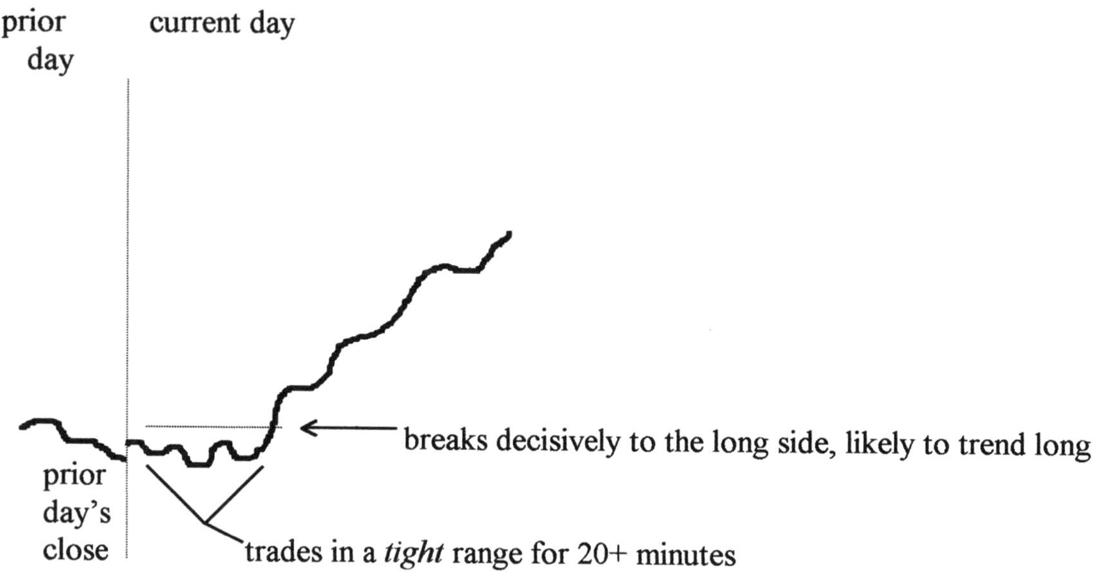

Once again, simply invert the above diagram to see how the index could have broken down through its lows for a potential trend down.

(opening near prior day's close, non-trending)

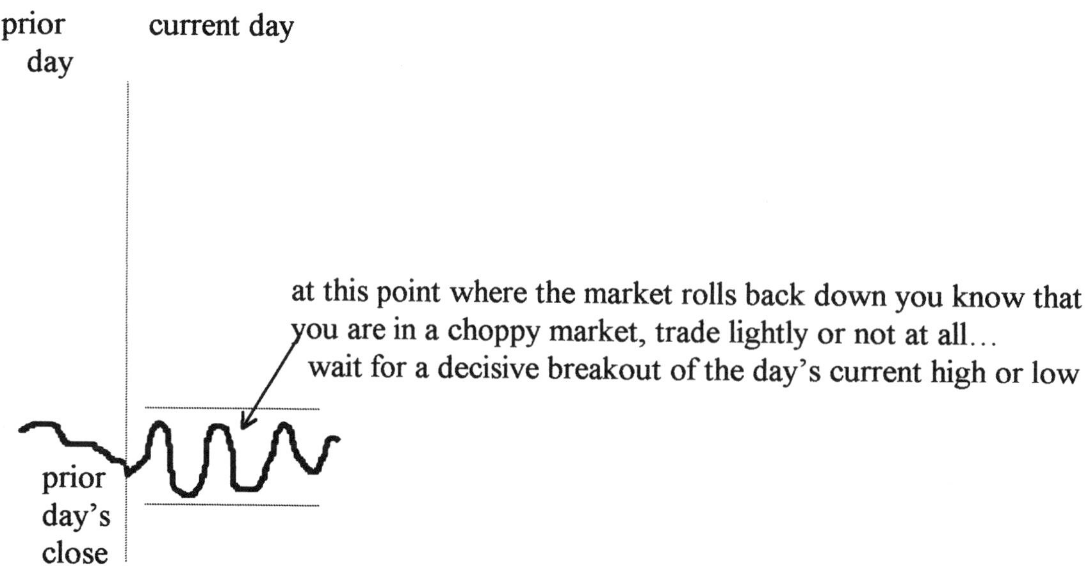

To recognize a choppy market as soon as possible is imperative. A market like this will have most stocks faking long, then short, then long etc. Even stocks with good price pattern setups won't provide much follow-through. You will save yourself money by backing away and simply not trading unless the market picks a direction.

ONE FINAL SCENARIO

There is one final scenario that has become more prominent recently. Sometimes the market will blast off from the open strongly up or down within the first 30 to 45 minutes of the session and then trade sideways in a tight range for an extended period of time. It's as if the market shot all of its bullets early and quickly. Instead of trending up or down to where it was likely headed, it ran right off of the open to that level and upon arrival began sitting stagnant for a while.

The money in this type of market is made early in the morning on the initial strong move up or down. This is how it looks.

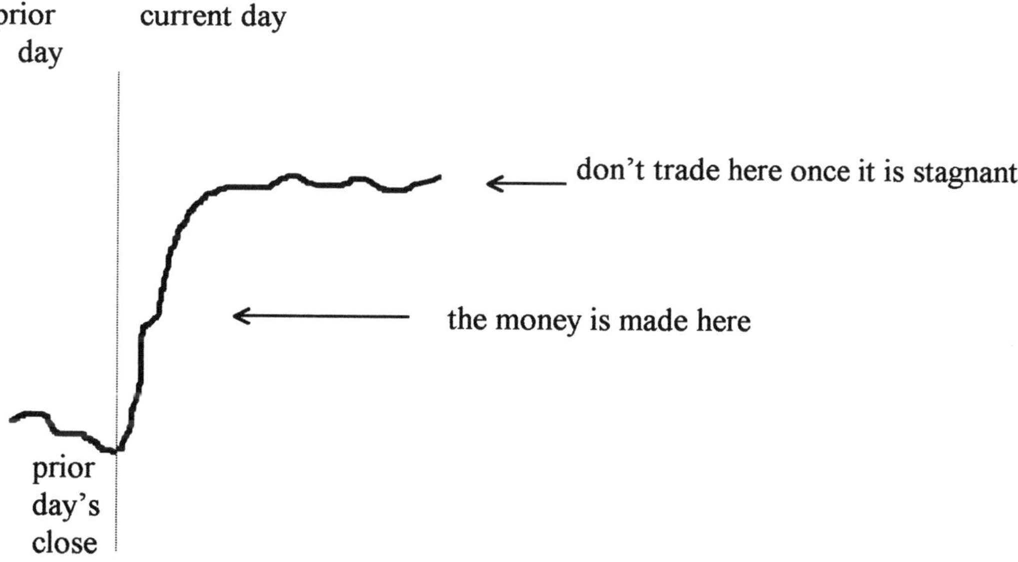

Never forget the significance of trading in the direction of the market indices. These scenarios give you an "expectation" of typical market behavior patterns. But remember, do not prematurely trade based merely upon the *anticipation* of one of these scenarios following through. You must always *react* to the market. Having a grasp of typical market index behavior provides a backdrop for your trading. It will key you into what trades to look for and enhance your timing and ability to enter them at the price that you want.

INTRADAY INDEX SUPPORT AND RESISTANCE

As a day trader, one of the most important factors that shapes your trading decisions is the overall market's intraday trend and direction. Trading in the direction of a stock's corresponding market index puts you on the right side of the market and path of least resistance.

The immediate direction of an index is different from its trend. Immediate direction is which direction (up or down) the index is currently moving during the most recent few minutes. Trend reflects a bit longer time frame (30+ minutes).

A stock index may be making higher highs and higher lows on the 5 minute bar chart as it works its way up. This "established" intraday uptrend means you will probably want to take only long trades in stocks. A downtrend is the opposite with lower highs and lower lows on the 5 minute bar chart pointing you to look for short trades.

If the market index establishes a trend then it helps you know which direction to trade and helps hone your timing as you enter stock trades. For an uptrend, wait for a pullback that stalls and as it begins to resume the upmove, look to stocks that have set up as buy candidates. The converse is true for a down trending index as you look to enter stocks short. Knowing the typical market index behavior patterns will provide you additional guidance for where and when to be looking for long or short trades to enter.

The indices do have typical patterns of behavior that are recognizable on the 5 minute chart. But you should also be aware of the prevalence of intraday support and resistance in this same 5 minute bar chart time frame. You'll see indices react to these support and resistance levels during each trading session. Also, intraday S/R from the prior several days tends to affect the current trading day.

The indices intraday market direction, trend and its "micro" support and resistance will strongly influence my stock trading decisions from minute to minute as the day unfolds. You can best gauge immediate market direction, overall trend, and support and resistance by constantly monitoring a screen showing 3 days or so of intraday activity. At a glance, these market tendencies help guide your stock day trading decisions.

Support and resistance are prominent in halting an index move. When penetrated, they often provide additional follow-through in that direction.

Consider an index that has quickly moved up or trended strongly upwards and is nearing a prior swing high set by the index earlier in the session or recent prior sessions. You probably should not jump into a long trade in a stock since it is likely that the market will react back down off of the prior resistance.

If the index traded up to this resistance level and held there for a while (15+ minutes) without selling off much, then a penetration of resistance is usually a green light to consider buying stocks out of price pattern setups. The resistance, when penetrated, should provide decent follow-through with the index as well as the stock.

The same halting effect works on intraday index support after a selloff. Wait for the index to languish at the support level for a while. If it breaks to the downside then consider entering new stock trades that have formed a good trading pattern short.

On the other hand, if the index appears to react strongly off of resistance, consider short trades. Just don't wait too far into the down move of the index before you enter a trade.

Once again, the same effect plays out on index bounces off of intraday support. If it appears that the support is turning the index back to the long side for a while, look for good buy setups to enter in stocks.

Since index direction is so important, I've included many annotated charts showing several different indices and their activity.

*$INDU
Fri Dec 11 19:43
Intraday (Left) $INDU (5-Min) Bar
12/02
12/03
12/04
12/07
12/08
RESISTANCE
RESISTANCE FROM 12/2 & 12/3
SUPPORT/RESISTANCE ZONE
RESISTANCE
SUPPORT
SUPPORT
RESISTANCE
SUPPORT

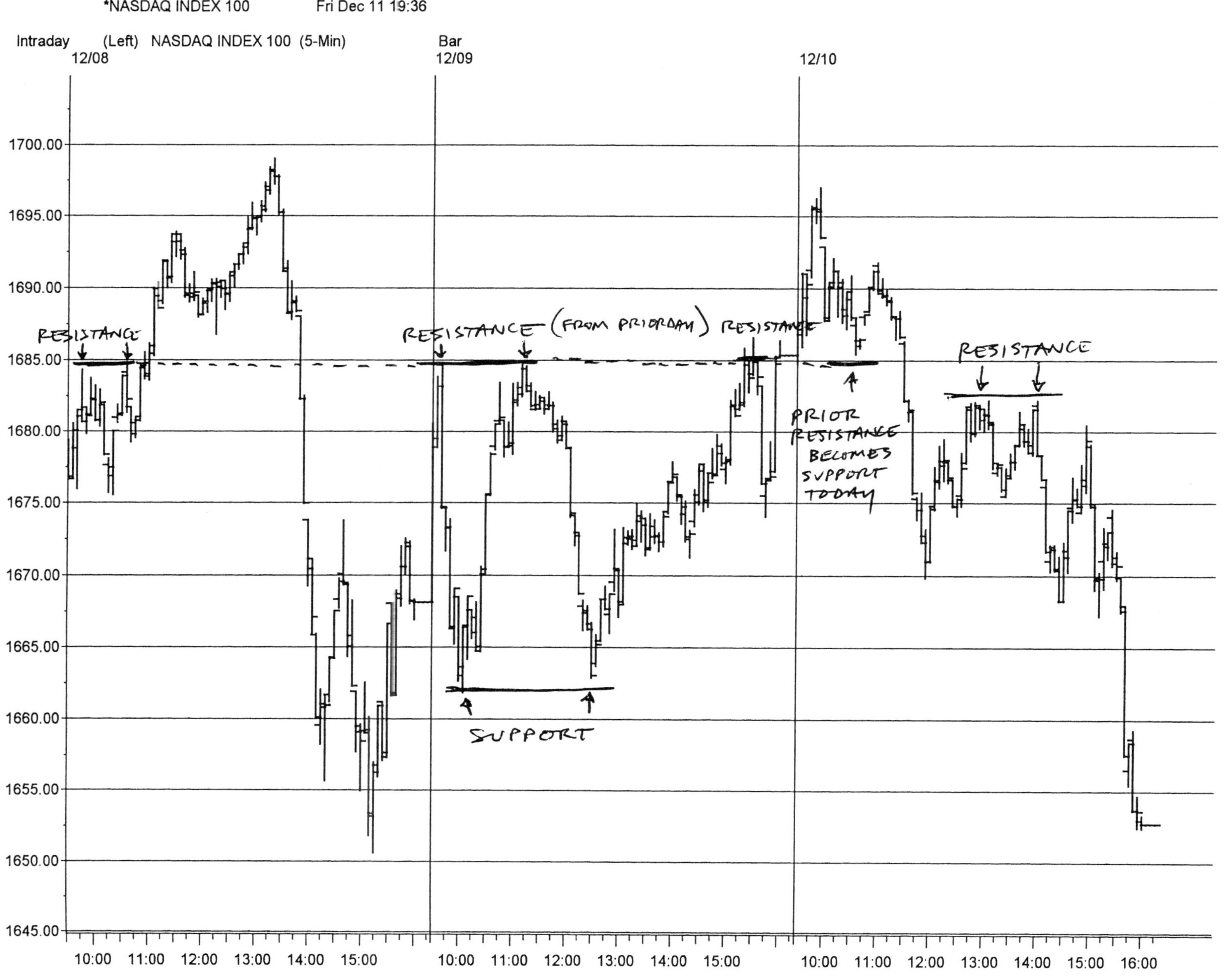
*NASDAQ INDEX 100
Fri Dec 11 19:36
Intraday
(Left) NASDAQ INDEX 100 (5-Min)
Bar
12/08
12/09
12/10
1700.00
1695.00
1690.00
1685.00
1680.00
1675.00
1670.00
1665.00
1660.00
1655.00
1650.00
1645.00
10:00
11:00
12:00
13:00
14:00
15:00
16:00
RESISTANCE
RESISTANCE (FROM PRIOR DAY) RESISTANCE
SUPPORT
PRIOR RESISTANCE BECOMES SUPPORT TODAY
RESISTANCE

*NASDAQ INDEX 100
Fri Dec 11 19:35
Intraday
(Left) NASDAQ INDEX 100 (5-Min)
Bar
12/10
12/11
1700.00
1695.00
1690.00
1685.00
1680.00
1675.00
1670.00
1665.00
1660.00
1655.00
1650.00
1645.00
1640.00
10:00
11:00
12:00
13:00
14:00
15:00
10:00
11:00
12:00
13:00
14:00
15:00
16:00
SUPPORT
RESISTANCE
RESISTANCE
SUPPORT AREA

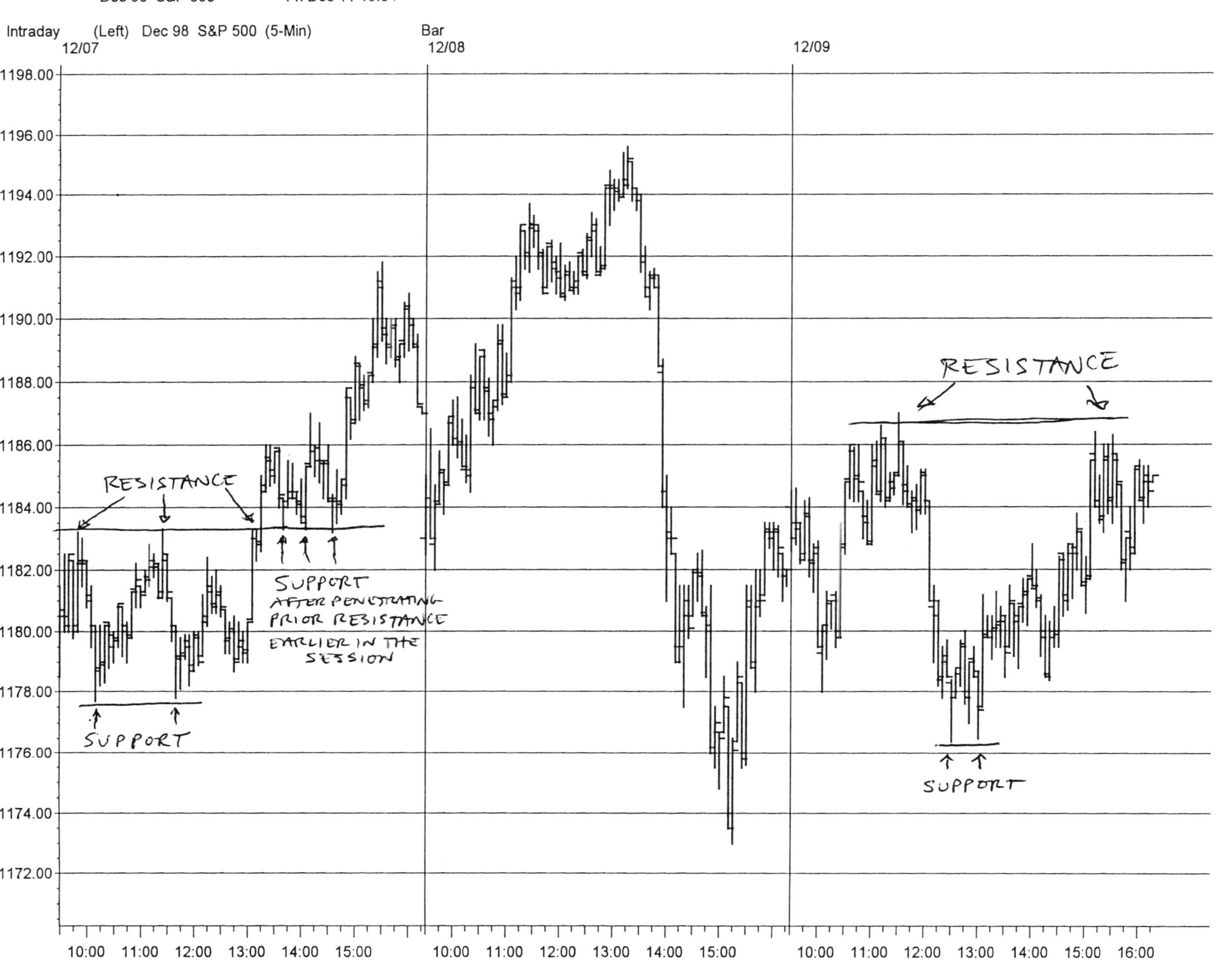
*Dec 98 S&P 500
Fri Dec 11 19:34
Intraday
(Left) Dec 98 S&P 500 (5-Min)
Bar
12/07
12/08
12/09
1198.00
1196.00
1194.00
1192.00
1190.00
1188.00
1186.00
1184.00
1182.00
1180.00
1178.00
1176.00
1174.00
1172.00
10:00 11:00 12:00 13:00 14:00 15:00
10:00 11:00 12:00 13:00 14:00 15:00
10:00 11:00 12:00 13:00 14:00 15:00 16:00
RESISTANCE
SUPPORT
SUPPORT
AFTER PENETRATING
PRIOR RESISTANCE
EARLIER IN THE
SESSION
RESISTANCE
SUPPORT

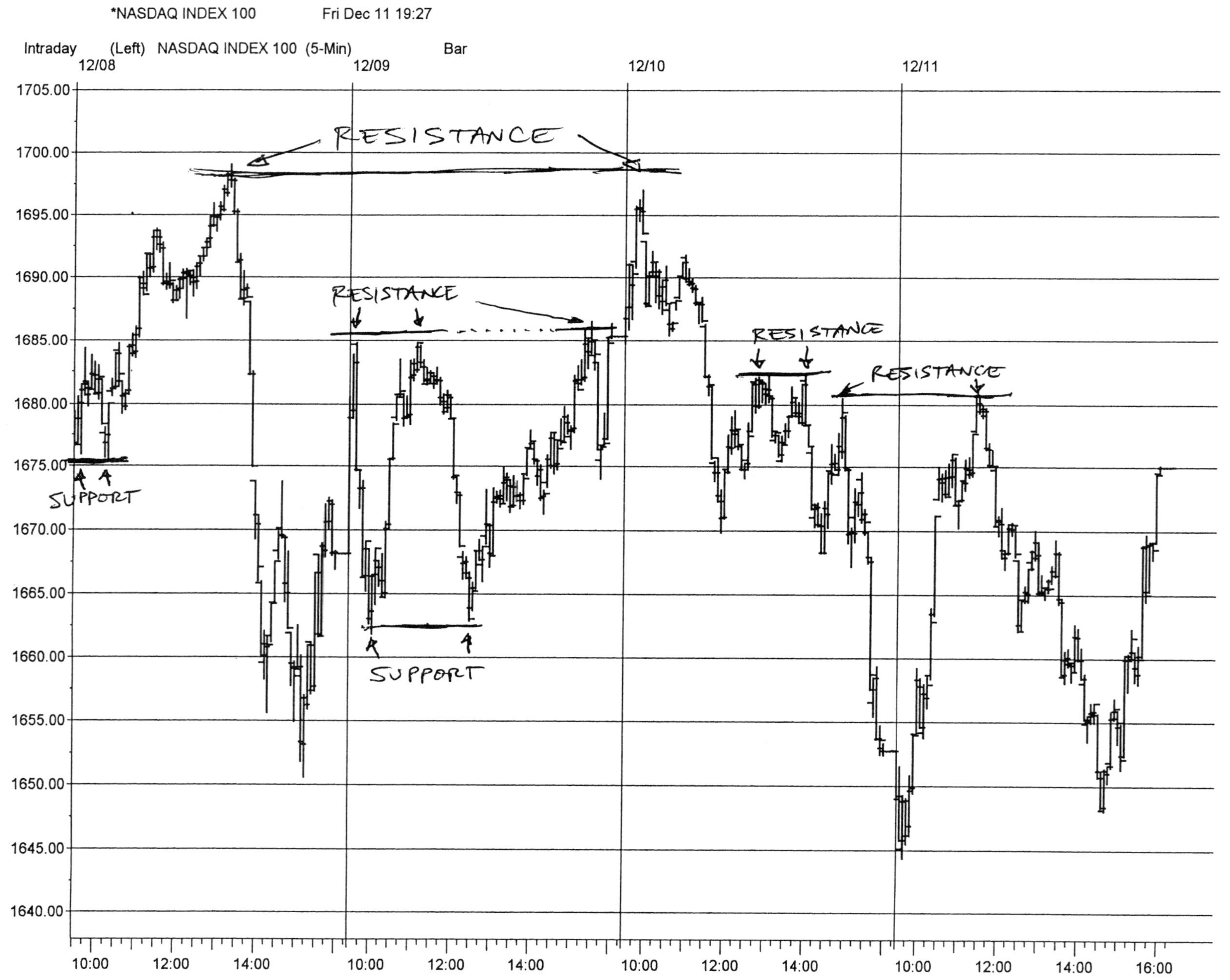
*NASDAQ INDEX 100
Fri Dec 11 19:27
Intraday (Left) NASDAQ INDEX 100 (5-Min) Bar
12/08
12/09
12/10
12/11
1705.00
1700.00
1695.00
1690.00
1685.00
1680.00
1675.00
1670.00
1665.00
1660.00
1655.00
1650.00
1645.00
1640.00
10:00
12:00
14:00
10:00
12:00
14:00
10:00
12:00
14:00
10:00
12:00
14:00
16:00
RESISTANCE
RESISTANCE
RESISTANCE
RESISTANCE
SUPPORT
SUPPORT

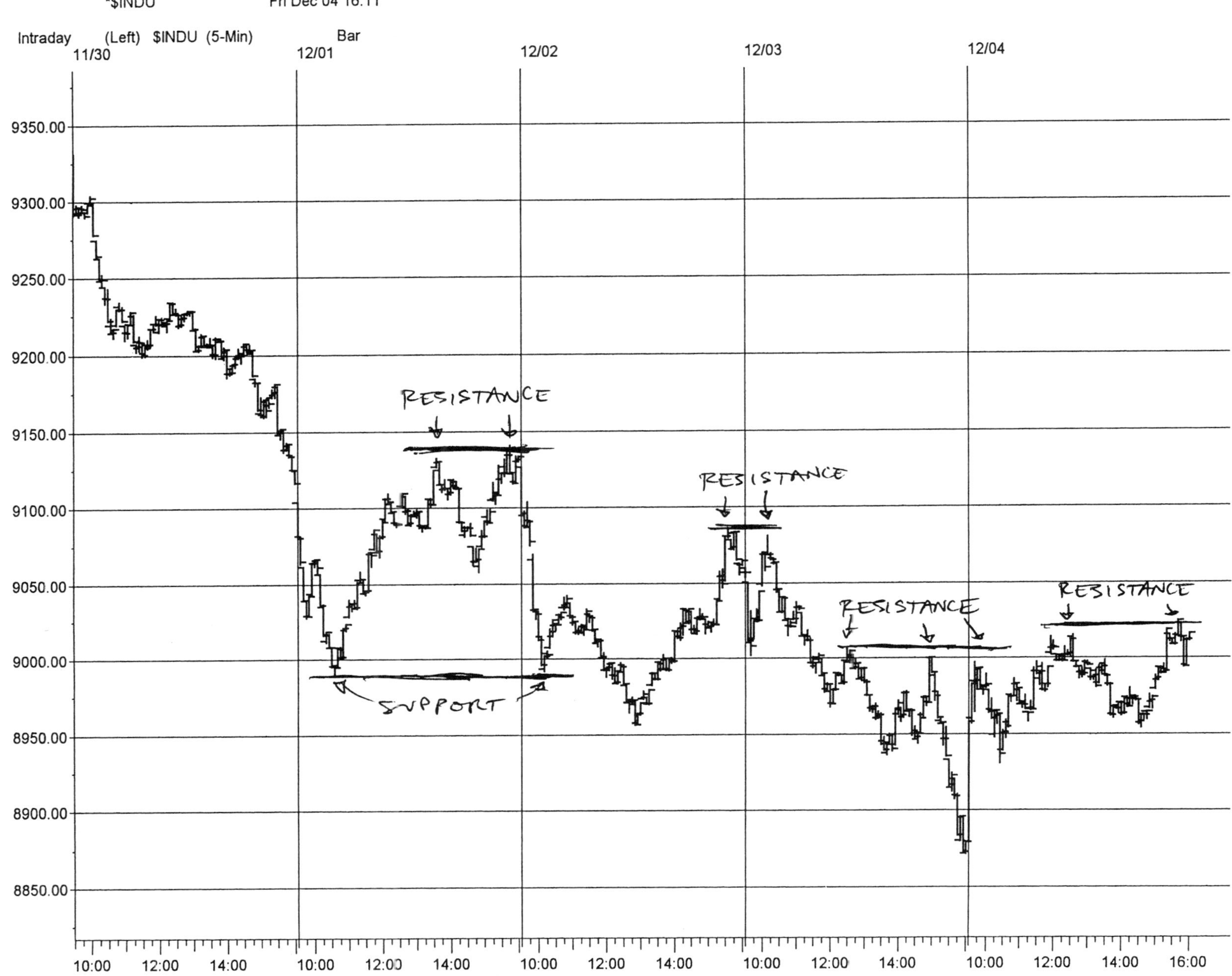

*$INDU
Fri Dec 04 16:11
Intraday
(Left) $INDU (5-Min)
Bar
11/30
12/01
12/02
12/03
12/04
9350.00
9300.00
9250.00
9200.00
9150.00
9100.00
9050.00
9000.00
8950.00
8900.00
8850.00
10:00
12:00
14:00
16:00
RESISTANCE
RESISTANCE
RESISTANCE
RESISTANCE
SUPPORT

*Dec 98 S&P 500
Fri Dec 04 16:09
Intraday
(Left) Dec 98 S&P 500 (5-Min)
Bar
11/30
12/01
12/02
12/03
12/04
RESISTANCE
RESISTANCE
RESISTANCE
RESISTANCE
SUPPORT

*Dec 98 S&P 500
Fri Dec 04 16:05
Intraday (Left) Dec 98 S&P 500 (5-Min) Bar
12/01
12/02
12/03
12/04
RESISTANCE
RESISTANCE
RESISTANCE
RESISTANCE
SUPPORT
SUPPORT
SUPPORT
1182.00
1180.00
1178.00
1176.00
1174.00
1172.00
1170.00
1168.00
1166.00
1164.00
1162.00
1160.00
1158.00
1156.00
1154.00
1152.00
1150.00
1148.00
10:00
12:00
14:00
16:00

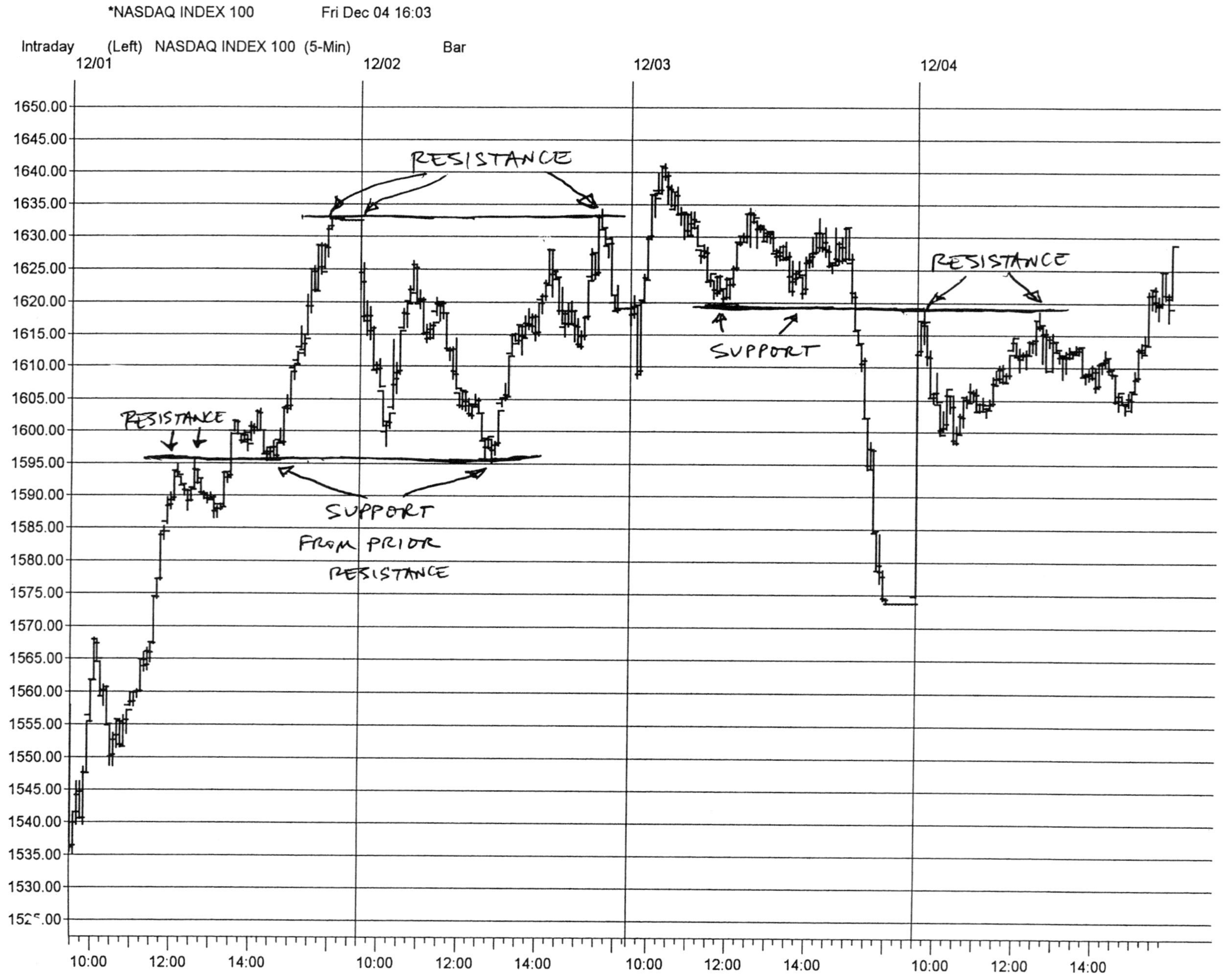
*NASDAQ INDEX 100
Fri Dec 04 16:03
Intraday (Left) NASDAQ INDEX 100 (5-Min) Bar
12/01
12/02
12/03
12/04
1650.00
1645.00
1640.00
1635.00
1630.00
1625.00
1620.00
1615.00
1610.00
1605.00
1600.00
1595.00
1590.00
1585.00
1580.00
1575.00
1570.00
1565.00
1560.00
1555.00
1550.00
1545.00
1540.00
1535.00
1530.00
10:00
12:00
14:00
RESISTANCE
RESISTANCE
SUPPORT FROM PRIOR RESISTANCE
SUPPORT
RESISTANCE

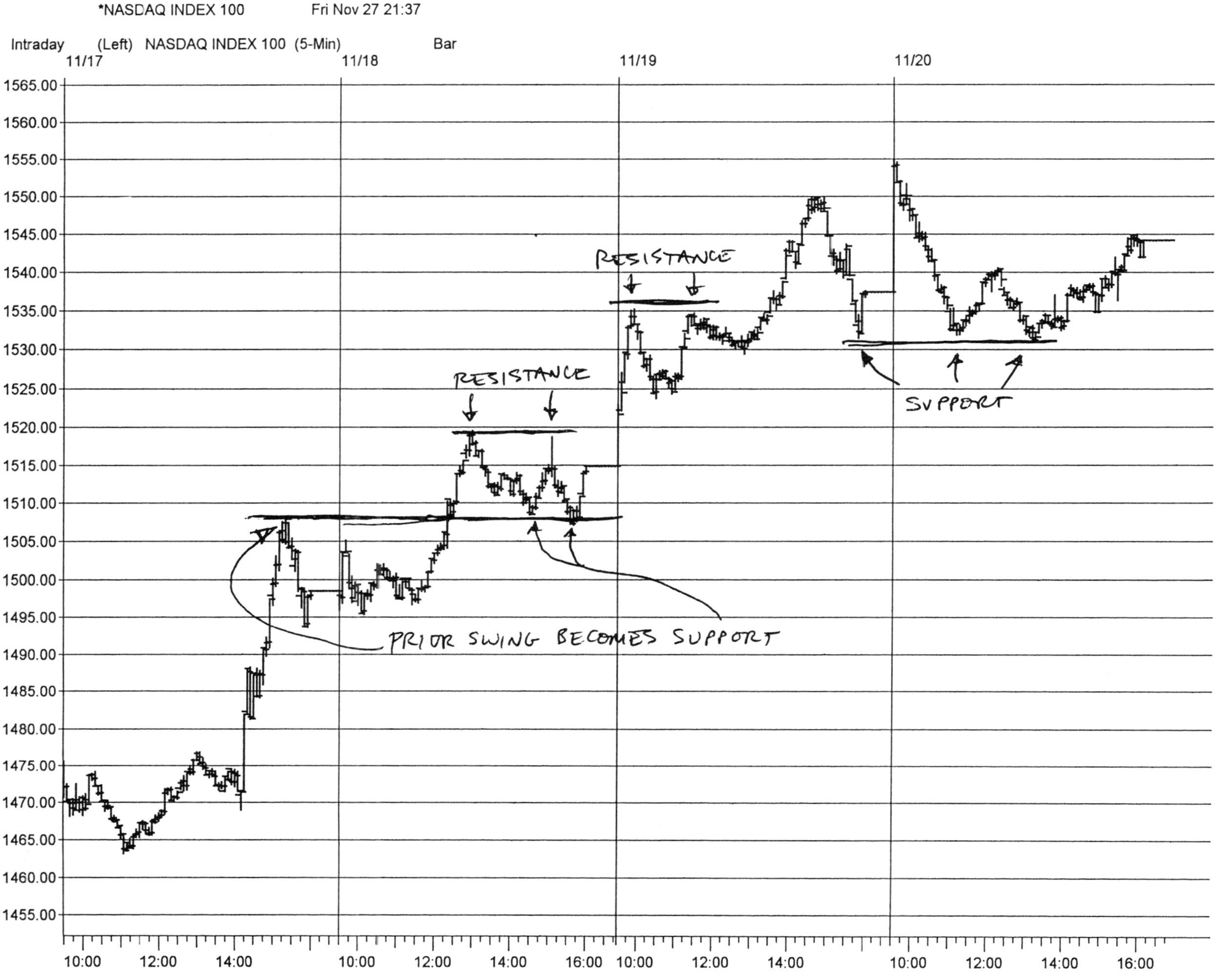
*NASDAQ INDEX 100
Fri Nov 27 21:37
Intraday
(Left) NASDAQ INDEX 100 (5-Min)
Bar
11/17
11/18
11/19
11/20
1565.00
1560.00
1555.00
1550.00
1545.00
1540.00
1535.00
1530.00
1525.00
1520.00
1515.00
1510.00
1505.00
1500.00
1495.00
1490.00
1485.00
1480.00
1475.00
1470.00
1465.00
1460.00
1455.00
RESISTANCE
RESISTANCE
SUPPORT
PRIOR SWING BECOMES SUPPORT
10:00
12:00
14:00
10:00
12:00
14:00
16:00
10:00
12:00
14:00
10:00
12:00
14:00
16:00

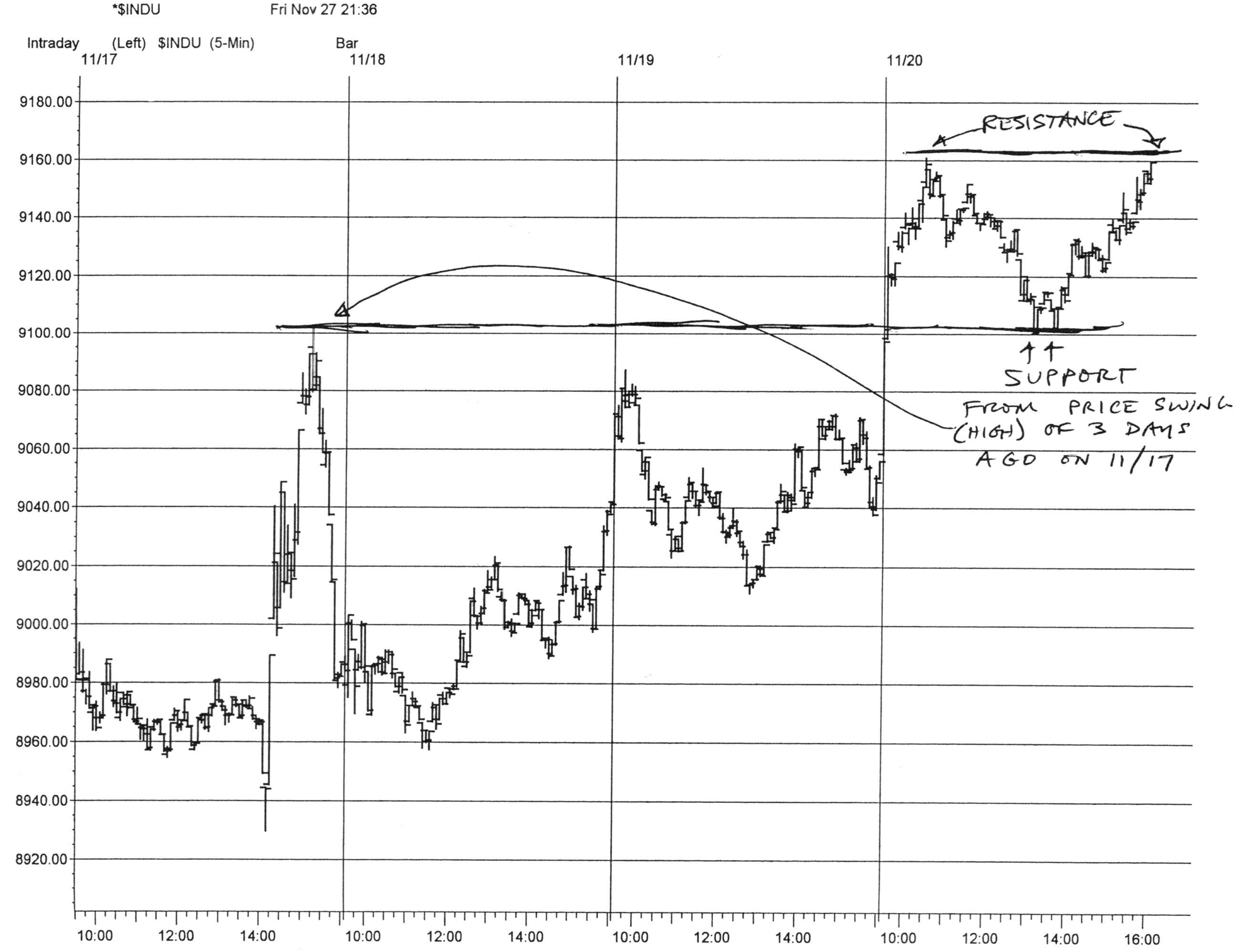

*$INDU
Fri Nov 27 21:36
Intraday
(Left) $INDU (5-Min)
Bar
11/17
11/18
11/19
11/20
9180.00
9160.00
9140.00
9120.00
9100.00
9080.00
9060.00
9040.00
9020.00
9000.00
8980.00
8960.00
8940.00
8920.00
10:00
12:00
14:00
16:00
RESISTANCE
SUPPORT
FROM PRICE SWING (HIGH) OF 3 DAYS AGO ON 11/17

*$INDU
Fri Nov 27 21:35
Intraday
(Left) $INDU (5-Min)
Bar
11/23
11/24
11/.
11/27
RESISTANCE
RESISTANCE
RESISTANCE
RESISTANCE
SUPPORT
SUPPORT ZONE
9400.00
9390.00
9380.00
9370.00
9360.00
9350.00
9340.00
9330.00
9320.00
9310.00
9300.00
9290.00
9280.00
9270.00
9260.00
9250.00
9240.00
9230.00
9220.00
9210.00
9200.00
9190.00
9180.00
9170.00
9160.00
9150.00
9140.00
10:00
12:00
14:00
10:00
12:00
14:00
10:00
12:00
14:00
10:00
12:00
14:00
16:00
18:00

*NASDAQ INDEX 100
Fri Nov 27 21:33
Intraday
(Left) NASDAQ INDEX 100 (5-Min)
Bar
11/23
11/24
11/25
11/27
1635.00
1630.00
1625.00
1620.00
1615.00
1610.00
1605.00
1600.00
1595.00
1590.00
1585.00
1580.00
1575.00
1570.00
1565.00
1560.00
1555.00
1550.00
1545.00
1540.00
1535.00
10:00
12:00
14:00
16:00
18:00
RESISTANCE
SUPPORT

TIME OF DAY

THE TICKER

CHOOSING YOUR BASKET OF STOCKS

THE TICKER

"How to use the ticker, and choosing your basket of stocks"

The ticker is the computer window which you have open with your other windows such as the daily bar chart, 5 minute bar chart, market maker screen etc. It shows market makers adjusting their bids and/or offers up and down (upticks and downticks) in real time for your stocks. Most software that provides a ticker will allow you to assign a specific color for upticks and another for downticks. As the stock symbols scroll by you can more easily identify an uptick or downtick at a glance based on its color.

You will "load" all of the stocks that you wish to track into your ticker so that you can easily monitor them throughout the day. Basic information on the ticker is covered in the *"Stock Patterns"* book beginning on page 99. Take time to review that information since this section builds upon it.

CHOOSING YOUR BASKET OF STOCKS

You will want to choose a group (basket) of stocks that fit certain criteria. It would be impossible to monitor all traded stocks on U.S. exchanges. Besides, most stocks out there are either too illiquid (low volume) or have outrageous bid/ask spreads. So what criteria should you employ to pick your basket of stocks?

I will describe the simple process by which I choose mine. You may wish to vary some of the criteria that I use. Also, everyone has a few "pet stocks" that they have followed for a long time and are very familiar with. These may be included as well.

I trade primarily NASDAQ stocks and so I screen the NASDAQ stock market with one of thc many computer programs available. The parameters that I apply include only a few and are listed below.

- Average volume greater than 200,000 shares traded per day
- Stock price should be 15 or higher
- That's it!

But we're not through yet. Once I have generated the list of NASDAQ stocks from this screening process, the final and most important evaluation comes from viewing the daily bar chart, 5 minute bar chart, and **level II market maker screen** for every stock on that list. So what traits am I looking for to classify a stock as one of my own that I will watch daily and trade when appropriate?

First, I'm looking at the market maker screen for an inside bid/ask spread of 1/8 to 1/4. I also want to see several market makers at each price level. Each price level should typically be in 1/8 increments. This is the most important part of the screening. It fits my own personal risk parameters. I do not like to risk more than 1/4 loss (occasionally 3/8) on any stock that I trade.

In other words, if I enter a trade in this stock and am wrong and immediately have to exit, where am I likely to get filled? The characteristics I'm looking for on the market maker screen allow me to stay within my risk parameters in this worst case scenario. It is my safety net.

I next look at the daily bar chart to see what the average range from high to low is for a typical day. I'm wanting to find stocks that span a range of a full point or more on a regular basis. I can't consistently make any money on a dud that doesn't move much.

Finally, I look at the 5 minute bar chart for several days back. I like to see trading activity, not a scattershot look to it. Somewhat consistent activity throughout the day is preferred. This is simply a visual inspection.

From the original list generated from my stock screen, I then hand-pick each stock that passes my criteria on the daily chart, 5 minute chart and market maker screen. This becomes my ticker of stocks. Every day I watch how each stock's chart moves and the dynamics of how the market makers move about on the market maker screen. Each has its own "personality" that I come to know intimately. I learn their quirks and subtleties and trade them more effectively from this continual learning by observing and trading my basket.

Occasionally, I add to or take out a stock since maintaining a good basket of stocks is important to my trading success. Each stock will tend to cycle in and out of a "trader friendly" mode which is typically reflected on the daily bar chart as congestion (unfriendly) and price swinging activity (friendly). Therefore, I focus on those stocks on my ticker that are currently in the trader friendly mode. Once they cycle out into congestion or choppiness I leave them alone until they become friendly again. There are always more than enough stocks on my ticker that are currently in the trader friendly mode for me to trade successfully.

EFFECTIVE USE OF THE TICKER

Now that you have your basket of stocks chosen and loaded into your ticker, how do you employ the ticker in your activity of day trading? I primarily use it as a reminder to type in a stock and look at my "big 4" (daily chart, 5 minute chart, market maker screen, and time and sales screen). This is just to see if one of the price patterns is beginning to set up. Due to the fact that I cannot remember all of the 130+ stocks that are on my current ticker, each time a stock symbol comes across, I type it in and look for a potential price pattern setup. I do this continually, typing through and evaluating up to 30 stocks per minute. This is not a leisurely pace by any means. But it is my trading style for searching out and finding good setups and being there when it's time to trade them and nail down the price that I want. I call it "speed-burning" through my stocks. It helps me keep my fingers on the pulse of the market. In a way it is an internal view of how stocks are moving. Are price pattern setups following through or stalling out?

Just because "speed-burning" is my style of trading does not mean that it is the only way or most effective way to hunt for good trading candidates. Nor does it mean you have to use your ticker this way. You can have as many or as few stocks on your ticker as you are comfortable with and can reasonably follow. Some trading partners of mine have more of a sniper approach. They hunt and peck each symbol and identify potential trading candidates early in the process of setting up in a price pattern. They do very well!

When I find a stock that looks like it is forming up into a good trade setup on the chart, I earmark that stock mentally (you can also write it down if it helps you to remember it). This is when I keep an eye out for the color coded upticks and downticks on that stock. If it is a short setup and a downtick (red coded for me) scrolls across my ticker, I type in that stock as fast as I can so that if it is breaking short out of the pattern, I'm going to be one of the traders out there who shorts that stock at the price where I want to sell it...no lower! Vice versa on a long setup with an uptick (green on my computer). This is when the color coding comes in handy for quick reaction time.

When the move out of a trade setup appears imminent, the market maker screen movement and prints on the time and sales screen are used to *time* the entry. There is an art to this that comes through experience. It is beyond the scope of this manual as it cannot be effectively communicated in writing. Paper trading and watching other live traders is the best way to learn before you go live yourself. If you are currently an active trader, then you know what I am talking about. I have taught methods and techniques to traders who have several years of experience trading. At that point they usually have trade entry and exit timing down to an art form.

Effective use of the ticker is another important component (puzzle piece) to incorporate into your trading. Consult with your day trading firm or software provider to learn the mechanics and options of creating and customizing your own personal ticker.

You should now have a fuller understanding of how to utilize your ticker. I have also explained a reasonable way for choosing your own personal basket of stocks that you will follow on your ticker. Over time you will come to know each stock as if it has its own personality...because it actually does.

III

REAL-WORLD TRADE ANALYSIS AND MONEY MANAGEMENT

TREND TRADING

VS.

SCALPING

TREND TRADING VS. SCALPING

"Intraday trend trading and scalping - which is right for you?"

Both intraday trend trading and scalping based on price pattern setups are covered in the *"Stock Patterns"* book. Pages 15-17 and 25 address intraday trend trading and the "wiggle" that is an integral part of this style. Page 163-165 covers the scalping methodology. Review each of these sections because you need to determine which style fits your personality the best and which style you actually trade most successfully. Both styles are effective. This manual obviously incorporates more techniques such as "fading" which usually is a scalping approach. But you have to decide upon a primary style for yourself that is the core of your trading methodology.

To hybridize the two is a recipe for disaster. You will invariably scalp trades that run another point and hold onto those trades that should have been scalped. This does not mean you have to do either one or the other 100% of the time. Rather, settle on the approach that you can comfortably and effectively trade the best. Trade that style primarily - roughly 80% of the time. Other trades may be taken from the fading techniques and the style that you are less suited to for the other 20% of your trading endeavors. That 20% should be "cherry picked" just as each trade from your primary style should be.

Let me give you an example. My background prior to stock day trading was actively day trading futures contracts such as the S&P, currencies, and bonds. I learned to scalp as my own personal style over several years of trading. Now, what style do I primarily use for day trading stocks? You guessed it, scalping. Do I also intraday trend trade? You bet! But typically only for a small portion of my trading. This matches my personality. If anyone attempts to trade a style that does not fit his or her personality, they are most likely doomed to fail in the long run. Some self-introspection and analysis will help you to determine what is right for you.

It is not necessarily a static process. Your trading style will evolve over time just as the markets are constantly changing and evolving. This is why I've tried not only to give you techniques and patterns in the *"Stock Patterns"* book and this manual, but to also explain the why's behind every component (or puzzle piece) of these methodologies. If I only give you a template to lay over the market stating that if "A" happens then do "B," it might work for a while. But by understanding the techniques fully, you can grow in your abilities as a trader and customize these methods into your own personal, effective style of trading that will grow with the market.

This is one of the primary reasons why I included so many charts with detailed commentary in the *"Stock Patterns"* book and some in this manual. It's the "roll up your sleeves and get down and dirty with the market" mentality...because that is the way the market is, and that is what works. All you need are a few simple techniques, a decent money management strategy, and **the discipline to strictly adhere to them - no exceptions!**

Are you someone who needs immediate feedback and spikes a blood pressure of 230 over 160 as you watch a 1/8 pullback in an already profitable trade? Do you tense up and tend to hyperventilate when you have a quick open profit in a trade of 3/4 on 1000 shares ($750) as it pulls back 1/4 ($250)? Then maybe intraday trend trading is not for you. You'll have to be comfortable giving 5/8 and 3/4 pullbacks as the overall strategy of the wiggle and intraday trend trading work for you.

On the other hand, do you go into vapor lock at the precise timing and frenetic activity of executing your quick entry and exit for scalping small profits from the market? Then maybe intraday trend trading better fits your personality style. You decide. You'll know after experimenting with both styles on paper, and especially if your are trading live, risking real dollars. But decide soon and focus on your strengths.

Part of being a well rounded trader is to accommodate different markets as a day trader. Some days will trend, which dovetails with intraday trend trading. Others are choppy and lend themselves to scalping. This is a reason to at least be versed in both styles of trading. You will adapt to the current market character as it plays out through the day. You'll be capable of coping with any trading environment. Sometimes that may mean trading lightly or not at all if the market is dead on arrival.

Whether you are new to stock day trading or are a seasoned trader of years, trading these strategies which fit your personality and fit the current market conditions can only enhance your success. Learn to incorporate them into your trading style and make them your own.

TRADE

ANALYSIS

TRADE ANALYSIS

"Managing your trading vs. simply managing a trade"

Once you have settled upon your own style of trading, you're just halfway there. You have a sound methodology at your fingertips now. What else do you need to succeed? A sound money management plan and the drive and ability to analyze your trading. This section deals with effective ways to analyze your overall trading activity. Money management is covered in the next section as your safety net while you walk that tightrope of day trading.

To be honest, I hate analyzing how I trade. I just want to trade (and make scads of money of course). But neither you nor I will ever succeed in the long haul unless we expend the effort to evaluate our trading. If I inundated you with tons of analysis material, you would simply ignore all of them. I know that I would. On the other hand, I'm going to provide you with just the few important approaches to improve your trading.

Commit yourself to this worthwhile endeavor. Otherwise you'll never excel in stock day trading. These tools will help you uncover your weaknesses and strengths. Adjust around your weaknesses and focus on your strengths to maximize your effectiveness as a trader. Constantly keep in mind how you can improve the quality of your trading with the feedback from the following analysis routines.

Three components for managing your trading include:

1) Religiously filling out your trading sheet throughout each day
2) Evaluating what times during the day you trade the best
3) Tracking which stocks you regularly trade profitably, & which ones are usually losers

1) TRADE SHEET

Refer to *"Stock Patterns"* pages 157 and 158 for a copy of the trading sheet (or log) to write down and track each stock trade. A blank trading sheet is also included in this section for you to photocopy and put to good use on a daily basis.

Make sure you fill it out completely with the stock symbol, buy and sell prices and exact time of entry and exit. Also indicate whether it was a long or short trade. All of this information will function as the raw data for analyzing your trading and also for helping you implement your money management plan which is covered in the next section.

Writing down your trades as you go visually reminds you where you stand on the day. It provides you vital information:

- Your current gross profit (or loss)
- Your net profit less commissions you've paid so far
- The number of trades you've taken (are you overtrading?)
- Whether your cumulative profit and loss column is increasing steadily, remaining the same (just racking up more commissions), or decreasing
- How many winning trades you've had vs. the number of losing trades (is it a bad market or are you simply not trading well?)
- Whether most of your winning trades are smaller than usual
- How many losing trades you've had in a row

Your trading sheet is the piece of paper giving the feedback you need. It functions as your road map throughout the day. Constantly check your "trading status" with a quick evaluation of your trading sheet as you assess the bullet points listed above.

It is your early warning system alerting you to a potential problem. Most often it will give you a sense of how aggressive you should trade, and whether it's time to back off or stop. The main warning signs to look for are:

1. Overtrading and just racking up commissions
2. If you've had 3 to 4 flat or losing trades in a row
3. Making sure your cumulative profit/loss column is increasing
4. If it's just not a very good trading day (stop trading)

I CANNOT OVER EMPHASIZE HOW IMPORTANT IT IS TO MAINTAIN AND EVALUATE YOUR TRADING SHEET THROUGHOUT THE DAY, EVERY DAY!

Another integral part of managing your trading is to evaluate each individual trade after the session is over. Set your trade sheet in front of you and type back through each individual stock trade. Evaluate the trade based on:

1. How good the price pattern setup was
2. If you entered at the appropriate point
3. Were the indices currently moving in the direction of the trade
4. Did you exit based on your trading rules, or did you exit prematurely

Jot down brief notes next to each trade. When you're finished evaluating the whole day's worth of trades, look back over your notes. Is there a common theme that emerges? Maybe you were not trading the best setups. Perhaps you were entering the trade too late into its move. Whatever theme you uncover, consider it a serious problem to be dealt with immediately. Focus on actively correcting that specific issue the next trading day and until you eliminate its negative impact on your trading.

Keep your trade sheets in a notebook chronologically. The above simple and rather quick exercise will vastly improve your trading over time. It's what trade analysis is all about isn't it?

2) EVALUATE WHAT TIMES OF DAY YOU TRADE THE BEST

After you've collected enough trading sheets, they can be put to further use. Since you logged the times in and out for each trade, you can isolate the times during the trading session when you tend to trade more effectively. On a sheet of paper make a column for each hour of the trading day. I recommend an additional column for the first 30 minutes due to the heavier volume and strong price moves off of the open. The "worksheet" should look something like this:

WEEK OF: ______________________

C.S.T.	8:30 - 9	9 - 10	10 - 11	11 - 12	12 - 1	1 - 2	2 - 3
# winning trades							
# losing trades							
net profit or loss							
rank best & worst times							

Each column is to be calculated only for trades initiated within that hour of trading. Tally these up for each week of trading. You'll be surprised to find that you consistently trade well during certain times of the day and poorly during others. So what is the message here? It's simple. Capitalize on trading during your best times of the day and either back way off or stop trading during the losing times.

Over weeks and months this can add thousands of dollars to your bottom line. But you have to do the analysis to know. And more importantly, you must have the discipline to put your analysis into action.

Feel free to make photocopies of the above template and put it to good use regularly.

3) TRACKING STOCKS YOU REGULARLY TRADE (PROFIT VS. LOSS)

Analyzing the stocks that you consistently trade well (and the ones that you don't) tunes you in to which stocks to continue trading actively and which ones to avoid. As mentioned earlier in this manual, every stock tends to cycle in and out of a "trader friendly" mode. In addition, you may just have a knack for trading some stocks better than others. So how do you track this? Buy an accounting ledger, or construct a grid and list all of the stocks on your ticker on the left. It might look something like the following:

AMGN	+1/8	0	+3/8	-1/8								
AAPL	0	+1/4	+1/8									
AMAT	-1/16	0	-1/8	+1/4	-1/4	-1/16	0					
BBBY	+7/8	-3/8	-1/8									
BMCS	+1/2	-1/4	+1 ¾	0								
CATP												
CNTO												

After each trading session, open your notebook and fill in win and loss amounts for each trade for each stock from left to right. After a week or two of trading you'll see which stocks are giving you good, consistent profits and which ones seem to always knock you for a loss or break-even (as well as the whole spectrum in between). It is a real eye opener!

Some stocks you thought were lining your pocket actually will show you at a net loss as you sum the trades from left to right. If you record the trades daily or set aside a time on the weekend then you won't find yourself with tons of trade analysis work staring at you due to procrastination. Besides, you need to keep up with this at least weekly to alert you to which stocks are paying out and which ones are biting into your wallet.

This is all of the analysis you need. And it is all based on the data from a completed trade sheet. So make sure you are filling out your trade sheet every day. Don't overanalyze, just do these few things. It really doesn't take much time if you keep up with it. And that time is well spent. Managing your trading will make you a more effective and more profitable trader progressively over time. Money flies if you don't analyze!

Trader: ______________________ **Date:** / /

	Stock	In	Out	Buy	Sell	G/L	Cum G/L
1							
2							
3							
4							
5							
6							
7							
8							
9							
10							
11							
12							
13							
14							
15							
16							
17							
18							
19							
20							
21							
22							
23							
24							
25							
26							
27							
28							
29							
30							
31							
32							
33							
34							
35							

RISK/REWARD RATIO

SCALING

RISK/REWARD RATIO

For any trade that you consider, it should provide you a decent risk/reward ratio. In other words, the dollar amount you are willing to risk on a trade should be offset by the reasonable potential of profit equivalent to several times the amount risked. Typically a 1 to 3 or 1 to 4 risk/reward ratio is required to give you good odds of profitability over time with both winning and losing trades.

This means that if you are risking 1/4 point on a 1000 share trade, the stock should have good potential to provide at least a 3/4 point to 1 point profit. If not, then it is probably not a very good trade simply based upon the need for a risk/reward ratio of at least 1 to 3.

When trading you must overcome the bid/ask spread, commissions and losing trades with the profit from your winning trades. With these costs associated with day trading, you can see why a reasonable risk/reward ratio is imperative to your success over time. This is especially true for intraday trend trading. Thus the old adage… "cut your losers and let your winners run."

A scalping style requires a different approach since you are looking for small quick profits. Since you are limiting your profit per trade, you must limit your risked amount even more. Be willing to take only a 1/8 loss or 1/16 loss…and a break even trade if you perceive that the stock is not going to follow-through with the anticipated small, quick price move.

In addition, scalping requires a higher percentage of successful trades…somewhere near 70%. If you think about it, your risked amount on a trade and the commission and the bid/ask spread represent a greater percentage of profit for each winning trade. Therefore, you need more winning trades to profit over time.

Let me give you a prime example of how the risk/reward ratio and percentage of winning trades can affect your overall trading. Here is the scenario based on a round-turn commission rate of $30 and 1000 shares per trade. Six successive trades are taken with the first 5 profitable to the tune of +1/16 each. The sixth trade is the only loser and only a loss of -1/8. Sounds like you'd have some money in your pocket doesn't it? Well, you don't! At least not much anyway.

In this case +1/16 equals $62.50. Five of these winning trades equals $312.50, but don't forget to take out commissions of $150 leaving you up $162.50. You then take a -1/8 loss equal to $125.00 which also incurs another commission. Do the math. 5 winning trades and only 1 relatively small losing trade netted you a mere $7.50 (pocket change).

Pay attention to your risk/reward ratio and percentage of winning trades to enhance the odds of your trading success.

SCALING INTO AND OUT OF A TRADE

Scaling into and out of trades refers to adding to or getting out of (covering) a portion of the shares which you are trading in a stock. Scaling out could consist of buying 1000 shares of a stock and at a certain point, selling out of 1/2 of your position (covering 500 shares). For instance, If you bought 1000 shares of a stock at 50 and it moved up to 50 1/2 , you could sell 500 shares to book 1/2 point profit and ride the remainder of the trade with the other 500 shares using the "wiggle."

Booking a portion of your profits like this helps you to more easily hold onto the other 500 shares with the "wiggle" and not be "shaken" out of your trade. This creates a profit buffer while still allowing you to participate in what may be a strong move in the stock for several points.

Scaling into a position is a bit different. If you bought 1000 shares of a stock and it subsequently formed another trade setup such as a breakout pattern on the 5 minute chart, you might wish to add to your position if more potential profit seems forthcoming. In this case you should already have a decent profit of at least 1/2 point or more before "adding size." You don't want to get caught in a quick move against the direction of your trade while you have significant size on.

Scaling out of a position is usually done more often than adding to a position. Avoid risking too much on one trade. The scaling into and out of a position can be a powerful tactic to help you better maximize the net dollars you are able to pull out of a stock while day trading.

More importantly, scaling out of 1/2 of your shares with profit does wonders for your trading mentality. If the remaining shares do not follow through for an intraday trend trade, you may decide to cover them at your initial entry point to break even.

Just knowing you've already booked a partial profit will *mentally* help you weather the pullbacks on the rest of your shares since the trade may offer a multi point move.

MONEY

MANAGEMENT

MONEY MANAGEMENT

"Your safety net: specific strategies to keep losses small and book profits"

You are a trader. You will have losing trades and losing days. You will have losing weeks. Accept it! It's part of the day trading game. But with a good methodology, regular trade analysis, unwavering discipline and strict money management, you will likely come out a winner over time. This is the nature of trading.

Don't get too emotional about it and bolt down the street to your favorite pub just because you lost money. If you cannot cope with losses then it's probably better for you to get a salaried job and punch in and out on the time clock.

It is interesting how the winning days tend to take care of themselves, but an unmanaged losing day can destroy your ability to trade effectively. That's what this section is all about: How to manage your net profits and losses during the day with a specific set of rules that you decide upon and make your own.

THE BASIC MONEY MANAGEMENT PLAN (your safety net) has 3 components.

1. A maximum net loss that you will not exceed on any given day
2. A point where you are net profitable enough that you will not continue to trade if you draw back down to net break-even on the day
3. A "profit booking" strategy to lock in some of your profits but still risk a certain portion of those profits to continue trading if you are in a good market

This is your basic safety net and must be implemented with the utmost discipline! Your trading sheet plays an important role here. It quickly tells you where you are in your money management strategy. ***It must always be net dollars after fees and commissions***.

Here is my own plan as an example for intraday trend trading.

- I will never lose more than $1000 in one day. If I get there I stop and go home.
- If I have a $500 net profit on the day, then I will not trade back below break-even. If I lose back to net $0, then I quit trading that day
- Once I exceed $500 net profit on the day, I start booking profits. If I'm up $800, I will not go below $400-$500 for the day. If I'm up $4000 then I will not go home with less than $3300 in my pocket that day. If I reach that draw down point I simply quit trading.

These are my numbers. You have to choose your own numbers that you are comfortable with and which are reasonable. It is a very straightforward plan. But it's hard to stick to. You must enforce discipline on yourself in this area of your trading above all others. It is what will keep you in the game and give you the chance to be profitable over the long run. Does that make sense to you? I hope so. You will fail if you do not write your safety net numbers down and strictly adhere to them no matter what!

Your numbers will be very dependent upon your trading strategy. If you are scalping then you must have a lower maximum loss amount than someone intraday trend trading. Craft your money management plan around your chosen trading method.

COMPLEMENTARY MONEY MANAGEMENT STRATEGIES

These are techniques that guide your trading activities by telling you when to back off from the market and slow down even before you encounter your safety net numbers. Don't for a moment think that these additional guidelines for money management are secondary. They are your first line of defense to protect yourself and your trading account.

You will key off of your trading sheet for these red flags (just another reason why keeping a good trading sheet is imperative). Each money managing factor is listed below and then described in more detail.

1. Layering your trades
2. A combination of 3 losing or break-even trades in a row
3. An increasing cumulative profit/loss column on your trading sheet

LAYERING pertains to intraday trend trading where you may have multiple positions open at the same time. Don't get into several trades at once. Enter a good trade and let it move to where you have some open profit in it before considering another trade. When you enter the next trade, let it too show a paper profit before entering a third trade. This is "layering." You are layering your trades with profit so that you have some breathing room in each one before you expose yourself to the risk of another trade.

This prevents you from taking several quick losses by entering too many trades at the same time. Also, if the market suddenly turns against you, you can exit with a small profit or break-even and not suffer much damage. Layering is like buying insurance. It protects you against unforeseen events in the market. It is a strong money management strategy for intraday trend traders.

THREE LOSING OR BREAK-EVEN TRADES IN A ROW should alert you that the market is not giving you money. You will likely continue losing for one of two reasons. Either there is not much directional follow-through in stock price movement, or you are out of synch with the market. It just may not be your day. In either case, this is your wake-up call to back off and reassess if you should continue trading or if you should wait until later in the session when the market shows a definite direction.

A CUMULATIVE PROFIT/LOSS COLUMN THAT IS DECREASING means you are slowly dwindling away your profits on the day and adding up more commissions. Maybe you are overtrading, or the market is getting choppy. It is a signal for you to back off and re-evaluate why you are losing money.

Always have these three money management tactics on your radar screen to isolate potential danger early. These strategies complement your basic money management safety net and will improve your overall trading. Once again, discipline to recognize and *act* on what they are telling you will be your key to success or failure.

So now it's your turn. Decide upon and write down your basic safety net strategy of maximum draw down, break-even point and profit booking amounts. Remember to calculate them in *net* dollars. Better yet, type them out and tape it to your computer monitor. Respect them. They are your own rules and will be your savior some days.

Here is what I've had taped to my computer monitor for guidance when I'm scalping:

Money Management
(all $ amounts are net)
1 Max drawdown $650
2 If $500 profit, never go below $0
3 Booking profits:

profit	book
600	250
700	350
800	450
1000	600
1200	800
1500	1000
2000	1500

There you have it. These are specific money management strategies designed exclusively for the stock day trader. Decide on your own parameters and put them on paper in some form. Make it a contractual agreement with yourself. It's the best contract you will ever agree to. Honor it and your trading abilities will be enhanced, as well as your bottom line.

What? Only three pages on money management. Folks, it's all you need. If you're wanting more paper with words on it, then you're looking in the wrong place. Finding good money management has more to do with looking inside yourself. Are you afraid you cannot stick to your basic rules? Then find some way, somehow to do it. If I can fit my rules on a 2 inch by 3 inch piece of paper then so can you. Look for the day trader cheer leading section somewhere else. It's all up to you, and you know what to do! The next few pages provide your own money management contracts to be filled out.

MONEY MANAGEMENT CONTRACT ***"EXAMPLE"***
for SCALPING

TRADER'S NAME: Billy Bob Moneymaker

All amounts are "net" dollars after commissions and fees!!

1) My maximum draw-down amount for the day: $ 650

2) My amount of profit achieved where I will not trade my account back below break-even on the day: $ 500

3) Profit amounts achieved on the day where I begin "booking" profits which I will not trade my account back down below:

current net profit		net amount booked	
$ 600		$ 250	-350
$ 700	100	$ 350	350
$ 800	100	$ 450	350
$ 1000	200	$ 600	-400
$ 1200	200	$ 800	-400
$ 1500	300	$ 1000	-500
$ 2000	500	$ 1500	500
$ etc.	AVG 233	$ etc.	AVG 407

SIGNATURE This is just an example for scalping. Fill out your own contract for both scalping and intraday trend trading on the blank forms on the next 2 pages. Also, type the amounts on a tiny sheet of paper and tape it to your computer monitor as a friendly reminder to yourself.

MY MONEY MANAGEMENT CONTRACT
for INTRADAY TREND TRADING

TRADER'S NAME:____________________________

All amounts are "net" dollars after commissions and fees!!

1) My maximum draw-down amount for the day: $____________________________

2) My amount of profit achieved where I will not trade my account back below break-even on the day: $____________________________

3) Profit amounts achieved on the day where I begin "booking" profits which I will not trade my account back down below:

current net profit	net amount booked
$____________	$____________
$____________	$____________
$____________	$____________
$____________	$____________
$____________	$____________
$____________	$____________
$____________	$____________
$____________	$____________

SIGNATURE____

MY MONEY MANAGEMENT CONTRACT
for SCALPING

TRADER'S NAME:______________________________

All amounts are "net" dollars after commissions and fees!!

1) My maximum draw-down amount for the day: $____________________________

2) My amount of profit achieved where I will not trade my account back below break-even on the day: $____________________________

3) Profit amounts achieved on the day where I begin "booking" profits which I will not trade my account back down below:

current net profit	net amount booked
$____________	$____________
$____________	$____________
$____________	$____________
$____________	$____________
$____________	$____________
$____________	$____________
$____________	$____________
$____________	$____________

SIGNATURE____

CONCLUSION

CONCLUSION

"Putting it all together"

If you are currently day trading, you should be able to incorporate these techniques into your activities rather quickly. If you are relatively new to stock day trading, don't rush through the material. Immerse yourself in the methodology and strategies contained in this manual and in the book *"Stock Patterns for Day Trading."*

Strive to fully understand each section of information and begin to mentally connect all of the ideas and how they relate to each other. Your goal is to see and comprehend the bigger picture as you put all of the pieces together. The process of evaluating potential trades will come more quickly with time and experience.

I believe this manual includes all of the trading strategies that you need to effectively participate in the stock day trading arena. If you put forth the effort and hard work to actively apply these trading concepts and tactics, you've gone a long way to increase your odds of long term success.

We've covered general trading methodologies, specific trading techniques with all of their nuances, as well as money management and trade analysis. The only other component that is vital to trading success revolves around the psychological and discipline factors unique to the day trader. These issues are addressed in *"The Psychology and Discipline of Day Trading."*

Roll your sleeves up and get your hands dirty with the market. Learn the price personality of different stocks and how the market moves. You'll detect when the odds are stacked in your favor while you recognize the most effective price pattern setups. This is the best way to approach the market, to take it's pulse…and learn what makes it tick.

Whether you trade as an avocation or as a career, I hope all of the instructional material that I have put together improves your trading. Never forget that you are in the market to make money, not to toss the dice. Treat your endeavors with seriousness, but by all means have fun!

The next pages outline a typical day's activities for high-probability trading.

A TYPICAL DAY - THE CHRONOLOGY

1. Review your list of stock picks from the daily setups and get your trading sheet out.

2. Review any market news or reports that are coming out prior to the market's open, and note the time of any significant scheduled reports due out that day that might affect the market.

3. Find out what the SP-500 futures and bond futures are doing prior to the open.

4. When the market opens focus on your hit list of daily setups and any stocks that gap significantly up or down on the open.

5. Consider waiting 10+ minutes into the market for the "noise" to shake out and for stocks and the market to pick a direction.

6. Look to play the w/r days and reversal setups in the first 30 minutes to 1 hour.

7. After 15 minutes, begin isolating any 5 minute consolidation setups that may provide potential breakout trading opportunities.

8. Begin evaluating whether price pattern setups are following through well and which techniques fit the market character best.

9. Be aware of the morning move's direction or if the indices are simply chopping sideways.

10. As you come into the 10:30-11:00 a.m. (C.S.T.) time frame, look for the typical slow down in price moves and adjust your trading accordingly.

11. If you trade during the dead zone, consider scalping and taking profits quickly.

12. At 1:30 p.m. (C.S.T.) start reviewing the 5 minute chart for each stock on the day. Also, watch how each stock moves as you near the power hour to isolate some of the best potential trading candidates.

13. As volume kicks in around 2 p.m. (C.S.T.) for the power hour, be aware of the direction of the market and its "afternoon move" as you look for trades.

14. During the last 15 minutes of the session, consider taking profits and looking for quick scalping opportunities for issues with heavy buying or selling volume coming into the close.

15. Exit all remaining positions into the close; you are a *day* trader.

16. After the close, review each individual trade from your trade sheet. Also evaluate what the overall market was like, its volume, and the number of stocks that followed through from trade setups.

17. Update your trade analysis by filling in your time of day and stock trades analysis sheets from the templates provided in this manual.

18. Decide if you need to adjust anything about your trading to improve the next day. Determine the specific actions you will take.

19. Review your daily trade setups for the next market day.

20. Get away from the computer…go out (or home) and have a good time. Let your mind take a break from the market so it's fresh to trade tomorrow.

APPENDIX

TECHNIQUE SUMMARY SHEET

TRADE SETUPS

W/R Day - opens even with the close
W/R Day - slight gap inside
W/R Day - slight gap outside
W/R Day - big gap outside
Reversal setup
Delayed Reversal setup
5 minute consolidation breakouts
5 minute consolidation breakouts - alternative entry on initial pullback
5 minute "L" pattern
The flashback
Failed morning rally
Shotgun pattern
Close at high or low of daily congestion
Price spike fade
2 waves up or down fade
Tagging
Big stack and a rainbow
Profit target reaction
Double roll-over
Double turn-up

FILTERS/ENHANCEMENTS

Too near a profit target
Intraday trend of indices not in direction of intended trade
Congestion on the daily bar chart
Watch the price-legend on the daily bar chart
Relative strength
Nearby high or low of the prior day or two - micro support/resistance
Support or resistance on the daily bar chart
The 50 or 200 day simple moving averages
Series of days with the same highs or lows

PROFIT TARGETS

Support or resistance on the daily bar chart
Retracement of a wide range day
The 50 or 200 day simple moving averages
The closing of a price gap
The profit target for the reversal setup
A price spike
A significant reversal in market index against the direction of your open trades

TRADE CHECKLIST

"For consolidation breakout setups on the 5 minute chart"

TRADE CHECKLIST

1 Look at 5 minute chart…is consolidation hugging high or low for roughly 20 minutes
2 Then look at daily chart for nearby support/resistance & 50 day moving average for room to run 1+ pt
3 If so, then make sure you are not in "congestion" on the daily chart
4 Make sure stock has a large enough typical daily range for a reasonable price move
5 Evaluate market maker screen bid/ask spread and depth of mkt makers at each price level
6 Check the trend of the indices, they must be moving in the same direction of the considered trade
7 Enter the stock on a separate market maker screen to keep an eye on it
8 When the market maker screen begins to move for the price breakout, enter the trade
9 The trade must be entered at the consolidated price or 1 price level into the actual breakout
10 Risk no more than 1/8 point when scalping, ¼ point when intraday trend trading
11 Once the trade is entered, bid or offer out into momentum if scalping
12 If intraday trend trading, use the wiggle to exit you out of the trade
13 When intraday trend trading and a profit target is reached, consider exiting the trade
14 Keep watching your ticker and cycling through your basket of stocks looking for trades setting up

DO THIS FOR EVERY TRADE TO MAXIMIZE THE ODDS OF SUCCESS!!

THE 10 COMMANDMENTS OF TRADING

(FOR INTRADAY TREND TRADING)

1) NEVER LOSE MORE THAT $1000 NET PER DAY (GO HOME)

2) LAYER YOUR TRADES BEGINNING WITH THE FIRST ONE (I.E. MAKE SURE EACH TRADE HAS AN OPEN PROFIT BEFORE YOU ENTER ANOTHER TRADE)

3) TAKE 10 TRADES OR LESS EACH DAY - UNLESS YOUR CUMULATIVE P/L IS INCREASING

4) "CHERRY PICK" ONLY THE BEST TRADES

5) DO NOT EXECUTE A TRADE IN THE FIRST 10 MINUTES OF TRADING

6) DO NOT RISK MORE THAN 1/4 POINT LOSS PER TRADE

7) ONCE YOU HAVE A GOOD PROFIT ON THE DAY, BOOK SOME $$$$ - EX. IF YOU HAVE $1500 NET PROFIT – POCKET $1000 AND USE $500 FOR MORE TRADES & COMMISSIONS

8) IF YOUR WELL PICKED TRADES ARE NOT CLEARING, OR YOU HAVE 3-4 LOSSES IN A ROW, STOP TRADING AND REASSESS IF YOU SHOULD BE IN THE MARKET

9) GIVE A GOOD TRADE THE "WIGGLE"

10) TRADING IS 90% MENTAL DISCIPLINE

THE 10 COMMANDMENTS OF TRADING

(FOR SCALPING)

1) NEVER LOSE MORE THAT $650 NET PER DAY (GO HOME)

2) ONLY OPEN 1 TRADE AT A TIME. CLOSE IT OUT BEFORE YOU ENTER ANOTHER TRADE

3) CONTINUE TRADING ONLY IF YOUR CUMULATIVE P/L IS TRENDING UPWARD

4) "CHERRY PICK" ONLY THE BEST TRADES

5) DO NOT EXECUTE A TRADE IN THE FIRST 10 MINUTES OF TRADING

6) DO NOT RISK MORE THAN 1/8 POINT LOSS PER TRADE - AND- REMEMBER, A FLAT TRADE IS YOUR BEST FRIEND IF THE ALTERNATIVE IS A LOSS

7) ONCE YOU HAVE A GOOD PROFIT ON THE DAY, BOOK SOME $$$$ - EX. IF YOU HAVE $1000 NET PROFIT – POCKET $700 AND USE $300 FOR MORE TRADES & COMMISSIONS

8) IF YOUR WELL PICKED TRADES ARE NOT CLEARING, OR YOU HAVE 3-4 FLATS / LOSSES IN A ROW, STOP TRADING AND REASSESS IF YOU SHOULD BE IN THE MARKET

9) BE QUICK TO TAKE A PROFIT WHILE MOMENTUM IS STILL MOVING IN YOUR FAVOR

10) TRADING IS 90% MENTAL DISCIPLINE

IF YOU CANNOT ADHERE TO THESE RULES, YOU WILL LOSE MONEY, AND YOU WILL FAIL!

THE PSYCHOLOGY AND DISCIPLINE OF DAY TRADING

"Or, how to tame that thing they call a brain"

Barry Rudd

THE PSYCHOLOGY AND DISCIPLINE OF DAY TRADING

Hello, and welcome to Hell! At least that's how most folks feel about literature that smacks of mumbo jumbo, get in touch with your trading-self psycho babble. I don't blame them. I have a psychology degree and still recoil at most books aimed at my inner trading child and co-dependent trading strategies.

I don't want to fill out forms about my goals, fears, likes, dislikes and why I want to trade. Don't get me wrong. I believe these are noble and valuable endeavors, but let's get serious. We want to trade don't we?! If perusing the skeletons in the closet of my mind soaks up more than a few minutes of my time, then my attention span quickly shrinks to that of a gnat.

Is this type of analysis important? Definitely. Will I or you actually expend the time and effort engaged in a full scale mental trading check up? Not likely. So why did I write a manual about the psychology and discipline of trading?

BECAUSE, IT IS THE SINGLE MOST IMPORTANT FACTOR TO YOUR SUCCESS AS A TRADER!

I've crafted the information in bite-sized chunks so that you will actually read it. Chew on each topic as you decide how it relates to you, your trading ideas and activities. This is not your typical trading psychology manual. I'll wager that you will easily find yourself described on several of the pages that follow. All I ask is that you recognize what issues apply to you and more importantly DO SOMETHING ABOUT IT.

BEFORE WE BEGIN

LEAVE YOUR EGO AT THE DOOR

I don't care if you were God's gift to the stock brokering industry. All previously successful people pay attention. If you have been a screaming success in your career and can tackle any of life's challenges with ease, you are likely a highly intelligent and capable human being. Does the market care what you've done or how smart your are? No. And it will reward you daily with both the pain of being wrong and a lighter wallet if you attempt to bend it to your will.

It's not just about winning. Winning will come over time if you trade with a decent strategy and leave your ego at the door. *Sometimes* you may be right about a trade. But remember, the market is *always* right no matter what your ego leads you to believe. To ignore this simple maxim will frustrate you to no end. The only end will be the conclusion of your trading career. The market will conquer you, not vice versa.

I know plenty about egos because I have one too. But I've come to learn that the market doesn't care. If I approach trading in the same way that I've approached everything else I've accomplished in my life (by forcing it to respond to *my* logic), then I am headed down the path to ruin. Remember to always leave your ego at the door.

COMMON PITFALLS AND MENTAL TACTICS

CASINO CHIP SYNDROME

When you day trade with a computer, don't forget that pressing a buy or sell key on your computer keyboard represents money at risk. It's like casino chips. If Las Vegas let you put cash down on the table, would you still play the same way? Probably not. Casino chips are uniquely designed to numb you to the fact that it is actual money you are risking. Your money.

A buy or sell keystroke on the computer lulls you into the same false perception of value. You do not see the actual green paper tossed out at the market in the high-tech, sterile environment of computerized trading. If you lose sight of this analogy, you will trade as if money doesn't really matter.

The trading and risk you are willing to incur changes. It's a matter of perception. Never forget that both a casino chip and an execution key on your computer are one and the same. They represent your hard earned money that you are putting at risk.

GUNSLINGING

I hope that by now most of you have in mind a trading method that you are confident with. When you depart from your method you become the equivalent of the old time gunslingers of the wild west, firing off trades with a six shooter in each hand.

There are all kinds of reasons that you might indiscriminately blast away with a quick series of trades. You'll have to figure them out and eradicate them. Gunslinging involves no methodology, only flair. Each bullet (or trade) loses significance in the barrage.

Focus instead on the silver bullet approach. Make sure each shot counts. You need a good target, exceptional aim, and a smooth pull of the trigger at just the right moment based on your training and experience.

Gunslingers typically enjoy the notoriety and reputation associated with the mystique of their showmanship. They take great risks and sometimes score big. It is merely luck. Over time the odds will catch up with them, and they will eventually find themselves on the wrong end of the barrel.

CHASING

These are the folks that get excited and "caught up in the moment" when a stock rockets in a direction either long or short. They almost forget their name as they throw caution and their methodology to the wind. All they want is to get into that stock…and do so usually at the end of its move.

Stay focused on your trading strategies and techniques. Enter trades based on your rules, not because a stock is simply ripping in a direction, and you are afraid to miss out on the big bucks. The big bucks will usually be the ones coming out of your pocket as you try to get out of the trade, since you probably bought the top or sold the bottom. Never chase a stock.

TOSSING THE DICE

I'm not talking about the random walk theory of the markets here. I'm talking about gambling, pure and simple. If you have no legitimate reason for taking a trade, but still find yourself buying or shorting a stock, go to the horse races…it's cheaper and more fun.

Reject the gambling mentality outright. Take pride in your abilities as a market speculator who knows when and what to trade based on a methodology strictly adhered to. You are a professional. You are an important participant in the marketplace.

Don't toss the dice, because odds favor snake eyes over the long haul. Every time you trade, you incur commission, the bid/ask spread, and the risk of being wrong. With this type of overhead expense you must make every trade count.

REVENGE TRADING

So you took a hit on a stock and lost money. The single worst thing that you can do is to try and "get that money back out of the same stock." Revenge is sweet, but not to you. The market will gladly take your money once again.

Your judgment will be clouded and risk exaggerated by holding a grudge against a stock or its market makers. They don't care about you. They don't even know who you are. But they like your money, and you will invariably hand it over to them when revenge is on your mind.

Leave the stock alone. Wait for a good pattern to setup before even considering another trade in the same issue.

MIDAS TOUCH SYNDROME

After a day or few of exceptional trading, you are on top of the world. Everything you touch (the buy or sell keys) turns to gold. But something begins to go awry. The next day you lose on your first few trades. Not to worry though, it's just an aberration because you've been trading so incredibly well.

Guess what? You are likely to keep trading and keep losing for one of two reasons. Either the market is not in a very tradable mode, or you are now out of synch with the market. In either case you will find yourself steadily dwindling down all of the hard earned profits of the past few days.

A series of successful days often breeds a continued aggressive trading style since you've been right consistently…until now. Recognize that something has changed, and reevaluate how your trades are unfolding.

The trading police are here and have their guns drawn on you. They are asking you to step away from the keyboard so that no one gets hurt, including yourself and your trading account.

The golden touch comes and goes. When it goes, reduce your level of trading activity. Don't give back all of your hard won earnings just because you think you still have the Midas touch.

HAPPY FINGERS - ARE YOU BORED?

Fingers on a keyboard
typing in a stock,
looking for a trade
but nothing's setting up.
Fingers getting happy,
buying shares of stock.
Bored with inactivity,
some dollars you will drop!

No iambic pentameter here. If you are bored or want activity for activity's sake, get the hell away from your computer. If the market is dead on arrival, go run some errands, call someone on the phone for a visit, run home and floss your cat's teeth, analyze your trading. Do something, but don't trade just to pass the time.

Any trade that you ever enter should be taken based on good market conditions and your proven methods and techniques. To do otherwise courts needless losses and commissions. If you sense that you are coming down with a case of "happy fingers," you'll be happier yourself by taking a break from trading for a while during the day.

SNAKE BIT

So much for the Midas touch. Sometimes you'll feel like every trade you pick is tainted by the fact that *you* chose to trade that stock. It's as if all the world of market makers said, "Okay, Bob just went long, let's take it down a point and screw him out of his money." Eventually you get snake bit. In other words, you're afraid to go near the buy or sell button because you know the trade won't work. The market venom seeps into your confidence and paralyzes your ability to trade.

It's time to take inventory of your method and technique. Are you trading the right stocks that are moving enough to offer a decent profit during the day? Are you trading "cherry picked" setups and getting filled at the price you want. If not, then back away...something evil this way comes.

If, after reviewing your trades, they are not quite up to snuff to be deemed "best setups," then something is amiss with your analysis and activity. This you can do something about by adjusting your trading technique.

Snake bites don't have to be lethal. Realize what is wrong with your trading or wrong with the market and take the appropriate action. You're not doomed by a bad string of trades. If you trade your methodology and pay close attention to your money management strategy then eventually odds will favor your success. Don't be scared off from the market. Losing trades and losing days are a fact of life in the day of a trader...as long as they are managed appropriately.

TUCK 'N ROLL

Remember when you climbed trees as a kid? If you ever fell then you know how it feels to hit the ground. It hurts. Consider a trade that isn't working out for you. It hurts too. If you agonize over every tick against you then you aren't trading your plan. It's like grabbing at every tree branch on the way down as you plummet toward the ground. You'll only break more bones, gather more bruises and extra cuts...but you are still going to end up in the same place - on the ground.

So don't fight it, tuck 'n roll. Make the fall more manageable and less drastic. Don't fight your way out of a trade by agonizing over every move against you. Get the hell out…simply tuck 'n roll out of the trade. Flailing away before your imminent demise only scars your trading mentality for the next opportunity. This is all about mechanically implementing your risk management to keep the fall from hurting too much and negatively affecting your future trades.

HANGING ONTO HOPE - A LOSING TRADE

Any trade that moves against you should be exited immediately based on your predetermined bail out point. But once it gets there you start wondering if maybe just another eighth will hold it. All of a sudden you find yourself staring a full one point loss in the face; that's a thousand dollars on a 1000 share trade!

"It will come back…won't it? At some point it has to, doesn't it?" Sure, after the multi-day 40 point move steadily grinds against your position and knocks you out of the day trading game. "I'll just average down my cost by picking up more shares." If your mind works this way then call me and I'll notify the undertaker. My hand will carve the inscription on your trading tombstone: "He couldn't take the loss."

I've never met a loss I couldn't take, as long as it was a small one. Waiting and hanging onto hope demoralizes you. It saps your ability to day trade by sucking all of your focus and energy into a progressively losing trade.

Woe to those who have done this and actually had a trade come back to breakeven or a profit. The worst possible trading habit has just been reinforced in your mind. All it takes is one trade where you let the losses get away from you to destroy your day trading ability and your trading career.

Believe me, I have seen it happen. I actually anguished over another trader's demise day after day. I wanted to run over to his computer and push the parachute button myself. But it's not up to me. It was his own fault. He knew better.

Like a little child who knows better, he hung onto hope. In the end the market hung him on the end of a rope. It is not a pretty sight. If you've already violated your initial exit strategy for a losing trade then *get out!*

A one point loss looks very attractive once it becomes a four point loss. A four point loss looks even more attractive once it becomes a ten point loss, ad infinitum. Never say to yourself "I can't take that loss." You sure as hell can and you had better do it quickly. Keep hoping and I'll see you on the street corner with a cardboard sign: "will trade for food."

TRAINED MONKEY EXIT

The prior two topics lead us to a way of reacting to a losing trade. You should already have your risk amount set in stone for every trade in advance. When the stock gets there, just punch the little button on your keyboard and you're out. No more worries, just a loss which is part of trading.

It doesn't always work that way though does it? You hesitate and do the worst thing possible, you *think* about it. This is just another recipe for disaster. Instead, be like a trained monkey. I know it sounds silly, but what does a trained monkey do? He simply reacts. He doesn't think about what he's supposed to do, he just does it.

Be like the trained monkey (kind of a Zen thing isn't it?). When your exit point for a loss is reached, reject all thought and act like the trained monkey. Punch that button and move on to greener trading pastures.

IT DOESN'T TAKE A ROCKET SCIENTIST

I've known a 19 year old who made substantial money day trading stocks. Almost anyone has the potential to make money no matter what their background may be. Sometimes it seems that the smarter a person thinks they are, the worse their odds of success. Read the interviews with some of the great traders. They will often relate how intelligence can be an inverse predictor of a trader's potential success.

If you bring to the table preconceived trading ideas from prior experience, they will often become your stumbling blocks to day trading success. Free yourself of all this mentally handicapping garbage…tabla rasa, a blank slate, is the way to begin.

Start fresh. Stock day trading is a totally different game with totally different rules and different players. Success comes to those who find a few decent strategies and incorporate good money management with the strictest discipline. They are the ones who in the future will be telling the old tales of how they made their money in the markets.

LOOK IN THE MIRROR

CONFIDENCE

You must have developed a reasonable dose of confidence to trade with consistent success. This confidence is not an arrogant cockiness and cavalier attitude toward the market. I'm talking about confidence in yourself and your decision making ability.

You'll definitely need confidence in your trading method. Develop this through paper trading. Over the course of days and weeks, watch how your trading approach yields a consistent and upward sloping equity curve. Even though it's only paper trading, that monopoly money goes a long way in buying your confidence that your trading technique will profit you over time.

The primary confidence factor to trade successfully relies upon your ability to take the right actions at the right times during the day. Are you sure that you are capable of pushing that button on a losing trade to close it out at the appropriate exit point *every time?* Can you count on yourself to "cherry pick" only the best setups, or will you waver in your stringency and start getting sloppy?

You must actively make these types of decisions in advance. They reflect your willpower to enact your trading technique and money management strategies without fail. You must find a way to rigidly adhere to all components of your trading plan. You cannot afford to trade without confidence in your ability to act.

PULLING THE TRIGGER

This differs from getting snake bit by the market. Many traders who have found a great setup to trade, eagerly await the moment when the stock begins to make its move. They're going to jump on board, get their price, and enjoy the satisfaction of a trade well done.

But they don't. For some reason they go into vapor lock when the moment comes to act. Off the stock goes while they stare at the screen wondering why they couldn't execute. Meanwhile the missed profits steadily pass before their eyes.

Several reasons may be at the root of your inability to "pull the trigger" (enter) on a good trade. Perhaps you are too afraid of losing money. Maybe your ego simply doesn't want to risk being proven wrong.

Are you looking for the stock to move far enough in the intended direction before you're comfortable entering? If so, then you'll enter too late into the move and probably get stopped out on the initial pullback.

Fear of pulling the trigger can be destructive. You will anguish over all of the potential profit you are missing out on as you punish yourself by watching the stock continue its move. After a few of these missed opportunities, aggravation sets in and you finally decide to take a trade that invariably will go against you. Now look what happened. Not only have you missed out on the good ones, but you got whacked when you finally acted.

What kind of cruel world is this anyway? It's not the world my fellow trader, it's you! Excuse yourself to the restroom and take a good long look at the man (or woman) in the mirror. Ask *that* person why you are gun shy on the trigger pull. Be honest with yourself and ferret out the primary reason for this shortcoming. Once it is isolated, develop a practical strategy for you to short circuit your way around this trading block.

ANALYSIS PARALYSIS

On one hand the importance of analyzing every trade before entry cannot be overstated, but don't overanalyze every detail to the point where you cannot act. It's like using too many technical indicators. Let's see…the MACD and intermediate trend point long. The Stochastic oscillator is oversold and turning back up. But the stock is just below its 50 day moving average, bearish divergence is present with the RSI and the market is going down.

"Do I go long or short?" Neither. You're looking at too many different varied criteria for a trade signal. This can happen with whatever trading strategies you employ. The fewer and simpler (such as pure price patterns), the better. If any of your criteria are conflicting, then you are not "cherry picking" your trades and should do nothing. Requiring too many variables to line up together for a trading signal will lead to consistent analysis paralysis. You'll never take a trade.

KISS: Keep it simple stupid. Do not lose yourself on a quest for the holy grail, it's a myth. And do not seek to reinvent trading. Your goal should instead be to re-invent yourself as a trader. Create and cultivate your abilities through self analysis and brutal honesty. As mentioned before, a decent trading method and a good money management approach are all the tools you need. The final ingredient is you. Don't fall prey to analysis paralysis like a deer caught in headlights.

AA FOR TRADERS

This is not intended to denigrate the impact that AA has had on improving the lives of those in need. But I have known many traders who could have benefited from a 12 step program. I would reduce it to two steps to make it simpler for the trader (I said simpler, not easier). Step one: Recognize that you have a problem (1% of the equation). It could be large or small and easily found in one or more of the topics discussed so far. Step two: Do something about it (the other 99% of the equation)! Don't just suffer away and whine about your lack of success. And for heaven's sake don't blame it on someone else. Any finger pointing should be at the fellow in the mirror.

Take responsibility and take action to correct the problem. If "happy fingers" regularly plagues you, figure out a practical way to circumvent it. Here would be some straightforward options. Get up from the computer and take a break. Go grab a bite to eat. Switch your computer to a "demo" mode and go off-line so that if you are tempted with a trade, it will take you too long to switch back over to live mode to enter it.

Think practical. Ask yourself: "What can I do to solve the problem?" If you can't just change it, then find a way to play tricks on yourself to short circuit that particular weakness.

More serious problems require more serious thought. Maybe your mental make-up is not designed for you to be a trader. It is very difficult to reroute a lifetime of hard-wiring. Let me give you an actual example from someone that I have trained.

He was a gambler at heart. When having a bad day, he would actually leave early and travel out to a nearby city full of casinos. Major red flag! I pleaded with him to forget about the money and action of trading, and to focus on just implementing quality method and quality money management.

He knew the stock setups well. He knew where to get in and out. He also knew what not to do…but he did it anyway. He simply couldn't help himself. He was a very likable person but not equipped with the necessary mental make-up to succeed in stock day trading.

Make sure you do not have a mental hurdle that cannot be overcome before you launch into a trading career.

So instead of AA, think of TA (Traders Anonymous). It's the two step program for day traders. *Recognize* a problem or weakness and *act* to negate its impact on your trading. Focus on your strengths.

MARKET PERCEPTION

DOING BATTLE WITH THE MARKETS

Although we like to talk about trading this way, it's really an unproductive characterization. If anything we are engaged in a battle with ourselves. Let's look at it differently. If you can quell the mental and emotional war taking place up there in command control central (your noodle), then a paradigm shift can take place.

Stop fighting. I know emotions of fight and/or flight seem to spring up automatically. It is the grinding together of greed and fear that instinctively give way to a smashed keyboard. Don't misunderstand me. It's far better to vent your emotions in a good old fashioned Freudian catharsis (in a productive way, of course), than to sit there and silently digest your stomach lining.

Change your way of thinking; shift your paradigm. Stop the psychological bloodshed of believing you are armed with mental and technological weapons to conquer the enemy of the market.

Don't get pissed off at the market. It's just that, a market. And don't get pissed off at the market makers who you know are deviously mapping out your demise. They are just doing their job by making a market and also trying to make money just like you. If you don't like the fills you are getting, don't bitch about it, adjust your trading and your way of thinking.

I guess the message here is: *Just let go of what you cannot control! Focus on what you can control*. You control which trading techniques to employ. You control your money management strategy. You choose when to and not to trade. You can recognize your weaknesses (some of which you've already read about). Most importantly, you can change and adjust any of these factors in any manner that you choose.

You see, it's all you. How often can someone take their avocation that they love and make it their vocation, their life's work. Enjoy your trading. It's hard work, and you have to evolve with the market as it changes. But by all means have fun with it.

Also, maintain realistic expectations. You're not likely to become an overnight millionaire. If you place this kind of demand on yourself then readjust your expectations. Be optimistic yet realistic.

IT'S REALLY SIMPLE - AND REALLY HARD

As mentioned earlier, the theme is to have just a few simple strategies and a straightforward money management plan and adhere to them strictly. Sounds easy enough doesn't it? But it isn't actually that easy.

It's really simple, and really hard. Funny, isn't it. You've got simple rules and strategies, but it's damn hard to make yourself stick to them. Discipline makes or breaks you in this game of day trading. We are human. We are not perfect.

Do I adhere to all of my rules all of the time? No. Why not? Because it's human nature. I know that if I did so, I would make more money. So what action must I take to overcome how hard it is to stick to my simple rules?

I believe one useful way of approaching this problem is to rate yourself on a percentage basis of how disciplined your trading has been. Scale it from 0% to 100% effective discipline. Don't fool yourself into thinking it's a static number either.

If I rate myself at 95%, that's not too bad in my book (as long as the other 5% doesn't include *major* mistakes). But that was for today's trading. What about tomorrow's and the next day's? Like I said, it's a dynamic number and constantly changing with a natural propensity in which direction? You guessed it. Back towards zero!

Therefore, actively visualize yourself constantly pushing that discipline factor as fiercely as you can back up to 100%. If it seems you've reached a plateau, you're wrong. By the time you recognize a plateau, your discipline factor has already slipped back in the other direction. View this as a constant striving as you daily push your discipline factor closer and closer to 100%. If you think you've arrived, that's only a signal to keep on pushing.

It's amazing how this striving impacts your esteem, your trading ability, and your account. Like I said, trading is really simple and really hard - hard work.

HOW YOU HANDLE YOUR *DISCIPLINE FACTOR* WILL BE THE SINGLE MOST INFLUENTIAL INGREDIENT TO YOUR SUCCESS OR FAILURE AS A DAY TRADER!

Let me repeat myself.

HOW YOU HANDLE YOUR *DISCIPLINE FACTOR* WILL BE THE SINGLE MOST INFLUENTIAL INGREDIENT TO YOUR SUCCESS OR FAILURE AS A DAY TRADER!

I KNOW WHAT TO DO - BUT I CAN'T DO IT

"The stock already broke long out of it's setup and has run 5/8 of a point. I know that I was supposed to enter it no further than 1/8 of a point into the breakout, but I can't help myself. I've got to buy it. My God, I just bought the top! I knew I was tossing my strategy out the window even as I was pressing the buy key. It's ripping down against me, what do I do, WHAT DO I DO?!?"

First, exit the trade NOW!

Okay, so you're out of the trade and the fear and panic are starting to recede...leaving behind an empty void echoing back your own question of "Why the hell did I do that?"

Good question.

You knew what to do...pass up the trade since it was beyond your entry point according to your *own* rules. But you couldn't do it. This scenario underscores the message in the prior topic. Trading is really simple and really hard, primarily because your discipline factor just came unraveled.

In your overall market perception, focus on the role of discipline in your trading. Knowing what to do and doing it are entirely two separate issues. Remember the Traders Anonymous two step program? Step 2: Do something about the problem.

Enter the discipline factor, stage left. Make sure he is the star of your day trading show from the start.

DON'T FORGET TO BREATHE

How many times have you day traded a stock and labored over when and where to exit. By the time you closed the trade you let out a long breath of relaxation. Why? Because your whole body tensed during the stress of managing the trade and, wonder of wonders, you actually forgot to breathe.

This is common in stressful situations. Trading can be one of the most stressing endeavors you'll ever encounter. Become aware of how your body physically reacts during your trading. What is your posture? What muscles tense up? Do you breathe shallowly or not at all? You'd be surprised if you saw a video of yourself. Tune into your physical response. It gauges the state of mind you slip into when handling day trades.

Why is this important? Because you trade more effectively when your mind and *body* are relaxed. If you notice a physical gut-response as your abdominal muscles assume the rigidity of titanium, then maybe it's time to relax. Take a few deep breaths from the abdomen and dissipate that hampering cloud of stress that most traders never become aware of.

I traded in an office next to my brother for a time. He is a very good trader. One afternoon I noticed he'd become very quiet for several minutes. Then, as if the world had been lifted off of his shoulders, he let out a huge sigh of relief. It turns out that he was in a trade that had unknowingly gone against him for over 2 points on 1000 shares. It finally rallied back to near break-even and he exited.

He sighed afterward because he'd forgotten to breathe as he lost himself to the stress of the market. Constantly do a physical checkup on yourself. It really doesn't take much time and it's very productive. Simply reflect on whether you are breathing or not. You'll be surprised.

Another more important result of this negative physical response during trading is a thing called "silent ischemia." Latin translation: "You're going to die soon!" As your body tenses continually throughout the day a certain phenomenon occurs. Blood flow to your heart is greatly reduced, depriving this vital organ with the oxygen and nutrients needed to sustain the trading organism that you are.

I'm dead serious. No one wants to find you slumped over your keyboard, even with an open winning trade. Do yourself the kindest favor and don't forget to breathe deeply, and evenly. Let the stress flow out of you with each smooth exhalation. Your body and mind will thank you.

LOSING FOCUS

Focus on trading your method and implementing your money management with a high discipline factor. It's so easy to forget this simple foundation for success when you're barraged with all of the information flowing through your computer and across your screen.

Getting wrapped up in "micro managing" one trade, whether it's a winner or loser, can constrict your focus. You'll no longer have your finger on the pulse of the overall market, and other potential trading candidates that are setting up. It's an issue of opportunity cost.

Keep your view broad. Know what the market indices are doing and cycle through the basket of stocks that you follow. They continually offer the subtle clues and subsequent insights about how trader-friendly current market conditions are. Also, your ringside seat offers an insider's peek at the internal price dynamics of multiple stocks as they unfold from minute to minute.

Break the habit of losing focus. When you realize you just missed three high-octane trading opportunities, it's probably because you spent all of your time watching the one trade you currently have open. Let your methodology take care of that trade for you.

Don't dance around like a cheerleader for a stock's every tiny move. Don't waste your time and concentration on just one stock by visually burning a hole in the computer screen. Look around. There's a whole world of trading opportunity and analysis available to you if you actively maintain a broad focus.

The status of your personal life also affects your focus. If you are angry, upset, sad or stressed by some event outside of trading, you may want to back off for a day and regroup. Don't allow negative events in your personal life damage your focus by bleeding over into your trading.

Focus-management is another one of those "recognize it and do something about it" patterns of behavior that traders occasionally fall into. Proper focus enhances market perception, which enhances quality trading decisions.

THE DEATH OF A TRADER

It happens. Not everyone climbs to the mountaintop. The slopes are scattered with the bones of those who've gone before and failed. No one likes to see it transpire or become one of the corpses of traders past.

It's very sobering to me when I reflect upon people who had the high hopes and right intentions but were eventually dashed against the rocks which litter the day trading landscape. The lush greenery and magnificent view lie at the top of the mountain of trading success.

This vista hasn't been reserved as hallowed ground for the millionaires and "big hitters." You too have a place reserved up there. And there is no check-in time. Just proceed at your own pace with your end goal in mind. And by all means enjoy the journey along the way.

Success is how you define it for yourself. Don't be lured or goaded into thinking the only way to the top mandates excessive risk and huge winning days. Understand who you are and make sure that your intermediate trading objectives are realistic. Decide what is reasonable for you as a trader in terms of success and income. It is a very personal subject and one not to be judged by others, only by yourself.

If you want to average $250 per day, then that is success when achieved. If your initial goal (as it should be) is to not lose money, then you have effectively accomplished your mission and should take pride in it.

Losing sight of what is right for you - losing sight of *your* mountaintop should be unacceptable in light of the esteem that you hold for yourself as a person and as a trader.

So how do traders die?...let me count the ways. Lack of discipline is at the top of the list. But in the big picture, two primary scenarios usually tend to play themselves out. Read them and avoid them through quality method, quality money management and quality discipline.

BLOWING OUT

Sometimes a trader will blast away at the market, exposing themselves to obscene risk from the start. Unless they have a seven figure account, they will be gone within a few days to a few weeks. Multi-thousand losses day after day exact a heavy toll. A trader should be taking it easy, learning and keeping their market "tuition" low. Never recognizing what is happening or not knowing to simply stop and reevaluate, they "blow out" their account and are gone.

What a waste of energy and money to have finished yourself off only as you've just begun. All of the prior planning, hopes and dreams slip down the drain before you know it. Shell-shocked! It's already over and there's nothing left to savor but the bitter taste. If you've just begun day trading or are about to embark on the day trader's journey, don't victimize yourself like this. There are plenty of other ways to inflict pain upon yourself that are a lot less expensive.

The problem is that you don't realize the mental pain until it's already too late. Pain can be your friend by telling you something is amiss. Fix it. If pain barely has time to register, then nothing can be done. This is the quick death.

DEATH OF A THOUSAND CUTS

Other folks enter the day trading arena more timidly and rightly so. But they never really "get it." Either they are without a basic trading method, money management safety net, or are suffering one of the afflictions covered in this psychological expose on the basic mental trading goofs. They make a little money, lose a little money, make a little money, lose a little mon…you get the picture. Bit by bit their account balance dips further and further into the red by small degrees.

If you find yourself on this path then refer to the "traders anonymous" topic. Obviously it's time to tweak some aspect of your trading. Analyze your method, your money management and your mental trading fitness. Find the squeaky wheel and grease it up good.

The amusing part of this is that while the little (or big) wheel is squeaking, you are usually deaf to it. Someone else observing your trading will hear it loud and clear. But since trading is akin to a lone wolf game, it's imperative that you lend an ear to the squeaks. Only you can solve them.

Like a tiny blade that cuts you once, you'll slightly notice it. But day after day, more cuts appear, virtually painless. As time goes by the blood flows, and before you know it, you are covered in red. Staunch the bleeding early. Negate the blade that whisks across your skin with each day that you've not tuned into possible problems underlying your lack of trading success.

This is the slow death.

SELF ANALYSIS

WHAT ARE YOU SAYING TO YOURSELF?

Don't you just love the psycho babble term "self-talk"? I actually do appreciate and understand the concept, but shy away from bogus sounding terms. Whether you know it or not, you do have a constant ongoing dialogue with yourself in your mind. We're not talking multiple personalities here, only the normal chatter. It refers to what that disembodied voice that is your own keeps saying to you in anger, happiness, empathy or self misery.

That voice impacts your thinking and actions way beyond what you perceive. You may not even be aware of its continual feedback on your decisions and activities, but be assured that it's definitely whispering in your ear. Most people don't even recognize its existence. We have learned to turn it off, or more commonly, press the "mute" button.

Why tune into the background "noise" in your gray matter? I'll let you in on a little secret. That voice is the soul of your salvation or destruction in trading and in daily life. Listen to yourself. What are you saying? The subconscious commentary permeates and affects everything you do, how you act and how you perceive yourself.

So what do you think about this proposition? Change the way you mentally talk to yourself and change who you are. Anthony Robbins would love this stuff. But so do I. Only for one reason: it impacts your trading ability and discipline. More than that, it sets the stage for your typical modus operandi throughout your life. If you choose day trading as an engaging and hopefully profitable component of your life then listen to that voice in your head (but not indiscriminately).

What you say to yourself is not always right or productive to guide you in your day trading endeavors. Do what momma said to never do: Talk back! Whatever me says that I deem a hindrance to me will be silenced and reprogrammed. Don't just "think positive." Take control of what you say to yourself.

"I will only take the best trade setups...I will not enter a stock past my get-in point according to my rules...I'm short and will hold the stock based on my trading rules and exit base on those same rules...So I took a loss, it was based on my rules, I've got the discipline to do it...I missed a trade setup, but that's okay others will come along, I'm not going to chase it...I cannot pick a winning trade no matter what I do!"?????

You get the idea. The last comment by the way wasn't very productive. Instead restate to yourself that you've had several losing trades. Then ask "Is the market not very tradable or is my timing off?" This is more productive. Picture yourself successful. Walk through a winning trade in your mind and hear what you would be saying to yourself as you managed it and finally closed it out for a profit. Do the same with a losing trade scenario.

It doesn't have to be positive talk, only productive talk...but never negative or berating to yourself, the market, the market makers or other outside influences. Listen to how you talk to yourself and make it work for you!

TRADE YOUR PERSONALITY

Learn from books, from training, from watching a good trader in action. Take any and everything in and process it. You must begin your trading with effective, proven strategies. But recognize who you are, what your personality is.

If you can't function because you hate giving back open paper profits then scalping is probably your shoe size. If you enjoy the ride of entering a trade that will wiggle all over the place as it hopefully keeps up the good fight in the direction of your trade, then intraday trend trading may fit you better.

A whole spectrum of trading styles spans the activities of market participants. Find what style of trading fits your personality and craft whatever training you've received to match what works for you. To do otherwise will not be in your nature and lead you down one of the many paths to failure. It reminds me of a story.

Once a scorpion asked a frog to take him across the pond on his back. The frog said, "But you're a scorpion, and you will sting me." The scorpion said, "No, I promise you that I won't sting you, you are the only way that I can get to the other side of the pond."

So the frog took the scorpion on his back and began to swim across the pond. As he neared the middle, the scorpion stung the frog with its deadly sting. The dying frog implored, "Why, why did you sting me scorpion?" The scorpion replied, "I couldn't help it, it is my nature."

The message is: Know your nature. If you engage in a trading style or situation that you have not crafted to fit your personality, then you will sink into the pond and die. Trade your personality.

DISCIPLINE

Am I beginning to sound like the "department of redundancy" department? Discipline, Discipline and more Discipline! That is what trading is actually about. You've already read all of the stories, descriptions and scenarios regarding the supreme importance of you're ability to enact ultimate discipline in all areas of your trading.

Of all of the day traders I have trained, I can honestly say to you that the primary reason any have failed has little to do with the trading methods and money management techniques I've imparted to them. They all knew how to effectively trade when I got through with them. And they knew I cared deeply about their success since I was in their shoes once upon a time.

So why have some failed in the grand pursuit of trading? They could not find gumption enough to force discipline on themselves…or should I say, to integrate strict discipline into their world trading view and into how they talked to themselves.

I've agonized over this issue above all others. What can I do to impart the ability to actively apply discipline in every area of trading? How do I get them to bow down to the goddess of discipline?

I've tried pleading. I've tried the "I'm disgusted with your lack of discipline" marine drill instructor approach. I've had sit-down "come to Jesus" talks with them. But in the end, I realize that it is up to them.

If they want to succeed and are willing to let themselves succeed, then they will swear allegiance to the goddess of discipline in their trading. They will constantly strive to continually push their *discipline factor* towards 100%, to *attempt* perfection. We are not perfect as traders; it is the undying effort of discipline that will make or break us, both you and me!

This I promise you is the most important part of self analysis. Discipline!

THE ART OF TRADING

Let us now depart from the cold hard facts of rules and regulations regarding trading methods and the mental gymnastics involved in trading. What about the *art* of trading? It's an intangible derived from experience.

My theory is that our little hard drive in our head sifts trading experiences and information over time, cataloging them in abstract but legitimate ways. At some point this subconscious, which hides out just below our awareness, whispers to us yes or no.

It complements our left brained analysis with a gut-feeling as it's often called. Learn to listen to this gut-feeling once it has developed over time and through experience. Consider it a confirming factor for a trade setup that you have isolated. Allow it to surface, don't push it aside. It is your innate ability telling you yes or no. If it ever tells you "I don't know" then consider passing up that particular trade.

The art of trading is difficult to describe and more difficult to teach. Watch a successful trader to see it at work. Gather insight through experience. Let the art enhance your trading ability. Never rely simply upon "a feeling." Incorporate this phenomenon as a confirmation in your decision making process for finding, entering, managing and exiting trades.

You will develop your own *art of trading* as part of a day trader's self analysis. It's not a license to go nuts and take any trade that "feels right." Scrutinize and evaluate its effect on your trading, but never ignore it.

PROTESTANT WORK ETHIC

I grew up in a very fundamentalist and conservative backdrop which I've since tried to ignore. But as a student of psychology, philosophy, and of course trading, I have concluded that there is a basic principle instilled in people which can significantly impact their trading activity. I call it the "protestant work ethic."

No disrespect is intended for your personal or religious beliefs. I'm coming from a more academic stance now. I think elements from our society's "world view" affect us to the very core of who we are. Therefore, as a trader, I deem it my job to alert you to its potential impact on how you view your career as a day trader.

We are ingrained with a very succinct formula for achievement and self worth which, I believe, is based on the good old fashioned work ethic. It's not overtly explained but rather intuitively learned and absorbed from our earliest years as we meander through this world in which we live and trade.

We are taught that to achieve results we must work. In our 90% agrarian society from the last century and before, this was very true. You were only as good as your work, which was mostly physical labor back then. This principle continues on today. But consider work as a synonym for *activity*. Work = results. If you (or someone else) is not satisfied with the results then it means you must work harder. Therefore, if work (activity) is not producing the desired result, then simply increase the work (activity) to improve the results. In other words, Increase your "activity."

Increased activity in most situations produces better results. *In the day trading environment it does not*. If you are trading and losing, your instinct tells you to trade more, trade harder (work harder)...increase your activity. Nothing could be further from the truth to succeed in day trading. But we have this little endless-loop audio tape playing in the back of our mind to "up" our level of trading activity, to work harder.

Step 1: Recognize the problem (sound familiar). Step 2: Do something about it. Temper your trading activity based not on this so called "protestant work ethic," but on what produces profits in the market. Usually, if you are not trading well you must actively pull back and lighten your trading or not trade at all. This is totally counter to how we've been programmed.

YOU MUST REPROGRAM YOURSELF AS A DAY TRADER THAT INCREASED TRADING ACTIVITY DOES NOT NECESSARILY LEAD TO IMPROVED RESULTS.

Any time that you must circumvent a pattern this ingrained in your psyche, it takes a constant act of will until it becomes habit, especially for your day trading. Trade smarter, not harder.

Once again, look in the mirror and ask yourself honestly, "Can I truly accept a new concept that increased activity does not necessarily yield improved results when I'm day trading?" If you can rewire yourself for this then profits await (as long as you employ the discipline factor).

Your primary focus as a day trader must be on self analysis. This is the area where increased activity will yield improved results. It incorporates discipline and an understanding of the mental issues which can and will impact your trading. Recognize and act to circumvent mental weaknesses and accentuate your strengths.

I think we've painted the overall self analysis picture as it should be seen. Don't cover your eyes. View it intently as a mirror to understanding yourself. With a few well placed brush strokes, you'll complete your own masterpiece.

WHERE DO I GO FROM HERE?

By now I think we've pried open your headbone and laid the wiring bare. I hope that we've also done a good job of reassembly. You'll know soon enough, I suppose.

Don't think you are finished with this manual and stuff it away on the shelf. It works best when it has a well-worn, dog-eared appearance. Read and reread it on a regular basis. Just like you take your car in for a tune up, your mind should be scheduled for regular maintenance. Consider this your very own psychological tune up manual.

As you travel down the road of trading possibilities, remember that you are always in the driver's seat. You make all of the decisions - good or bad. It's all up to you now, each and every trading day. I hope this material helps you create success and contentment in your trading endeavors.

See you on the mountain top!

DAY TRADERS COURSE

A real-time training course is available which offers both classroom style learning sessions as well as hands on guidance during "live" trading. This is best done with a group of several traders since the synergy will help foster the exchange of ideas. The one-on-one personal interaction brings alive the book's trading strategies in 10 plus hours of classroom training and 5 full days of market trading. You will understand and recognize the nuances of how to actually trade profitably. The goal is to raise your trading skills to a higher level. Additional materials and information are also provided.

Whether you trade from home or at a day trading firm, a week of on-site training is available to you. The only requirement is that you have access to NASDAQ level II quotes with price charting and order execution capabilities, and a week's worth of your time devoted to learning and sharing ideas.

Although I enjoy trading, I also enjoy teaching. If you are interested in serious training that is crafted to your needs, visit my website at **www.sceptretrading.com** or fax me at the phone number listed below for details and fees. Provide your name and phone number, and I will return your call as soon as possible.

SCEPTRE TRADING

E-MAIL: sceptre@flash.net
FAX: 214-827-9530

RESOURCES

Telechart2000 provides a very high quality, low cost software/data service for end of day stock charting. Analytics, stock grouping and chart scanning capabilities are all included. I use it daily in my own trading analysis. They may be contacted at **1-800-776-4940** or on-line at **www.tc2000.com**.

Pattern Smasher is a new and very unique software package from **Kasanjian Research**. It enables the trader to easily define both simple and complex patterns for daily bar chart analysis. No programming experience is necessary. I have found it an effective tool to scan groups of stocks for multiple patterns. **Kasanjian Research** may be reached at **1-888-220-9789** or on-line at **www.kasanjianresearch.com**.

For real-time level II stock quotes, analysis and execution software, *TradeCast* offers a top notch trading program. I currently trade with *TradeCast* software through a local trading firm in Dallas, Texas. To find out more about the program call *TradeCast* at **1-713-627-0488** or view their website at **www.tradecast.com.**

NOTES

NOTES

NOTES

NOTES